W9-DBJ-750

WOMEN OF THE BIBLE

the Smart Guide to the Bible series

Kathy Collard Miller
Larry Richards, General Editor

THOMAS NELSON
Since 1798

NASHVILLE   DALLAS   MEXICO CITY   RIO DE JANEIRO   BEIJING

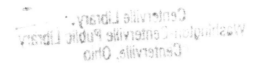

Women of the Bible
The Smart Guide to the Bible™ series

Published in Nashville, Tennessee, by Thomas Nelson. Thomas Nelson is a trademark of Thomas Nelson, Inc.

Thomas Nelson, Inc. titles may be purchased in bulk for educational, business, fund-raising, or sales promotional use. For information, please e-mail SpecialMarkets@ThomasNelson.com.

Originally published by Starburst Publishers under the title *Women of the Bible: God's Word for the Biblically-Inept.* Now revised and updated.

Scripture quotations are taken from The New King James Version® (NKJV), copyright © 1979, 1980, 1982, 1992 Thomas Nelson, Inc., Publishers.

General Editor: Larry Richards
Managing Editor: Lila Empson
Associate Editor: W. Mark Whitlock
Scripture Editor: Deborah Wiseman
Assistant Editor: Amy Clark
Design: Diane Whisner

ISBN-10: 1-4185-0989-2
ISBN-13: 978-1-4185-0989-7

Printed in the United States of America
07 08 09 RRD 4 3 2

Introduction

Welcome to *Women of the Bible—The Smart Guide to the Bible*™ series. This series is designed to bring God's encouraging and loving message to you in an easy-to-understand and relevant style. You are about to discover a new commentary that will change your outlook on the Bible forever.

What Is the Bible?

The Bible is like no other book. Written over a span of fifteen hundred years, it is a collection of sixty-six books written by at least forty different authors but with one message to tell: God loves you and wants the best for you!

The Bible is divided into two main sections: an "Old" Testament and a "New" Testament. The Old Testament was written between 1400 BC (before Christ) and 400 BC. The New Testament was written in about seventy years, between AD (anno Domini, "the year of our Lord") 40 and AD 100. The Old Testament deals with the old covenant that God had with his chosen people, the Hebrews, before the birth of Jesus Christ; the New Testament is about the new covenant: Jesus' birth, life, resurrection, and the spread of the early church by Jesus' followers.

Centuries later, experts divided the books of the Bible into chapters and verses. Thus Genesis 12:3 refers to the twelfth chapter and the third verse in the book of Genesis. If you know the name of the book and its chapter and verse number, you can locate specific Bible verses, stories, and teachings.

Who Wrote the Bible?

At least forty different people wrote the Bible, but all of them believed they were writing the Word of God. Some were educated; some were not. Some were mighty kings, and others were lowly shepherds. Moses, for example, was a prisoner and a slave before freeing the Hebrews with God's help. He is credited with writing the first five books of the Old Testament: Genesis, Exodus, Leviticus, Numbers, and Deuteronomy. King David, on the other hand, was Israel's greatest king and wrote many worship songs and poems in the book of Psalms. Four of Jesus' disciples, all from different backgrounds, wrote what are known as the New Testament "Gospels," which are titled by the names of those disciples: Matthew, Mark, Luke, and John.

The disciple John also wrote the book of Revelation under the guidance of its true author—the Holy Spirit, the third person of the Trinity. The word "trinity" is not found in the Bible, but we use the term to describe the three ways God reveals himself: God the Father; his Son, Jesus Christ; and the Holy Spirit. Think of the Trinity as three different expressions of God just as you express yourself in actions, spoken words, and written words.

The Languages of the Bible

The first books of the Bible and most of the Old Testament were written in Hebrew. Parts of the books of Daniel and Ezra, however, were written in Aramaic, a related language spoken by most Near Eastern peoples from about 600 BC onward. The people of Jesus' day also spoke Aramaic in everyday situations but studied the Bible in their ancient tongue, Hebrew. About one hundred years before Christ, the Old Testament was translated into Greek, because most people throughout the Roman Empire spoke Greek.

The New Testament was written in the Greek spoken by ordinary people. This meant that the New Testament was easy for all people throughout the Roman Empire to understand so the message of Jesus spread quickly.

Because the Old and New Testament books were recognized as holy, first by Jews and then by Christians, they were copied accurately and carefully preserved.

Why Study the Bible?

BECAUSE . . . For more than two thousand years, millions of people have improved their lives by following its wisdom. The Bible tells us repeatedly that when we study the Bible we will receive valuable blessings.

BECAUSE . . . Many people believe that God communicates with us through the Bible. Within its pages God tells us he wants us to know him and to follow his guidelines for how to live. Romans 15:4 tells us, "For whatever things were written before were written for our learning, that we through the patience and comfort of the Scriptures might have hope" (NKJV).

BECAUSE . . . All of us want to respond to life's challenges in a godly way. Even though the Bible was written many years ago in a totally different place and culture than ours, the Bible offers answers to the troublesome situations and the difficult questions of every generation.

Introduction

Why Learn About Women of the Bible?

The women of the Bible can show us how to live, what choices to make, and why. These women faced sticky problems and difficult situations just like we experience. No matter where we are in our lives, we can gain encouragement and wisdom from these women. They struggled through every sort of difficulty, yet most endured and built their faith. Eve, for example, lived thousands of years ago, but we too have been tugged by temptation just like she was. Sarah lived three thousand years ago and yet, as we read about her struggle to trust God, we can see our own struggles of faith.

God had a purpose for each woman in the Bible, from Priscilla, in her ministry, to Mary, in her motherhood of Jesus. God also has a purpose for each one of us. By studying the lives of the women of the Bible, we can know God, bring him into every area of our lives, build our faith and character, and be led to his purpose.

But what about the women who were not faithful to God? Can we learn anything from them? Sure we can! In fact, if we failed to look at why certain women rebelled against God, and only paid attention to those who are held up as good role models, we would be missing out on as much as half of the wisdom that the Bible has to offer. There are blessings for faithfulness, and there are consequences for disobedience; both principles are important.

How to Use Women of the Bible—The Smart Guide to the Bible™

You'll notice this book is divided into three main sections, as follows:

- Part One, "Bible Matriarchs" (chapters 1–5), discusses the most important women of the Bible: Eve, Sarah, Rebekah, Rachel and Leah, and Mary the mother of Jesus.
- Part Two, "Women of the Old Testament" (chapters 6–13), presents the wide variety of women whose stories are told in the Old Testament. You'll find the good, the strong, and the cruel here.
- Part Three, "Women of the New Testament" (chapters 14–18), shares the stories of women who were directly helped by Jesus.

Start the book with chapter 1. As you work through each chapter, use the sidebars loaded with icons and helpful information to give you a knowledge boost. Answer the Study Questions and review with the Chapter Wrap-Up. Then go on to the next chapter. It's simple!

Dates

Unlike any other book, the Bible was written over a span of fifteen hundred years! Because of this long period of time, biblical experts sometimes differ in the dates they give for various events. Thanks to archaeologists and their discoveries, however, the accuracy of these dates has improved. We can now accurately date many of the events in the Bible. See Appendix A for time lines that show when in history the women of the Bible lived.

A Word About Words

As you read *Women of the Bible—The Smart Guide to the Bible*™, you'll notice some interchangeable words: Scripture, Scriptures, Word, Word of God, God's Word, etc. All of these terms mean the same thing and come under the broad heading of "the Bible."

In most cases the phrase "the Scriptures" in the New Testament refers to the Old Testament. Peter indicated that the writings of the apostle Paul were quickly accepted in the early church as equal to the other Scriptures (2 Peter 3:16). Both Testaments consistently demonstrate the belief that is expressed in 2 Timothy 3:15–16, all Scripture is God-breathed.

One Final Tip

God gave us these stories of the women of the Bible so we could learn from them. With God's help, you can use the experiences of these women to improve and bless your life. Open your heart. Ask God to speak his Word to you as you read, and God will further your understanding and your life.

Understanding the Bible Is Easy with These Tools

To understand God's Word you need easy-to-use study tools right where you need them—at your fingertips. The Smart Guide to the Bible™ series puts valuable resources adjacent to the text to save you both time and effort.

Every page features handy sidebars filled with icons and helpful information: cross references for additional insights, definitions of key words and concepts, brief commentaries from experts on the topic, points to ponder, evidence of God at work, the big picture of how passages fit into the context of the entire Bible, practical tips for applying biblical truths to every area of your life, and plenty of maps, charts, and illustrations. A wrap-up of each passage, combined with study questions, concludes each chapter.

These helpful tools show you what to watch for. Look them over to become familiar with them, and then turn to Chapter 1 with complete confidence: You are about to increase your knowledge of God's Word!

Study Helps

The thought-bubble icon alerts you to commentary you might find particularly thought-provoking, challenging, or encouraging. You'll want to take a moment to reflect on it and consider the implications for your life.

key point

Don't miss this point! The exclamation-point icon draws your attention to a key point in the text and emphasizes important biblical truths and facts.

go to

death on the cross
Colossians 1:21–22

Many see Boaz as a type of Jesus Christ. To win back what we human beings lost through sin and spiritual death, Jesus had to become human (i.e., he had to become a true kinsman), and he had to be willing to pay the penalty for our sins. With his <u>death on the cross</u>, Jesus paid the penalty and won freedom and eternal life for us.

The additional Bible verses add scriptural support for the passage you just read and help you better understand the <u>underlined text</u>. (Think of it as an instant reference resource!)

How does what you just read apply to your life? The heart icon indicates that you're about to find out! These practical tips speak to your mind, heart, body, and soul, and offer clear guidelines for living a righteous and joy-filled life, establishing priorities, maintaining healthy relationships, persevering through challenges, and more.

This icon reveals how God is truly all-knowing and all-powerful. The hourglass icon points to a specific example of the prediction of an event or the fulfillment of a prediction. See how some of what God has said would come to pass already has!

What are some of the great things God has done? The traffic-sign icon shows you how God has used miracles, special acts, promises, and covenants throughout history to draw people to him.

Does the story or event you just read about appear elsewhere in the Gospels? The cross icon points you to those instances where the same story appears in other Gospel locations—further proof of the accuracy and truth of Jesus' life, death, and resurrection.

Since God created marriage, there's no better person to turn to for advice. The double-ring icon points out biblical insights and tips for strengthening your marriage.

The Bible is filled with wisdom about raising a godly family and enjoying your spiritual family in Christ. The family icon gives you ideas for building up your home and helping your family grow close and strong.

something significant had occurred, he wrote down the substance of what he saw. This is the practice John followed when he recorded Revelation on the **Isle of Patmos.**

What does that word really mean, especially as it relates to this passage? Important, misunderstood, or infrequently used words are set in **bold type** in your text so you can immediately glance at the margin for definitions. This valuable feature lets you better understand the meaning of the entire passage without having to stop to check other references.

the big picture

Joshua
Led by Joshua, the Israelites crossed the Jordan River and invaded Canaan (see Illustration #8). In a series of military campaigns the Israelites defeated several coalition armies raised by the inhabitants of Canaan. With organized resistance put down, Joshua divided the land among the twelve Israelite

How does what you read fit in with the greater biblical story? The highlighted big picture summarizes the passage under discussion.

what others say

David Breese
Nothing is clearer in the Word of God than the fact that God wants us to understand himself and his working in the lives of men.[5]

It can be helpful to know what others say on the topic, and the highlighted quotation introduces another voice in the discussion. This resource enables you to read other opinions and perspectives.

Maps, charts, and illustrations pictorially represent ancient artifacts and show where and how stories and events took place. They enable you to better understand important empires, learn your way around villages and temples, see where major battles occurred, and follow the journeys of God's people. You'll find these graphics let you do more than study God's Word—they let you *experience* it.

Chapters at a Glance

PART TWO: Women of the Old Testament

PART THREE: Women of the New Testament

Part One
Bible Matriarchs

Chapter 1 Eve

Chapter Highlights:
• Garden of Eden
• Creation of Eve
• Temptation by Satan
• Disobedience
• Confession
• God's Consequences

Let's Get Started

Eve! The name conjures up all sorts of images. Apple tree. Temptation. Snakes. She has quite a reputation. Yet it all started out so wonderfully when Adam yelled, "Yippee! She's here!" Adam and Eve were innocent creations of God who knew God personally. Everything was perfect in their intimate Garden, but their love for God was not truly love until it was tested . . . and that's where it all started.

created
Genesis 2:7

Wow! What a Place!

GENESIS 2:15 *Then the LORD God took the man and put him in the garden of Eden to tend and keep it. (NKJV)*

Eve's story begins even before she was <u>created</u> (see Appendix A). God created the heavens and the earth (Genesis 1:1–23), and then formed Adam ("the man") from the dust of the earth. God knows Adam needs purpose in his life, so he places him in a pristine environment, the Garden of Eden (see Illustration #1), and tells him to care for the Garden. Now God has given purpose to his new human creation, but Adam will soon find purpose alone cannot meet all his needs.

God gave Adam (and later Eve) work to do to give him purpose, because God created men and women to achieve goals. The fact that Adam's God-given work was in the Garden before there was even an opportunity to preach about God lets us know that any and all work we do by God's design is "service." That includes working in a factory, selling a product, or taking care of children. As long as God has called us to that job, we are serving him, and it becomes our act of worship.

Illustration #1
Garden of Eden—
While we don't know
exactly where the
Garden of Eden was,
we do know four
rivers ran through
Eden including the
Tigris and the
Euphrates Rivers.
The first human civi-
lizations developed
here, now the pres-
ent-day location of
Iran and Iraq.

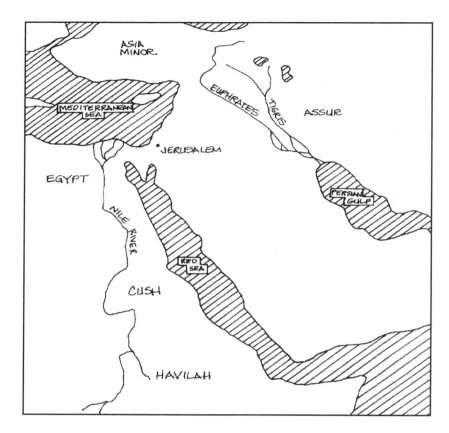

said
Psalm 34:1

activity
1 Corinthians 10:31

Why Not That One, God?

GENESIS 2:16–17 *And the LORD God commanded the man,
saying, "Of every tree of the garden you may freely eat; but of
the tree of the knowledge of good and evil you shall not eat, for
in the day that you eat of it you shall surely die."* (NKJV)

God is a God of "yes." So many people picture God as always negative, always saying no. We need to know that God gives us commandments to keep us from doing some things. He gives **commandments** for our safety and allows us great freedom to do all the things that will not harm us. God's commandments are always meant for our good.

God sets limits in order to **test**, not tempt, his creation. His desire is to reveal who a person really is inside and give us an opportunity to really love him through our obedience. Love is not love if there are no opportunities to disobey. So God gives one no-no: the fruit from the **Tree of the Knowledge of Good and Evil** must not be eaten. Just think, there is only one thing Adam and Eve couldn't do and a whole garden of things they could do!

meant for our good
Joshua 1:8

tests
James 1:13–15

instructions
Deuteronomy
30:11–20

commandments
God's directions for living

test
a way of revealing who a person really is

Tree of the Knowledge of Good and Evil
Its fruits signified the ability to know good and evil by personal experience.

what others say

Jill Briscoe

Although we usually consider temptation in negative terms, God allows us to be tempted in order to provide us with a chance to be obedient....Saying no when you want to say yes strengthens you, produces endurance, and builds character—Christian character.[2]

The motive behind testing is different from the motive behind tempting. Testing is done to reveal the truth. Tempting is done to make someone fail, become discouraged, and give up. Satan is the initiator of temptation and wants us to fail. God tests us to find out the truth about our weaknesses and strengths. God has also developed instructions for his people to follow, and we have the opportunity to choose whether to obey or disobey. We grow spiritually and emotionally when we are tested. Even though we wish for a problem-free life, we wouldn't crave or need God if our lives were always without problems.

Still Not Happy

GENESIS 2:18 *And the LORD God said, "It is not good that man should be alone; I will make him a helper comparable to him." (NKJV)*

God notices that Adam is not content. Adam has his work, his purpose, and the Garden, but Adam feels something or someone is

creative
Genesis 1:21, 25, 31

helper
Psalms 33:20; 70:5;
115:9

missing. What a contrast to everything else God created. Over and over again, God saw that his <u>creative</u> results were "good." But now the Lord God says, "This isn't good. I will correct it."

The word "<u>helper</u>" isn't meant to be demeaning. God himself is also called a "help." The word "suitable" can also be expressed as "a help, as opposite him" or "corresponding to" and can be thought of like a man's suit; it's tailored, taken in or let out, to fit exactly according to his body. The words "a helper comparable to him" also refer to how the description of Adam in Genesis 2:7 would also apply to this new creation. These two will have the same nature, similar to God's nature.

Adam and Eve are both created for marriage with God's intention for them to complement each other. What the man lacks, the woman provides. What the woman lacks, the man supplies. God intends for them to learn from each other and consider the differences of the mate as a benefit, not a detriment.

God intends to provide for Adam exactly according to Adam's needs. But first God needs to show him some of the other things that ultimately will not satisfy, because the things of this world never satisfy.

Naming the Animals

GENESIS 2:19 *Out of the ground the LORD God formed every beast of the field and every bird of the air, and brought them to Adam to see what he would call them. And whatever Adam called each living creature, that was its name. (NKJV)*

God has already formed the beasts of the earth and the birds of the air. Now it is up to Adam to name them. God doesn't correct Adam at any point. Whatever Adam says, goes! What freedom God gives Adam. Like a doting parent, he smiles in joy as Adam uses his creativity to fulfill this assignment from God.

God could have named everything himself, just as he powerfully had called all into existence. But God delegates this task to Adam. This shows how God loves to involve us in his work. He wants us to be involved—even if we do it imperfectly.

Still Alone!

GENESIS 2:20 *So Adam gave names to all cattle, to the birds of the air, and to every beast of the field. But for Adam there was not found a helper comparable to him.* (NKJV)

Even as Adam names the animals, he seems to be actively seeking a helper suitable for him. We can imagine Adam saying, as each animal stands before him, "Nope, that's not my helper." Of course, God doesn't expect a zebra or an eagle to become Adam's mate. God has a much bigger plan: a woman!

Only in relationships do humans truly find fulfillment. "Work" doesn't satisfy. "Things" won't bring a sense of completeness. It is only in "relationships" that God designed humans to be fulfilled: in relationship with the Creator and other human beings. Ultimately, the most fulfilling relationship is our relationship with God. For even if all of our human relationships fail, we can still count on God to bring satisfaction and completion.

What a Gal!

GENESIS 2:21 *And the LORD God caused a deep sleep to fall on Adam, and he slept; and He took one of his ribs, and closed up the flesh in its place.* (NKJV)

God performs supernatural surgery and removes one of Adam's ribs. He administers his own brand of anesthesia, and the operation is painless. Because none of us lack a rib, the removal of one from Adam obviously doesn't affect the anatomy of a human body.

Marriage, like the removal of Adam's rib without anesthesia, isn't meant to be painful. But disobedience makes it seem like surgery has been performed on a wife's or a husband's heart. God wants marriage to be a blessing through a husband and a wife giving sacrificially to each other. Adam didn't have a choice whether or not to give up his rib, but he still benefited from the loss of it. God wants marriage to offer the benefit of companionship.

for your marriage

what others say

Naomi Rhode
Families need time together for proper maintenance and growth. Nothing else can substitute for daily, personal interaction.[3]

What a Rib

GENESIS 2:22 *Then the rib which the LORD God had taken from man He made into a woman, and He brought her to the man. (NKJV)*

God turned something of little value into a precious treasure: a woman. The fact that she isn't created from the dust of the earth like Adam but from his rib suggests the special bond between these male and female creations of God. They will always be linked in a special way.

what others say

David and Claudia Arp

The creative task of marriage requires a day in, day out process of hard work and mutual adjustment. In a successful, growing marriage both the husband and the wife share their lives, support one another, and continually seek to fulfill their duty to one another.[4]

Finally, Someone Like Me

GENESIS 2:23 *And Adam said:*
"This is now bone of my bones
And flesh of my flesh;
She shall be called Woman,
Because she was taken out of Man." (NKJV)

We can only imagine Adam's joy when he saw a human being like himself. He had named all sorts of animals, fish, insects, and birds, but these were not like him. He could talk to these creatures, but they couldn't talk back. No wonder he felt lonely.

But now he sees before him someone like himself: similar in body, yet she has some added features. She is similar in desires, able to talk, and shares similar emotions. He takes his own designation from God, man, and gives the word a slight twist to represent the small differences between male and this female. He continues his naming process: she's a woman!

Maybe he lets out a "wolf whistle" to accompany his saying for the first time: "Woman!" At the least, he must have given a deep sigh, for now he has experienced completeness and fulfillment. She is the suitable helper he sought.

Together We Are One

GENESIS 2:24 *Therefore a man shall leave his father and mother and be joined to his wife, and they shall become one flesh. (NKJV)*

go to

At this point, there isn't even a "family" (or in-laws!). Yet, God distinguishes an important principle for marriage. The new bride and bridegroom will leave their respective families and set up their own households.

marriage
Matthew 19:4–6;
Mark 10:6–9

physical joining
1 Corinthians 6:16

principles
Ephesians 5:31

what others say

Bill Hybels

The sexual bond that occurs between a man and a woman in the **covenant** of marriage—what the Bible refers to as "oneness"—is very much like the intimacy God desires between himself and his people....God and sex are connected. God created sex. For a man and a woman in the bond of marriage, sex is designed as a good and powerful gift.[5]

covenant
promise, contract, a binding agreement

apostle
one of Jesus' original disciples, plus Paul

As Adam and Eve consummate their marriage, they become one "flesh," their bodies joined together in intercourse. And in God's sight, they are no longer two individuals, but one unit. Since God designed marriage to be such a bonding experience, to break up a marriage in divorce creates pain and conflict. Jesus spoke about marriage when he was on earth. The **apostle** Paul also gave ideas from God about the wrong use of physical joining and other important principles.

No Clothing Budget

GENESIS 2:25 *And they were both naked, the man and his wife, and were not ashamed. (NKJV)*

Adam and Eve are not self-conscious about their bodies as we often are today. They probably don't compete with each other or think of the other person as inferior. They completely accept each other just as they are, unlike so many newly (and not-so-newly) married couples who try to change each other.

Adam and Eve felt at ease with one another without any fear of being hurt by the other. When we are self-conscious about our body or focused on our own emotional neediness, we are concentrating on ourselves and not on the needs of our spouses. God wants us to focus on loving others.

something to ponder

Here Comes the Bad Guy

shepherd
John 10:14

GENESIS 3:1 *Now the serpent was more cunning than any beast of the field which the LORD God had made. And he said to the woman, "Has God indeed said, 'You shall not eat of every tree of the garden'?" (NKJV)*

Satan appears in the form of a serpent and wants to ruin the whole thing! Satan, who represents and encourages evil, can't stand the innocence and goodness of Adam and Eve. God tries to protect Adam and Eve by commanding them to stay away from the Tree of the Knowledge of Good and Evil, but Eve, encouraged by the serpent, is lured into wrong thoughts.

The serpent's clever comment makes Eve question God's command. Why, the serpent hisses, would God put such a stupid boundary on the freedom of this first couple? How can God give such a command to Adam and Eve, after creating them to enjoy everything in this perfect and beautiful place?

what others say

Rick Warren

There are certain situations that make you more vulnerable to temptation than others. Some circumstances will cause you to stumble almost immediately, while others don't bother you much. These situations are unique to your weaknesses, and you need to identify them because Satan surely knows them![6]

Jill Briscoe

The devil knows that fear can cause us to fail to follow the Shepherd, whether it be the fear of death, or even the fear of failure. He knows that if he can frighten us from the Shepherd, he can get hold of us and gobble us up with fear. It was not until I recognized the fact that inordinate fear is a lack of trust—and a lack of trust is sin—that I was able to let Christ deal with it.[7]

Scholar Merrill Frederick Unger defines temptation as the "enticement of a person to commit sin by offering some seeming advantage." Temptation seems to offer something good, but it never does.

We are being tempted when we have thoughts that question the validity of God's Word, the Bible. God wants us to study the Bible, so its words give us a <u>source</u> of strength during temptation. The first thought of a temptation is neither right nor wrong. At that point, we have not sinned. It only becomes sin when we give in to it and cooperate with Satan's <u>schemes</u>.

source
Ephesians 6:10–17

schemes
2 Corinthians 2:11

Jesus responded
Matthew 4:4–10

understand
Hebrews 4:14–15

Here's a New Twist

> **GENESIS 3:2–3** *And the woman said to the serpent, "We may eat the fruit of the trees of the garden; but of the fruit of the tree which is in the midst of the garden, God has said, 'You shall not eat it, nor shall you touch it, lest you die.'"* (NKJV)

Eve answers the serpent accurately with God's words . . . at least to start with. Unfortunately, Eve doesn't stop with the truth. She soon adds her own interpretation to God's loving intention. Eve is able to magnify God's requirement for obedience to make God's rule seem ridiculously strict, and this interpretation gives her a reason to disobey.

what others say

Beth Moore

Who are the chief targets of Satan's ever increasing fury? We are. Why? I believe Satan has two primary motivations: (1) to exact revenge on God by wreaking havoc on his children and (2) to try to incapacitate the believer's God-given ability to overcome him.[8]

When Jesus was on earth as a man, he also faced Satan and Satan's efforts to make him sin. <u>Jesus responded</u> to temptation with complete confidence and integrity. He endured temptation so that he would forever <u>understand</u> the temptation that humans face—and know what temptation feels like.

We should learn from Eve not to answer Satan at all. We shouldn't even listen to his scheming words, and if we answer, our words should indeed be the words of God—just like Jesus responded. We behave like Eve when we conveniently forget the love behind God's rules, and view his rules as a way to prevent us from experiencing something that we think we want or need.

Oh, Nothing Is Going to Happen

go to

Father of Lies
John 8:44

grow
Colossians 2:6–7

GENESIS 3:4 *Then the serpent said to the woman, "You will not surely die. (NKJV)*

Satan, the <u>Father of Lies</u>, refutes God's words by denying they are true. His hiss must have sounded so authoritative. Satan craftily reveals that Eve will not physically die on the spot. God never meant that she would immediately die physically. He meant a spiritual and emotional death.

Satan's Temptations of Eve and of Jesus[9]

Temptation	Genesis 3	Matthew 4
Appeal to physical appetite	You may eat of any tree (3:1)	You may eat by changing stones to bread (4:3)
Appeal to personal gain	You will not die (3:4)	You will not hurt your foot (4:6)
Appeal to power or glory	You will be like God (3:5)	You will have all the world's kingdoms (4:8–9)

Satan's assurances often sound reasonable, but Satan always twists the facts to his own advantage. He is telling Eve she can sin without paying the consequences God has established. We <u>grow</u> emotionally and spiritually when we take seriously God's consequences for sin as described by God in the Bible. These warnings can motivate us to obey God, even though God prefers we obey him out of our love for him. When we see the benefits of obeying God, we become more motivated by love than by the fear of the consequences.

what others say

Kay Arthur

Not listening to God is the way sin originally entered into the world. Adam and Eve did not listen to God. They listened, instead, to Satan and believed a lie. And what they did affected all future generations.[10]

You Can Be Just Like God?

GENESIS 3:5 *For God knows that in the day you eat of it your eyes will be opened, and you will be like God, knowing good and evil." (NKJV)*

Satan channels the focus onto Eve. He makes it sound like God is withholding something that Eve should really want. In effect, Satan is telling Eve that God is withholding "godness," the opportunity to become exactly like God. Satan portrays God as selfish, as someone who doesn't want anyone else to enjoy what he enjoys. We never need to doubt God's character and his loving desires for us.

Where is Adam at this time? Is he far away, so she can't call him? Or is he nearby, but Eve doesn't want to bother him? Is Eve afraid that Adam will argue against the snake's "wisdom" and stop her from getting what she wants?

Maybe Eve feels flattered by the attention of the serpent. Maybe Adam has been working too many hours in the Garden, and Eve has been spending too much time alone. Perhaps Eve feels hurt that Adam leaves her for so long and that he isn't giving her the same devoted attention that she first received from him. She might be pouting, and that's why she doesn't join Adam in the garden work. Since she is supposed to be helping Adam, her idleness gives Satan the opportunity to tempt her into disobeying God's command.

Both Adam and Eve seem to be in the wrong place, physically, spiritually, and emotionally. Whenever you and I put ourselves somewhere other than where God wants us, we also will be tempted. Running away, not confessing sin, or not spending time with God keeps us from God and his love.

In certain religions, becoming a "god" is presented as a possibility. But such a possibility is the age-old lie of Satan, who tries to tempt us by saying we can become like God. But only God can be God.

<u>And Now Comes Sin</u>

GENESIS 3:6 *So when the woman saw that the tree was good for food, that it was pleasant to the eyes, and a tree desirable to make one wise, she took of its fruit and ate. She also gave to her husband with her, and he ate.* (NKJV)

Eve makes the mistake of looking too closely at the forbidden fruit. It looks and smells so luscious, plus it represents wisdom. As a delighted Satan slinks away, Eve reaches up, plucks the fruit from the branch, and bites into the apple. A smile crosses her face. Adam now

go to

wisdom
Proverbs 1:7

fear of God
Job 1:8

appears, notices her joy, and doesn't want to be left out. He also eats. In heaven, there is a dull thud of disappointment. The first act of sin has occurred. If Eve had resisted the temptation, she would have grown in wisdom. The Bible tells us that the real source of <u>wisdom</u> is the <u>fear of God</u>.

> what others say
>
> **Kay Arthur**
>
> Sin is disobedience. To know the right thing to do and not do it is sin.[11]

The forbidden fruit described in Genesis is generally thought of as an apple, even though the Scriptures don't actually specify the fruit. Could the fruit have come from a tree found only in the Garden of Eden? Is such a tree or similar sources of sin and temptation around today? We will be successful in resisting temptation when we can identify false statements like:

- Everyone's doing it.
- Do it your way.
- Do your own thing.
- It doesn't hurt anyone else.

Our resistance to sin will be enhanced when we question anything that makes God seem unloving or anything that gives us an opportunity to be selfish.

Adam, Look the Other Way

> **GENESIS 3:7** *Then the eyes of both of them were opened, and they knew that they were naked; and they sewed fig leaves together and made themselves coverings. (NKJV)*

Their initial delight is replaced by a gnawing awareness that everything is different in an unhappy and uncomfortable way. What a disappointment, especially when they were expecting to become more "like God." Their perspective on each other, the Garden, and life itself is no longer innocent, but self-conscious and self-absorbed. Satan's promises are always a tremendous letdown.

Instead of humbly seeing life like a baby with no fears, they now view their surroundings with distrust and tension. They have been fed a <u>lie</u> by Satan, and already they are suffering the consequences. For example, they try to cover their bodies—representing their shame and awareness of their disobedience—with fig leaves.

lie
2 Corinthians 11:14

righteous
Romans 3:10

> **what others say**
>
> **Elizabeth George**
>
> In his Word we learn how to rekindle, rebuild, and rediscover intimacy. From God we can learn how to overcome the sin and tension that is now a factor in every human relationship—even that between a married couple—as a result of "the Fall."[12]

The fig leaves are an impractical and sorry attempt to hide their shame. Even though fig trees in the Middle East have large leaves, fig leaves could never cover the awareness of sin deep in Eve's and Adam's hearts.

Adam and Eve try to cover up their bodies to hide their uncomfortable self-consciousness. The covering of fig leaves represents a human effort to be in good standing with God. But, no one can be <u>righteous</u> in their own efforts. Later, God will provide his own solution.

We too try to run away from God when we do something wrong. We try to "cover up" our mistakes by telling ourselves that whatever we did wasn't so bad. Oftentimes, we would rather deceive ourselves than come clean with God. But God already knows our sins, so it doesn't make much sense to try and hide them. The sooner we confess to him what we have done, the sooner we will have peace.

Whenever we try to get our needs met by doing something other than God's perfect will for us, we will be disappointed. Nothing satisfies completely except God. Material things or the love people offer us seems to make us feel better, but only God fills the spiritual emptiness in our hearts.

Hurry Adam, Hide over Here

GENESIS 3:8 *And they heard the sound of the LORD God walking in the garden in the cool of the day, and Adam and his wife*

go to

undeserved love
Romans 5:8

knows everything
Romans 11:33

angel of the Lord
Psalm 34:7

forgiveness
sin no longer held
against us

hid themselves from the presence of the LORD God among the trees of the garden. (NKJV)

Before eating the fruit of the forbidden tree, Adam and Eve greeted God's presence with joy and anticipation. But now they question his <u>undeserved love</u> for them and fear his wrath. They hide themselves, as if the Lord God of the universe can't see them or doesn't already know what has happened. However, God <u>knows everything</u>. God wants to forgive them, but Adam and Eve do not yet know such a thing as forgiveness is possible. They can only focus on their own changes. Our spirit shrivels when we hide from God because of sin. But our spirit expands and develops when we quickly acknowledge sin, ask for **forgiveness**, and turn away from sin.

what others say

Jan Johnson

From God's perspective, enjoying his presence is perfectly natural—not lofty or difficult. God created us out of love and stamped us with his image. He chose for himself the role of parent, relishing human companionship as pictured by his walking in the cool of the day with Adam and Eve in a young creation. God delights in us and wants us to connect with who he is.[13]

Harold Ocknega

The half-truth which Satan told was fulfilled. They now were as God. They knew the difference between right and wrong, but they also carried with them the terrible sense of guilt because they had transgressed the commandment of God.[14]

Since God is a spirit, and without human form, how do you think Adam and Eve knew God was walking through the Garden of Eden? The Old Testament frequently refers to God appearing to people as the <u>angel of the Lord</u>, and that is usually understood to refer to an appearing of Jesus in human form before he was born as a human.

We Better Tell Him

GENESIS 3:9 *Then the LORD God called to Adam and said to him, "Where are you?" (NKJV)*

By calling to Eve and Adam, God initiated contact to show them his love had nothing to do with their performance. That's grace and mercy! God knows where they are, but he wants them to take the first step toward getting reconnected with himself by Adam and Eve revealing their location and coming out of hiding. God attempts to reach out to them with a question, most likely asked in loving gentleness—instead of a statement that could sound condemning. God does everything he possibly can to prove his <u>desire</u> to forgive them—for his sake—because he wants their company.

God already knew about Eve and Adam's sin, yet he wants to reach out to them. How does he reach out? With his grace and mercy. The only <u>condition</u> for forgiveness is acknowledging it and asking for it.

desire
Isaiah 43:25
condition
1 John 1:9

omniscience
knowing all
guilt
shame for doing wrong

Over Here, God

GENESIS 3:10–11 *So he said, "I heard Your voice in the garden, and I was afraid because I was naked; and I hid myself." And He said, "Who told you that you were naked? Have you eaten from the tree of which I commanded you that you should not eat?"* (NKJV)

Somehow Adam puts aside the torturous feelings of shame and fear and responds to God's call. Forever from that moment, mankind will first shrink from God before responding to his reach of redemption. God shows his gentleness by responding with a question. Instead of stating the facts gained through his own **omniscience**, he gives Adam and Eve an opportunity to begin healing by admitting their sin.

what others say

Patsy Clairmont
Whether false or genuine, **guilt** affects our connection with others.[15]

She Did It! He Did It!

GENESIS 3:12 *Then the man said, "The woman whom You gave to be with me, she gave me of the tree, and I ate."* (NKJV)

Blaming, a common response of mankind, gets exercised here for the first time. Adam points the finger at Eve and says, "It's all her

go to

deceived
2 Corinthians 11:14

fault. If only you hadn't given her to me, I wouldn't have done the wrong thing." Adam's voice must have stressed the "you" as he attempts to put the blame squarely first on Eve and then on God.

When we "pass the buck," we are not taking responsibility for our actions. Instead, we are creating a spiritual blindness to our own accountability. If we admit our wrongdoing and "come clean," we'll experience the peace that eluded Adam and Eve.

> ### what others say
>
> ### Barbara Johnson
>
> Beware of the blame game! It can cause the sin of one person to practically destroy the entire family. The mother blames herself, and sometimes the father blames the mother—or he may decide to blame himself. Soon everyone is caught up in the "blame game," which is destructive to any family.[16]

for your marriage

We may think we can motivate our husbands to change by blaming them for the difficulties in our marriages, but more often blaming will alienate our husbands. Husbands will actually be more motivated to change when we take responsibility for ourselves.

No, Satan Did It!

GENESIS 3:13 *And the LORD God said to the woman, "What is this you have done?" The woman said, "The serpent deceived me, and I ate."* (NKJV)

God again asks a question, this time of Eve. God is trying to encourage his human creations to take responsibility. But Eve doesn't see the logic or benefit of taking such a position, so Eve blames the serpent. Everyone is criticizing everyone else. But Eve is able to identify that Satan <u>deceived</u> her. Only through being honest with God and themselves will Adam and Eve find healing.

The fastest way to end deception is to acknowledge what we did wrong. Taking the blame can seem very difficult at first, but admitting a wrong gets easier each time we do it. That's because we experience peace and a renewed relationship with God, as we can sense God's favor once again.

go to

devil's works
1 John 3:8

redemption
Galatians 4:4–5

dying on the cross
Matthew 27:50

You Had It Coming

GENESIS 3:14 *So the LORD God said to the serpent:*
"Because you have done this,
You are cursed more than all cattle,
And more than every beast of the field;
On your belly you shall go,
And you shall eat dust
All the days of your life. (NKJV)

God questions Adam and Eve to give them an opportunity to clear their consciences, but God doesn't ask the serpent anything. Instead of asking the serpent questions, God immediately gives consequences to Satan, who is in the form of the serpent. He is cursed, above all other creatures, and isn't given an opportunity to say anything.

The serpent had always slithered along the ground since its creation, but now God gives that characteristic a new meaning. It will represent Satan's part in Adam and Eve's disobedience and remind us to avoid sin initiated by temptation.

Satan, though seemingly victorious in battles on earth, will ultimately be overpowered by God's omnipotence in an enormous spiritual war. Through his Son, Jesus, the <u>devil's works</u> are destroyed, and <u>redemption</u> is made available by Jesus' <u>dying on the cross</u> for our sins.

All-Out War

GENESIS 3:15
And I will put enmity
Between you and the woman,
And between your seed and her Seed;
He shall bruise your head,
And you shall bruise His heel." (NKJV)

go to

war
Revelation 12:17

Satan's purposes
Acts 13:10

Satan is powerless
Hebrew 2:14

saved by grace
Ephesians 2:8–9

God will ultimately win the <u>war</u>, but the battles will be fierce. This enmity—spiritual war—is between Satan and the offspring of the woman (Eve). <u>Satan's purposes</u> are to destroy humans, and he will seem to have victory as he "bruises the heel" of mankind in the skirmishes, but it is not complete victory. Since the head of someone or something is its controlling force, God is saying that Satan's power will be defeated in the end times. Satan doesn't have enough power to defeat God so all he can do is temporarily cripple humanity. <u>Satan is powerless</u> because of Jesus' death.

what others say

Barbara Johnson

The foundation for all joy for Christians is that we can live as though Christ died yesterday, rose today, and is coming tomorrow. It starts here and it's for everyone, no strings, no admission fee, because we are <u>saved by grace</u> and grace alone.[18]

Pain and Submission

GENESIS 3:16 *To the woman He said,*
"I will greatly multiply your sorrow and your conception;
In pain you shall bring forth children;
Your desire shall be for your husband,
And he shall rule over you." (NKJV)

Although Eve is destined to experience pain when she gives birth, God determines her consequence for sin will be the increase of that pain. She will also be required to submit to the leadership of her husband. Because her desires for the forbidden fruit have brought her to a point of sin, she needs her husband's protection from temptation.

A woman's greatest need is security: feeling loved. A man's greatest need is significance: feeling important. Those needs correlate to God's directions for husbands and wives. Husbands are to love their wives, giving them security, and wives are to respect their husbands, making them feel significant.

God's Principles for Marriage

1. Everyone is to be subject to everyone else. (Ephesians 5:21)

2. Wives are to be subject to their own husbands and to respect them. (Ephesians 5:22 and 5:33)

3. Husbands are to be the head of their wives, just like Christ is the head of the Church. (Ephesians 5:23)

4. Husbands should love their wives and be willing to give their lives, just like Jesus loved and sacrificed for the Church. (Ephesians 5:25)

God does not put Adam as the spiritual leader in order for him to be a dictator, but a loving protector. He is supposed to motivate his wife toward spiritual excellence, loving her unconditionally, as Jesus loves the body of Christ, which is every believer in Jesus.

And Now for You, Adam

GENESIS 3:17 *Then to Adam He said, "Because you have heeded the voice of your wife, and have eaten from the tree of which I commanded you, saying, 'You shall not eat of it':*
"Cursed is the ground for your sake;
In toil you shall eat of it
All the days of your life. (NKJV)

Adam and Eve thought they would become godlike. Instead, because they believed Satan's lie, they are held in the bondage of pain in childbirth and in the curse of hard work. God rebukes Adam for not discouraging Eve from eating the fruit, and Adam receives the consequences. The same Hebrew word, issaabon, is used for the "pain" Eve will experience and the "painful" toil Adam will suffer.

In disobeying God, Adam and Eve sought to fill their needs themselves, instead of seeking God to fill their needs. Not seeking God's ways only brings us greater pain.

Back to the Dust You Shall Go

GENESIS 3:18–19
Both thorns and thistles it shall bring forth for you,
And you shall eat the herb of the field.
In the sweat of your face you shall eat bread
Till you return to the ground,

more highly
Philippians 2:3

For out of it you were taken;
For dust you are,
And to dust you shall return." (NKJV)

Adam's work will now include pain and trouble, as he must now deal with the thorns and thistles of the land. Additionally, both Adam and Eve will die and return to dust. Before Adam and Eve ate the forbidden fruit, they could have lived indefinitely. Now, their mortality is described. God created Adam and Eve for lasting fellowship with him, but now because of their sin, they will die and quickly return to dust. As a consequence of sin, Eve suffers pain in childbirth and is subject to Adam; Adam must work hard and return to the earth as dust; and Satan will be ultimately defeated.

> **what others say**
>
> **Elizabeth George**
>
> As a result of the curse God placed upon the soil after Adam and Eve rebelled against him, men would struggle to extract a living from the soil. In other words, all their lives men would have to work and labor and "sweat" so they and their families could eat and live.[19]

God gives consequences that are related to Adam and eve's sin. Adam and Eve sinned by eating the forbidden fruit; therefore, they will now work hard to earn their own food in a painful way. Eve gave her husband the forbidden fruit, so she will be in subjection to him. Satan destroyed the human race, so he will be destroyed. God's consequences are not permission for a husband to abuse or be harsh with his wife. God wants both husbands and wives to think <u>more highly</u> of the other than they do of themselves.

God Gives Consequences Related to Sin

Biblical Figure	Sin	Consequence
Adam	Ate forbidden fruit	Painful toil
Eve	Ate forbidden fruit	Painful childbirth
Satan	Destroyed human race by introducing sin	Will be destroyed

<u>New Beginnings</u>

GENESIS 3:20 *And Adam called his wife's name Eve, because she was the mother of all living. (NKJV)*

Things changed after the Fall for Adam and Eve. For the first time, Eve is named and her name means "living." This first husband and wife are able in God's power to forgive each other and themselves. In time, they begin to see their future in a positive light. Thankfully, the first divorce doesn't occur after this first marriage's short existence.

Though Adam has just been given a death sentence, he takes the promise of God's future victory over Satan seriously: "You are cursed more than all cattle, and more than every beast of the field; on your belly you shall go, and you shall eat dust all the days of your life" (Genesis 3:14 NKJV). Adam focuses on the positives of life: the future birth of their children. Adam and Eve's children will never enter the Garden of Eden. They will be deprived of a perfect world because of their parents' sin. Likewise, when we disobey God, the consequences of our bad behavior can cause trouble for others, not just ourselves.

go to

redemption of sins
Isaiah 53:4–6

> **what others say**
>
> **Marjorie L. Kimbrough**
>
> Her former name was woman, taken out of man. Her new name is Eve, meaning life-giving. She will give life, but she will do so in pain. This is a part of her punishment for disobedience.[20]

Get Rid of Those Fig Leaves

GENESIS 3:21 *Also for Adam and his wife the LORD God made tunics of skin, and clothed them. (NKJV)*

Adam and Eve had tried to hide their shame with fig leaves, but God provides garments of skin. God kills an animal to clothe Eve and Adam, and this slaying of an animal gives a peek into Jesus' future sacrifice for the <u>redemption of sins</u>. God's ways are always better than man's feeble efforts to provide for his own needs.

> **what others say**
>
> **Jill Briscoe**
>
> It is hard to remember, when you're down physically and have blown it spiritually; when you are wiped out emotionally and feel ostracized socially, that failure is never final. Christians aren't made—they are in the making![21]

Banished!

Tree of Life
Revelation 22:2

cherubim
angels

GENESIS 3:22–23 *Then the LORD God said, "Behold, the man has become like one of Us, to know good and evil. And now, lest he put out his hand and take also of the tree of life, and eat, and live forever"—therefore the LORD God sent him out of the garden of Eden to till the ground from which he was taken. (NKJV)*

Now that Adam and Eve have eaten from the Tree of Knowledge of Good and Evil, they cannot eat from the other tree, the Tree of Life. They can no longer live forever, because God has determined that someday they will die. Adam and Eve must leave their idyllic Garden and struggle to make a living in a much more difficult place.

Gone Forever

GENESIS 3:24 *So He drove out the man; and He placed **cherubim** at the east of the garden of Eden, and a flaming sword which turned every way, to guard the way to the tree of life. (NKJV)*

God prevents Adam and Eve from ever returning to the perfect world of the Garden of Eden by placing angels to guard the entrance of the Garden. Adam and Eve must leave and never return. Their hearts must be breaking as they go. But when the first child is born, Eve honors God by exclaiming after Cain's birth, "I have acquired a man from the LORD" (Genesis 4:1 NKJV). Sadly, in time, they will experience more pain and heartbreak when their first son Cain kills their second son Abel.

The Process of Temptation: From reading Genesis 3 and learning about Eve's experience, we are alerted to how temptation leads to sin. By becoming aware of this process and watchful for temptation's presence in our lives, we can fight against temptation and sin. To overcome temptation, we must remember:

1. Temptation starts with questioning God's command. (Genesis 3:1)

2. Temptation works to change God's message. (Genesis 3:2–3)

3. Temptation means Satan is challenging God's wisdom while we are putting our focus on ourselves, not God. (Genesis 3:4–5)

4. Sin is conceived when we are deceived into believing temptation's deceptive "positives." (Genesis 3:6)

5. In our shame, we try to cover up our sin. (Genesis 3:7–11)

6. We try to shift blame and criticize others. (Genesis 3:12–13)

7. God gives consequences for disobedience. (Genesis 3:14–19, 22–24)

8. But God offers hope in the <u>covenant of Jesus</u>. (Genesis 3:15, 21)

covenant of Jesus
Hebrews 9:15

Chapter Wrap-Up

- Through the forbidden fruit of the Garden of Eden, God provided an opportunity for Adam and Eve to express their love for God by obeying his command. (Genesis 2:15–17)

- The animals could not meet Adam's needs, so God created a woman from Adam's rib. (Genesis 2:22)

- God designed men and women to bond together physically, emotionally, and spiritually in marriage. (Genesis 2:23–25)

- The serpent, representing Satan, tempted Eve by questioning God's command and suggesting God wanted to withhold something good from her. (Genesis 3:1–5)

- First Eve disobeyed God's command; then Adam disobeyed. Adam and Eve were so fooled by the fruit's attractiveness and by the thought of becoming like God that they thought about themselves, not God. (Genesis 3:6)

- After they had eaten of the forbidden fruit of the Tree of the Knowledge of Good and Evil, they lost their innocence and tried to hide their nakedness with fig leaves. (Genesis 3:7)

- Although God knew what had happened, he came to the Garden and asked Eve and Adam about their clothing to give them an opportunity to confess their sin. Instead of confessing, they blamed each other and the serpent. (Genesis 3:8–13)

- All three (Adam, Eve, and the serpent) were given consequences for the wrong choices they made. But God also symbolically referred to his Son Jesus' coming in the future to provide a permanent sacrifice for sin. (Genesis 3:14–19)

Study Questions

1. What instructions did God give Adam about the trees in the Garden?

2. Who named Eve, and why was that name chosen?

3. How did the serpent begin his temptation of Eve?

4. What three things were attractive to Eve about the forbidden fruit?

5. What consequences did God give Eve, Adam, and the serpent?

Chapter 2 Sarah

Chapter Highlights:
- God's Promise
- A Half-Truth
- Another Promise
- A Plan of Self-Effort
- Isaac's Promised Birth

Let's Get Started

Every woman who wants to draw closer to God will face the challenge of trusting him. The more she gets to know him, the more the Holy Spirit beckons her to let him be in charge of her life. In this second chapter, we'll look at the example of Sarai, who eventually became Sarah. The life of this biblical matriarch speaks to us today about believing and following God's directions. She had many winsome attributes and in the New Testament, she is described in a positive light. She also represents the truth that no woman is perfect. Women who are seeking to draw closer to God can learn from Sarai's strengths and weaknesses. Just as the Holy Spirit worked within Sarai, the Holy Spirit works within us for our transformation.

Holy Spirit
2 Corinthians 3:18

she is described
Hebrews 11:11

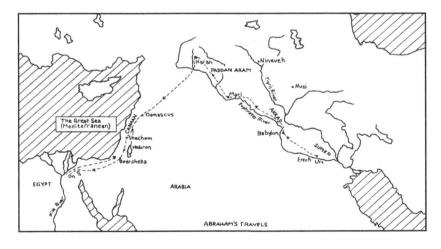

Illustration #2
Sarah's Journey—Abraham and Sarah traveled from Ur of the Chaldeans, through Haran and Egypt, to Canaan.

Get Up and Leave Your Home

GENESIS 11:27–32 *This is the genealogy of Terah: Terah begot Abram, Nahor, and Haran. Haran begot Lot. And Haran died before his father Terah in his native land, in Ur of the Chaldeans. Then Abram and Nahor took wives: the name of Abram's wife was Sarai, and the name of Nahor's wife, Milcah, the daughter of Haran the father of Milcah and the father of Iscah. But Sarai was barren; she had no child.*

Lot
Genesis 12:5

Terah
Abram's father

Haran
brother of Abram

Mesopotamia
present-day Iraq

And Terah took his son Abram and his grandson <u>Lot</u>, the son of Haran, and his daughter-in-law Sarai, his son Abram's wife, and they went out with them from Ur of the Chaldeans to go to the land of Canaan; and they came to Haran and dwelt there. So the days of Terah were two hundred and five years, and Terah died in Haran. (NKJV)

Sarai, whose name is later changed to Sarah, is first mentioned in Scripture as the wife of Abram, whose name is later changed to Abraham. Most significantly, Sarai is identified as being unable to conceive a child. In that culture, barrenness is a condition attributed to being cursed by the gods. Later it is revealed that Sarai is related to Abram. Some Bible experts believe she is his half-sister (the daughter of Abram's father **Terah** but not his mother), whereas some believe she may be his niece (the daughter of **Haran**). Sarai and Abram must have been married for a reasonable period of time before they moved out of Ur of the Chaldeans (see Illustration #2), because it becomes apparent she could not conceive.

Ur of the Chaldeans is an ancient, thriving commercial city located about 125 miles from the present mouth of the Euphrates River. The inhabitants used to worship the moon god, "Sin." Archaeologists have discovered glorious treasures from its buried ruins, some dating back to 3000 BC. Haran, an important city in ancient **Mesopotamia**, is located about 550 miles northeast of Ur. In ancient times, it was a principal center for the worship of Sin. Even today, it exists as a small Arabian village.

In ancient times, it was not unusual or immoral for relatives to marry each other, so long as those with the same mothers did not marry. Therefore, since Abram and Sarai had the same father but not the same mother, they were allowed to marry.

Here I Am, Abram

Genesis 12:1-9

the big picture

God appears to Abram and directs him to leave the country where he is living and go where God directs. God doesn't tell him exactly where to go. Instead, he is to follow God's directions along the way. God gives him some wonderful blessings and promises: he will be a great nation, and many blessings will come through his descendants. Abram responds immediately and leaves with his wife Sarai and his nephew, Lot, along with all his many possessions and herds.

Terah's Family

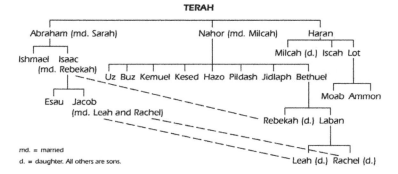

md. = married
d. = daughter. All others are sons.

As far as we know from the text, this is the first time God appears to Abram, but it will not be the last. According to Scripture, God appears to Abram seven times.

God's Appearances to Abram

Bible Passage	Circumstances	Promise or Challenge
Genesis 12:1–3	God's call for Abram to leave his home in Ur of the Chaldeans	I will make you a great nation. You will have blessings. I will make your name great. You will be a blessing to others. Those who bless you will be blessed and those who curse you will be cursed. All the families of the earth will be blessed through you.
Genesis 12:7	Abram arrives in Canaan	I will give this land to your offspring
Genesis 13:14–15	After Lot separates from Abram	This land will be yours.
Genesis 15:1–5	After Abram refuses reward from Melchizedek	You will have a child who is a blood heir. Your descendants will be as numerous as the stars in the sky.
Genesis 17:1–5	When Abram is 99 years old	You will walk blameless. God establishes his covenant with Abram and promises to multiply him into many nations. Abram becomes Abraham.
Genesis 18:1–33	At oaks of Mamre	Three messengers from God promise that Sarah will give birth to a child a year later. Abraham also is given an opportunity to pray for any righteous people at Sodom.
Genesis 22:1–12	Testing of Abraham's dedication	God asks Abraham to sacrifice his son, Isaac, but an angel intervenes, stopping the sacrifice.

go to

great nation
Numbers 2:32

covenant
Genesis 15:18

ancestral line
Luke 3:23–38

Abrahamic Blessing
Genesis 25:5;
27:27–29

theophany
God in human form

Abrahamic Blessing
specific promises
God made to
(Abraham) Abram.

In Bible language, this sort of personal appearance is called a **theophany**, which means God appears in a human, visible form. Below are some examples of Biblical Theophanies, which was God's way of revealing himself early in history.

Biblical Theophanies

Theophany	Scripture
God meets with Adam and Eve in the Garden of Eden.	Genesis 3:8–24
God speaks to Cain, warning him of possible sin.	Genesis 4:6–7
God appears to Abraham in the form of three men (possibly Jesus and two angels) to announce the destruction of Sodom.	Genesis 18:1–33
God calls to Hagar out of heaven in the voice of the "Angel of God" usually attributed to Jesus.	Genesis 21:17–18
God appears in a dream to Jacob.	Genesis 28:12–15
God appears to Jacob and wrestles with him.	Genesis 32:24–29

In God's first theophany with Abram, he doesn't tell Abram where to go—just to go. But in a step of faith, which is believing without evidence, Abram rounds up at least some of his family, including Sarai, and his belongings, and then leaves for unknown lands. Evidently, God directs him step by step because Abram doesn't have a map and doesn't know where he will be led. But what Abram counts on is the fact that God has promised him he will become a great nation. In those days, this covenant was very valuable and important because children were greatly valued to continue the ancestral line.

God also promises that he and his future family will bring great blessings to everyone on the earth. That's a tremendous promise from the living God. In Bible language, this promise of great blessings is called the "**Abrahamic Blessing**," because Abraham will later bestow the promise of blessings to his son, Isaac. Then Isaac will pass it along to his son, Jacob. Thus, it will get passed down from generation to generation, from father to eldest son.

what others say

Stormie Omartian

God has gold nuggets and diamonds everywhere in his Word, but we must dig them out. And, just like precious gems and metals when they are first pulled from the ground, the treasures of God's Word need to be polished and refined in us in order to have the brilliance they are capable of revealing.[1]

We cannot fully appreciate the step of faith that Abram and Sarai took without understanding that the religion of their culture was one of trusting in many gods—gods whom individuals tried to manipulate into giving them prosperity. Rejecting all of these gods, Abram and Sarai choose to believe in the one God, Jehovah. People of Abram's time worshiped the gods associated with their particular geographical area, so Abram takes a tremendous step of faith in believing in this "new" God. God had revealed himself to Abram as a God who transcends boundary lines and knows the whole earth. Abram is forced to believe that Jehovah is everywhere he goes. Sarai, the dutiful wife, agrees to follow her husband's lead. They are headed for a strange, distant land.

go to

Ishmael
Genesis 16:15

pharaoh
Egyptian king

Although Sarai and Abram cannot know the full consequences of the blessings to which God refers, we know now that Jesus would be among the ancestral line of Abram and would bring the greatest blessings to all: the gift of forgiveness of sins and renewed friendship with God for those who believe. When each of us believes in the God of the Bible, we take the same tremendous step of faith that Abram and Sarai did. Jesus is the ultimate blessing God promised.

Abram and Sarai had to trust God enough to leave everything they knew and were comfortable with—friends, culture, locale, family. God must have revealed himself in a special way, so that they could distinguish him from the common moon-god, "Sin." Because of Abram's step of faith, he is known and honored as a spiritual "father" by Christians, Jews, and Moslems. Moslems are people who practice the religion Islam, started by Muhammad, who was a descendant of Ishmael, in AD 570. Furthermore, Moslems consider Sarai their spiritual "mother."

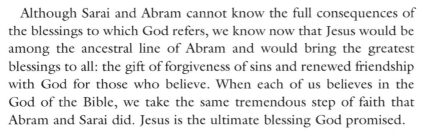

the big picture

Genesis 12:10-20

Abram lies about Sarai and says she is his sister instead of his wife, which is a half-truth. He lies because he is afraid that someone like the **pharaoh** will see Sarai's beauty, kill Abram, and take Sarai as a wife. Pharaoh does see her beauty and takes her into his harem but releases her after he learns she is really Abram's wife.

<u>Not My Wife</u>

Although Abram has recently taken a huge step of faith, faith retreats and fear invades when his life is potentially threatened.

go to

emulate
1 Peter 3:1–6

Abram asks Sarai to tell the Egyptians that she is his sister and not to mention that she is also his wife. Actually, as Abram mentions in Genesis 20:12, Sarai is indeed his sister—the daughter of his father but not of his mother. However, his actions are not of faith because he is not trusting God for his safety.

When Sarai and Abram arrive in Egypt to visit Pharaoh (the title of their king), Sarai is taken into his harem, and Abram is treated well because of it. But God brings judgment upon Pharaoh's household, and Pharaoh somehow learns that Sarai is actually Abram's wife. As a result, Abram must confess his fear. Sarai is rescued from the harem and leaves with Abram.

God does not want wives to cooperate with a husband's illegal or immoral activities in the name of submission. Just as a Christian is told to obey God even at the cost of disobeying the government, wives should not participate in evil even when commanded by a husband. But as Sarai's experience proves, God can rescue the obedient wife if God calls her to obey her husband.

> ## what others say
>
> ### Edith Deen
>
> As Sarah and Abraham journeyed through strange and perilous country, Abraham passed his wife off as his sister, which was a half-truth. Possibly it was because he knew that these ancient monarchs would employ any means, however cruel and violent, to get the radiantly beautiful Sarah into their harems.[2]

Sarai must have been very beautiful for Abram to think the Egyptians would want to kill him and let her live. A wife's beauty is often a source of pride for her husband, but in this case, Sarai's beauty was a source of major anxiety for her husband.

apply it

As the dutiful wife, Sarai goes along with Abram's scheme when his life is potentially threatened. In the New Testament Sarai is lauded by one of Jesus' disciples, Peter, as an obedient wife whom all Christian wives should <u>emulate</u>. Whether Peter is specifically referring to this situation we do not know, but overall, Sarai has an obedient spirit toward her husband. God wants all wives to have the same spirit as they work together with their husbands to make decisions.

Believe Me! You Will Have Children

go to

considered
Romans 4:5

promised
2 Peter 1:4

waiting
2 Peter 3:8–9

> ### Genesis 15:1–21
>
> **the big picture**
>
> In a fourth appearance, God speaks to Abram in a vision and reaffirms his promise that Abram will indeed have children. To seal his promise, he makes a covenant with Abram by accepting Abram's animal sacrifice.

God has already appeared to Abram three times. This time God tells him, "Do not be afraid, Abram. I am your shield, your exceedingly great reward" (Genesis 15:1 nkjv). As soon as God speaks to him Abram brings up the subject that is likely to have troubled Abram a great deal: why hasn't God made good on his promise of a child? Abram indicates that he has more or less given up on the promise—that his faithful servant, Eliezer, will become the heir. God tells him no and again tells Abram that his descendants will be as numerous as the stars. In an act of faith that is forever credited to Abram, Abram believes God. Abram "believed in the Lord, and He accounted it to him for righteousness" (Genesis 15:6 nkjv).

Abram is credited with believing God and therefore is righteous in God's eyes. You and I will be <u>considered</u> the same if we believe in God and in his provision for our deliverance from sin through his Son Jesus' death on the cross.

I'll Do It My Way

> **GENESIS 16:1–4** *Now Sarai, Abram's wife, had borne him no children. And she had an Egyptian maidservant whose name was Hagar. So Sarai said to Abram, "See now, the LORD has restrained me from bearing children. Please, go in to my maid; perhaps I shall obtain children by her." And Abram heeded the voice of Sarai. Then Sarai, Abram's wife, took Hagar her maid, the Egyptian, and gave her to her husband Abram to be his wife, after Abram had dwelt ten years in the land of Canaan. So he went in to Hagar, and she conceived. And when she saw that she had conceived, her mistress became despised in her eyes. (NKJV)*

When next we find Sarai in the Genesis account, 10 years have passed. God has <u>promised</u> Sarai and Abram a child, but they are still <u>waiting</u>. From a human perspective, based on the customs of the day,

go to

our own human
understanding
Proverbs 3:5–6

it is entirely reasonable for Sarai to suggest that her maid, Hagar, bear the promised child. In that society, a barren wife often offered her servant as a substitute and as a result, any child born of the union became the heir. Abram follows Sarai's advice and Hagar conceives a child. Hagar immediately looks down on her mistress, considering herself more important than Sarai, because she carries the master's child.

what others say

Stormie Omartian

Even if the dreams you have in your heart are from God, you will still have to surrender them. That's because God wants you clinging to *him* and not to your dreams. He doesn't want you trying to make them happen. He wants you to trust *him*, and *he'll* make them happen.[3]

It may be that Sarai's impatience is fueled by her pride. No longer able to stand the stigma of being barren, she devises a plan to make the disgrace disappear. Little does she know that her own efforts will only fuel bitter relationships and heartache. Ishmael, the child born to Hagar, becomes the father of those we know today as the Arabs. Over the centuries, the Arabs have often been enemies of the Jews (Isaac's descendants), and they have fought over possession of the same land in the Middle East.

Sarai's earthly way of thinking is not a plan based in faith. God wants to fulfill his promise his own unique way. We want to use <u>our own human understanding</u> to try to bring God's plan into fulfillment and then call it "success." But that is not God's definition of success. He wants us to depend on him, even when it means waiting on him for what seems a long time. When we take matters into our own hands, we invite bitter-tasting consequences.

It's All Her Fault

GENESIS 16:5–6 *Then Sarai said to Abram, "My wrong be upon you! I gave my maid into your embrace; and when she saw that she had conceived, I became despised in her eyes. The LORD judge between you and me."*

So Abram said to Sarai, "Indeed your maid is in your hand; do to her as you please." And when Sarai dealt harshly with her, she fled from her presence. (NKJV)

Although Sarai thinks up the idea of using Hagar as her substitute, she quickly ends up blaming Abram for the resulting disaster. She even calls upon God's judgment to make her point. Abram, not knowing how to handle the awful turn of events, wipes his hands of the whole mess and gives Sarai his permission to do whatever she wants. Her own grief and pride cause her to mistreat Hagar, who runs away.

admitting sin
1 John 1:9

healing
Psalm 51:10–12

> ### what others say
>
> **Patsy Clairmont**
>
> As I study Sarah's life, I see her triumphant faith and her dismal failures, which help me accept my own inconsistencies. I take heart at her courage, her charity, and her long-awaited answered prayers.[4]

When we aren't honest enough with ourselves to identify our responsibility in wrong choices, it's easy to begin blaming others. <u>Admitting sin</u> helps us to open our eyes to the truth and be accountable for our part of any error. God honors that and brings <u>healing</u>.

He Cares for All

> ### the big picture
>
> **Genesis 16:7–16**
>
> Hagar runs out into the wilderness and God speaks to her there. He tells her to return to Sarai and submit to her authority. But he also promises that she will give birth to a son, whom she should name Ishmael.

God, in his faithfulness, meets Hagar after she runs away. This is another example of a theophany—a personal appearance by God. God is no respecter of persons. He is concerned about a humble servant girl, just like the future parents of his chosen people. He comforts Hagar in her distress and promises to take care of her child. In obedience to God's instructions, Hagar returns to Sarai and eventually gives birth to Ishmael. God is faithful to respond to any who call upon him and seek him.

That Hagar is willing to return to more possible abuse in Sarai's home is quite remarkable. Yet directly speaking with God had an effect on her, as it certainly would anyone. When any one of us truly has an encounter with God, we will also have courage to do what we might not otherwise.

Do You Hear Me Now? You Will Have Children

the big picture

Genesis 17:1–27

In God's fifth appearance when Abram is ninety-nine years old, God changes Abram's and Sarai's names to represent the work he's doing in their lives. He also commands them to have all of the males in their household circumcised. And for the fourth time, God affirms his promise that a child will be born to Abraham and Sarah.

Even after Sarai and Abram have tried to fulfill God's plan in their own method and timing, God still intends to fulfill his own promise. Years pass, and he again reveals himself to Abram and sets up a covenant with him, instructing him about circumcision, which is the ceremony of cutting off a male's foreskin. God also changes Abram's name to Abraham, and Sarai's name to Sarah. Furthermore, he states in a firm way that Sarah will indeed bear a child one year later. Abraham is surprised and laughs with joy, amazed that his body, at one hundred years old, and Sarah's, at ninety, can create a child. God tells Abraham that the child shall be called Isaac, which means "he laughs." In blessed irony, the child will forever be a reminder that Abraham laughed at God's miraculous plan. Later, Sarah would laugh too, yet she laughs in doubt, not in amazement as Abraham did.

Sodom and Gomorrah
Genesis 13:10; 14:2

"Abram" means "exalted father," referring to his royal lineage. "Abraham" sounds similar to a Hebrew word that means "father of a multitude" or "father of many nations." "Sarai" and "Sarah" both mean "princess," but "Sarah" has a further meaning—"one whose seed would produce kings." The root idea of the name Sarah means "to rule."

Which Do You Want First: The Good News or the Bad News?

the big picture

Genesis 18:1-8

In a sixth appearance, three angels from God arrive at Abraham's tent. True to oriental custom, Abraham prepares a meal for them. Everything seems happy, but Abraham is about to get some rather unfortunate news.

God sends three angels (one is believed by many Bible experts to be the preincarnate Jesus) to communicate his plan for the destruction of <u>Sodom and Gomorrah</u>, a nearby city where Abraham's nephew, Lot, resides. But first, the Lord wants again to reiterate, primarily for Sarah's benefit, his intention of bringing Isaac into the world within a year.

what others say

Marie Chapian

I have had to learn that God doesn't have a designated day when he answers our requests. It's a mistaken notion that God should jump the instant we call. Some women I've spoken to have had the idea that God was like a lover or a kindly old soul who should come to our rescue anytime we are in distress.[7]

one hundred years old
Romans 4:19

God is faithful to assure us that he won't be late with his promises, even if he doesn't always send angels like he did with Sarah and Abraham. Although God does respond to our prayers, his ultimate plans will not be blocked by human mistrust or disobedience. He is powerful enough to do whatever he wishes.

I Can't Believe This

GENESIS 18:9–15 *Then they said to him, "Where is Sarah your wife?" So he said, "Here, in the tent."*

And He said, "I will certainly return to you according to the time of life, and behold, Sarah your wife shall have a son." (Sarah was listening in the tent door which was behind him.) Now Abraham and Sarah were old, well advanced in age; and Sarah had passed the age of childbearing. Therefore Sarah laughed within herself, saying, "After I have grown old, shall I have pleasure, my lord being old also?"

And the LORD said to Abraham, "Why did Sarah laugh, saying, 'Shall I surely bear a child, since I am old?' Is anything too hard for the LORD? At the appointed time I will return to you, according to the time of life, and Sarah shall have a son."

But Sarah denied it, saying, "I did not laugh," for she was afraid. And He said, "No, but you did laugh!" (NKJV)

When years before God appeared to Abraham as described in Genesis 17, Sarah was probably not a part of the interaction. We don't know whether Abraham told her about their new names and the circumcision covenant, but if he did, Sarah must have still been disbelieving God's great plan. In order to bring Sarah fully into the plan, the Lord converses with Abraham, knowing that Sarah is listening closely nearby. When God again states his promise to bring the child in a year, Sarah laughs. It's a laugh of doubt, not delight. Abraham is now fully <u>one hundred years old</u> and Sarah is ninety, completely past the usual physical ability to conceive. When confronted about her lack of faith, she denies it. God merely states the truth: she did indeed laugh.

Maybe Abraham has not told Sarah about the heavenly visitors' message of the coming pregnancy in Genesis 17, because he knows he wouldn't be able to convince her of something so incredible. Or maybe he did tell her and she still isn't convinced. Regardless, God thinks it necessary to visit them personally.

go to

mercy
Exodus 33:19

faithfulness
Exodus 34:6

motives
Proverbs 21:2

look on the heart
1 Samuel 16:7

accept
Romans 14:1

experience
Genesis 12:10–20

> ### what others say
>
> **Marie Chapian**
>
> Our moments of testing are occasions to stretch our faith and confidence in God's love.[8]
>
> **Anne Graham Lotz**
>
> Just as storms make it possible for eagles to soar, so suffering makes it possible for you and me to attain the highest pinnacles in the Christian life. Suffering develops our faith.[9]

God has told Sarah all along what he intends to do, but because he hasn't done it within her expectations, she laughs in unbelief. Her trust in God's power is at its lowest point. Yet God, in his <u>mercy</u> and <u>faithfulness</u>, intends to fulfill his plan regardless of her doubt. Although God does respond to our prayers, his ultimate plans will not be blocked by human mistrust or disobedience. He is powerful enough to do whatever he wishes.

Abraham laughs and so does Sarah, but their motives for laughing are not the same. Each of us can respond in the same way to God's workings, but the meaning behind our response may be different. God knows our heart and judges us not by our outward reaction but by our <u>motives</u>. God can <u>look on the heart</u>, but we humans can't judge a person's heart. It's up to God to evaluate a person's actions and motives. We must be careful to seek God's plan before confronting someone else. God may want us to <u>accept</u> the one who is weak in faith.

apply it

Here We Go Again!

> ### the big picture
>
> **Genesis 20:1–18**
>
> Abraham and Sarah travel to Gerar and there they again tell a half truth to the king of that area. It's the same half-truth as before: that Sarah isn't Abraham's wife but his sister. God reveals the truth to the king in a dream.

When we again come to Sarah in the Genesis account, Abraham is again tested about trusting God for his own safety. Unfortunately, he hasn't learned the lesson from his previous <u>experience</u> in Egypt.

Abimelech
Genesis 20:1–18

When another king, <u>Abimelech</u>, wants to make beautiful Sarah a part of his harem, Sarah must again cooperate with Abraham's plan of telling the half-truth about her being his sister. Now more than ever before, Abraham and Sarah's involvement in this lie threatens God's plan for the conception of the promised child, Isaac. Sarah is at the risk of having sexual relations with King Abimelech, but God steps in and again rescues her. The miraculous conception of Isaac is safeguarded again.

Finally, the Promised Child

> GENESIS 21:1–7 *And the LORD visited Sarah as He had said, and the LORD did for Sarah as He had spoken. For Sarah conceived and bore Abraham a son in his old age, at the set time of which God had spoken to him. And Abraham called the name of his son who was born to him—whom Sarah bore to him— Isaac. Then Abraham circumcised his son Isaac when he was eight days old, as God had commanded him. Now Abraham was one hundred years old when his son Isaac was born to him. And Sarah said, "God has made me laugh, and all who hear will laugh with me." She also said, "Who would have said to Abraham that Sarah would nurse children? For I have borne him a son in his old age." (NKJV)*

What God has said and promised all along is now fulfilled! After many years of waiting and learning to believe God, Sarah becomes pregnant and gives birth to Isaac. What laughter of faith overwhelms Sarah's heart and life. The long-awaited baby fills her home with joy and emotional fulfillment—exactly at the time God had intended all along. The delay makes the possibility even more impossible and when the miracle happens in God's power, no one can deny that God's incredible abilities are the cause.

what others say

Max Lucado

God does that for the faithful. Just when the womb gets too old for babies, [Sarah] gets pregnant.[10]

Barbara Johnson

Christians have the assurance that as long as Jesus is with them, they are more than conquerors. Jesus is our hope. He is God's gift of grace to us. Whenever we say that something is hopeless, we are slamming the door in the face of God.[11]

When God delays the fulfillment of a promise or a desire in your life, his power is revealed all the more as his plan is finally accomplished. Everyone acknowledges that you could not have made it happen and as a result, God receives the <u>glory</u> and praise. If we give up on trusting God, we're saying God doesn't have enough power.

Sarah's at It Again

> GENESIS 21:8–13 *So the child grew and was weaned. And Abraham made a great feast on the same day that Isaac was weaned.*
>
> *And Sarah saw the son of Hagar the Egyptian, whom she had borne to Abraham, scoffing. Therefore she said to Abraham, "Cast out this bondwoman and her son; for the son of this bondwoman shall not be heir with my son, namely with Isaac."*
>
> *And the matter was very displeasing in Abraham's sight because of his son.*
>
> *But God said to Abraham, "Do not let it be displeasing in your sight because of the lad or because of your bondwoman. Whatever Sarah has said to you, listen to her voice; for in Isaac your seed shall be called. Yet I will also make a nation of the son of the bondwoman, because he is your seed." (NKJV)*

glory
Philippians 4:20

apostle Paul
Galatians 4:21–31

Sarah's joy is diminished as she catches Ishmael scoffing at the new son. At the celebration of Isaac's weaning (usually around three years of age), the older son makes fun of the toddler. Ishmael was most likely around sixteen or seventeen years of age at this time. His behavior made Sarah furious. She may be jealous of Ishmael's status within the family, or maybe she fears the teenager may inherit what truly belongs to Isaac. She demands that Abraham cast Hagar and her son out of the family. Though this demand distresses Abraham immensely—for Ishmael had also been a child of his old age—God assures him Ishmael will be taken care of.

The <u>apostle Paul</u> identifies Hagar as a demonstration of fleshly efforts to fulfill God's plan. But Sarah represents the "free woman," a demonstration of living by faith in God's power and depending on him to fulfill his plan.

Sarah's desire to protect her son is certainly a natural one, but the way she goes about it shows both a lack of faith in God's plan and a lack of trust in Abraham's love for his new son, the rightful heir. But God chooses to use her faithless reaction for his own purposes, as we

go to

example
Hebrews 11:11

shall see. We mothers won't be able to protect our children in every instance, but God will work through their neediness to draw them to himself.

the big picture

Genesis 21:14–22:24

Abraham obeys God about casting Hagar and Ishmael out of his home. But then God challenges him even more by commanding him to sacrifice the life of the promised child, Isaac. He also obeys God in that, even though it seems to make no sense.

Although Sarah often fails to trust God, she is an <u>example</u> of faith. How like God's mercy and grace to forgive our moments of failure and remember our moments of belief. When you feel like your faith is small, remember Sarah. Through Christ, God remembers your faith and forgives and forgets your moments of distrust.

Did I Hear You Right, God?

In obedience to God, Abraham casts Ishmael and Hagar out of his home, and God keeps his promise to provide for this son who is a result of a plan gone bad. Then years later, God challenges Abraham to take the promised child, Isaac, and sacrifice him, saying, "Take now your son, your only son Isaac, whom you love, and go to the land of Moriah, and offer him there as a burnt offering on one of the mountains of which I shall tell you" (Genesis 22:2 NKJV). Abraham must be wondering if he is hearing God correctly. After all, this is the child he and Sarah had waited for and whom God had promised. Yet, Abraham obeys without question and takes Isaac to the mountain. Just as Abraham is about to kill him on an altar with a knife, God tells him to stop. Abraham and Isaac return in good health, for God is only testing the doting father. Needless to say, Abraham passes the test.

We are not told whether Sarah knows about God's challenge, but if she does, she must have wondered about her husband's sanity in hearing such a thing from God. "He has given us this child, how can he be asking for Isaac's death?" she may have asked. If she did know about the sacrifice, we can only imagine the relief in Sarah's heart when her husband and son return.

buries
Genesis 23:19

Carol Kent

Abraham knew the purpose of the trip was to worship his God by sacrificing his son, and he was so enthusiastic about following God's instructions, he started the trip early in the morning. If I had been in that situation, I would have left at the latest possible time, hoping God would tell me he changed his mind and we could cancel the trip.[12]

Lysa TerKeurst

Abraham walked away having experienced God in a way few ever do. God wants to know if we're willing to give up what we love to him who loves us more. He desires for us to open our fists and trust him with absolutely everything.[13]

A Ripe Old Age

GENESIS 23:1–2 *Sarah lived one hundred and twenty-seven years; these were the years of the life of Sarah. So Sarah died in Kirjath Arba (that is, Hebron) in the land of Canaan, and Abraham came to mourn for Sarah and to weep for her. (NKJV)*

At age 127, Sarah dies. Abraham <u>buries</u> her in Machpelah, which is Hebron (see Illustration #2) in the land of Canaan. Though beautiful for many years and able to bear a son in her old age, her life is concluded before Abraham's as a part of God's sovereign plan. Abraham carefully chooses a burial ground that will be remembered. Normally, he would have returned to his ancestor's home for her burial, but instead, he purchases land for her grave in the area that God called him to inhabit, though he does not own any of it. He knows by faith that he will also be buried there, having been promised by God that this present ground would one day be owned by his descendants. Of course, today we know that land as Israel.

Sometimes when God does great things for us, like God did in providing a miraculous child, we begin to concentrate more on his blessings than on him. God wants us to worship him because he's God, not because of what he does for us. Our worship of God must focus on who he is, while our thanksgiving can concentrate on what he does for us.

Abraham grieves deeply for the beloved wife with whom he has experienced so many heartaches and joys of life. Their marriage has survived many a crisis that would have crumbled other relationships. Their love endured through the test of time and challenge.

Chapter Wrap-Up

- God promises Abraham and Sarah that they will be the ancestors of a great nation through whom all the people of the earth will be blessed. (Genesis 12:1–3)

- When Abraham is afraid that Sarah's great beauty will cause his death, he tells her to say they are brother and sister. This is a half-truth because while they do have the same father, they have a different mother. (Genesis 12:10–20)

- God promises that even though Sarah is barren, Abraham will indeed have a child through Sarah. (Genesis 15:1–6)

- Because God delays his provision of a child for Abraham and Sarah, Sarah's maidservant, Hagar, is given to Abraham as a substitute. Hagar gives birth to Ishmael, Abraham's son, even though this is not God's plan. (Genesis 16:1–16)

- In keeping with God's long-awaited promise, Isaac is finally born when Abraham is 100 and Sarah is 90. (Genesis 21:1–5)

Study Questions

1. What does God first communicate to Abraham and Sarah?

2. Why does Abraham want Sarah to say they are siblings instead of spouses?

3. Who instigates the plan to have a child through Hagar?

4. When Sarah denies laughing about God's promise of a child, what does God say about his own power?

5. How old are Abraham and Sarah when their son Isaac is born?

Chapter 3 Rebekah

Chapter Highlights:
- On a Mission of Love
- God's Prediction for the Future
- The Twins Are Born
- Favoritism and a Sold Birthright

Let's Get Started

The Bible shows us the weaknesses of our spiritual ancestors to give us clear examples of what we should and should not do. Rebekah, one of our biblical matriarchs, provides us with both. She wrongly played favorites with her children and tried to secure God's plan through manipulation. As if God couldn't be trusted to fulfill his sovereign plan, she arranged things to make sure.

But Rebekah also offers many positive examples, especially the kindness and the energy she shows as an innocent young woman. She, for example, fetches water for a stranger and for the stranger's ten camels. Then she courageously agrees to leave immediately for a strange land and an unknown husband. From the honest portrayal of Rebekah, both in her youth and old age, we can learn from her life, its good and bad.

go to

marry
2 Corinthians 6:14

Eliezer
Genesis 15:2

I Must Find You a Wife

the big picture

Genesis 22:20–24; 24:1–11

Abraham hears news from his old neighborhood about his brother's family, which includes Rebekah. Later, Abraham sends his faithful servant, Eliezer, back to his home country, Haran (see Illustration #2), to find a wife for his son Isaac.

Abraham learns that his brother Nahor, who still lives back home in Paddan, has children and grandchildren. One of Nahor's grandchildren is a young woman named Rebekah.

Abraham does not want his son Isaac to <u>marry</u> a woman from the people in Canaan who don't believe in Jehovah, where Abraham and his family now live. Abraham tells his faithful servant, believed to be <u>Eliezer</u>, to go to Abraham's old home and find a wife for Isaac. What unfolds is the beautiful story of the meeting between Eliezer and Rebekah at the village well.

guidance
Matthew 21:22

promises
1 John 5:14–15

everything
1 Timothy 2:1–3

Abraham is right in wanting his son to marry a believer in Jehovah. God gives his children the same instruction. Christians should marry Christians. That way they have a better chance of having unity and security in their relationship.

Looking for a Sign

GENESIS 24:12–14 *Then he said, "O LORD God of my master Abraham, please give me success this day, and show kindness to my master Abraham. Behold, here I stand by the well of water, and the daughters of the men of the city are coming out to draw water. Now let it be that the young woman to whom I say, 'Please let down your pitcher that I may drink,' and she says, 'Drink, and I will also give your camels a drink'—let her be the one You have appointed for Your servant Isaac. And by this I will know that You have shown kindness to my master." (NKJV)*

Eliezer prays specifically for guidance to find Isaac's future wife in Abraham's former home. In the village, he feels led to a spot by the well. To know whether God is leading him, Eliezer asks God to help him choose the right wife for Isaac. Eliezer knows he will find young women at the well, since the young women of the village always get the water for their families. Rebekah sees Eliezer and cheerfully gives him and his ten thirsty camels water. Rebekah's actions, getting water for a strange man and for his ten camels, show extraordinary kindness. Her energy and willingness to get water for ten thirsty camels show Eliezer how special Rebekah is.

God delights in having us call upon him to provide his blessings and direction. Although he doesn't promise to say "yes" to all our prayers, he promises to answer, and his answers depend upon what he knows to be best for us. We sometimes think God is only interested in the "big" things of life, but he is actually interested in everything about our lives, big or small.

what others say

Jimmy Carter

God always answers prayers. Sometimes it's "yes" and sometimes the answer is "no," and sometimes it's "you gotta be kidding." But when prayers are not answered the way we want them, then we have an opportunity and an obligation to re-examine our own position. Maybe the things for which we are praying aren't God's will.[1]

go to

love
1 Corinthians
13:1–13

Rick Warren

Sometimes while you are praying, Satan will suggest a bizarre or evil thought just to distract you and shame you. Don't be alarmed or ashamed by this, but realize that Satan fears your prayers and will try anything to stop them. Instead of condemning yourself with "How could I think such a thought?" treat it as a distraction from Satan and immediately refocus on God.[2]

Camels drink huge amounts of water. A camel that has gone a few days without water can drink as much as twenty-five gallons. A water pot, used by any young woman at the well, might hold three gallons. That's more than eight trips to the well to bring water to one camel. Obviously, a woman willing to draw water for ten camels is energetic, industrious, and motivated. Interestingly, those are the very traits Rebekah's husband-to-be, Isaac, lacks.

God often draws a man and a woman together who complement each other's personality traits. While courting, these opposing traits seem fascinating and attractive; after marriage, these differences often become intense sources of irritation. God wants each spouse to recognize the value of having their personality's "rough spots" smoothed by someone with opposite characteristics. This way we will have God's kind of <u>love</u> for our spouse.

for your marriage

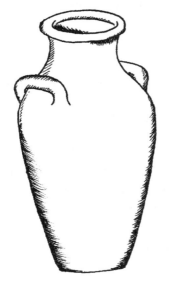

Illustration #3
Water Pot—Rebekah probably used a three-gallon water pot very similar to this one.

An Answer from God

love
Genesis 24:67

please
Genesis 27:6–17

GENESIS 24:15–21 *And it happened, before he had finished speaking, that behold, Rebekah, who was born to Bethuel, son of Milcah, the wife of Nahor, Abraham's brother, came out with her pitcher on her shoulder. Now the young woman was very beautiful to behold, a virgin; no man had known her. And she went down to the well, filled her pitcher, and came up. And the servant ran to meet her and said, "Please let me drink a little water from your pitcher."*

So she said, "Drink, my lord." Then she quickly let her pitcher down to her hand, and gave him a drink. And when she had finished giving him a drink, she said, "I will draw water for your camels also, until they have finished drinking." Then she quickly emptied her pitcher into the trough, ran back to the well to draw water, and drew for all his camels. And the man, wondering at her, remained silent so as to know whether the LORD had made his journey prosperous or not. (NKJV)

What a feast for old Eliezer's eyes, watching Rebekah, a beautiful young virgin, draw him water at the well. His simple request for water is answered instantly with cheerful agreement. Then his ears hear the words he wants to hear: "I will draw water for your camels also, until they have finished drinking" (Genesis 24:19 NKJV). What a young woman! Eliezer's heart must have risen with joy; God has answered his prayer quickly and exactly. For many minutes, Rebekah runs back and forth watering those thirsty camels, and the servant watches in awe at God's answer to his request (see Illustration #3).

> ### what others say
> #### Jill Briscoe
> If we could only learn not to isolate ourselves in times of deep trouble, we would receive ministry to our wounded spirits that would bless not only us, but also those who minister to us.[3]

Rebekah's name means "tied-up calf or lamb," suggesting beauty that snares or captures men's hearts. Throughout Rebekah's life, her great beauty does capture men, from winning Eliezer's attention and gaining Isaac's <u>love</u>, to motivating her son to <u>please</u> her.

God loves for us to serve him with cheerfulness and energy. Often we get discouraged, because we're not asking God for help, or we're

doing too much, or we're not doing what God called us to do. If we are obeying God and doing what he wants, we can serve cheerfully and energetically, because we will feel as if we're <u>serving him</u> directly. When we lose our ability to be cheerful in God's service, we need to allow others to help us. We must receive, as well as give, or we'll burn out.

serving him
Colossians 3:17

Now to Get Her Home

> **GENESIS 24:22–27** *So it was, when the camels had finished drinking, that the man took a golden nose ring weighing half a shekel, and two bracelets for her wrists weighing ten shekels of gold, and said, "Whose daughter are you? Tell me, please, is there room in your father's house for us to lodge?"*
>
> *So she said to him, "I am the daughter of Bethuel, Milcah's son, whom she bore to Nahor." Moreover she said to him, "We have both straw and feed enough, and room to lodge."*
>
> *Then the man bowed down his head and worshiped the* LORD.
>
> *And he said, "Blessed be the* LORD *God of my master Abraham, who has not forsaken His mercy and His truth toward my master. As for me, being on the way, the* LORD *led me to the house of my master's brethren." (NKJV)*

First Eliezer's heart jumped with joy. Now Rebekah's heart is filled with delight and surprise at her new gold nose ring and her two new gold bracelets. The nose ring weighed one-fifth of an ounce or half a shekel, and the two bracelets weighed about four ounces or ten shekels. Obviously, no matter how rich Rebekah's own family is, her family will be impressed by these expensive gifts. Eliezer, likewise, is thrilled to learn this wonderful young woman is the grandniece of his master, Abraham, making her the granddaughter of Abraham's brother. How wonderful! Eliezer worships Almighty God, who has made Eliezer's trip so successful.

At this time, jewelry was not only popular adornment but a way to store and display family wealth. Rebekah's two bracelets were worth about what a worker earned in a full year. Expensive gold bracelets, probably very similar to the ones Eliezer gave Rebekah, were discovered in the tombs of Rebekah's contemporaries. The remains of these women showed that they wore bracelets on their arms as well as their wrists.

But First We Must Meet the Relatives

clever
Genesis 29:26

GENESIS 24:28–32 *So the young woman ran and told her mother's household these things.*

Now Rebekah had a brother whose name was Laban, and Laban ran out to the man by the well. So it came to pass, when he saw the nose ring, and the bracelets on his sister's wrists, and when he heard the words of his sister Rebekah, saying, "Thus the man spoke to me," that he went to the man. And there he stood by the camels at the well. And he said, "Come in, O blessed of the LORD! Why do you stand outside? For I have prepared the house, and a place for the camels."

Then the man came to the house. And he unloaded the camels, and provided straw and feed for the camels, and water to wash his feet and the feet of the men who were with him. (NKJV)

Rebekah returns home, tells her family about the events at the well, and shows them her new gold jewelry. Her brother, Laban, quickly returns to the well to offer this rich stranger a place to stay, and the stranger accepts. Rebekah's family greets Eliezer. To their surprise, Eliezer brings greetings from their relative, Abraham. The family is very impressed. Rebekah's brother, Laban, realizes the worth of Rebekah's new jewelry and, being the <u>clever</u> person he is, does whatever he can to please this important stranger.

Look What God Has Done

> **the big picture**
>
> **Genesis 24:33–49**
>
> Eliezer is intent on telling Laban and his family the purpose of his mission. This faithful servant challenges this family to cooperate with Abraham's desires.

Eliezer wants to find out whether God has brought him to the right home and to the right woman for Isaac. So before sitting down to eat, Eliezer insists on telling the family the purpose of his trip. While the family listens, he recounts exactly what happened, beginning with Abraham's instructions and ending with his encounter with Rebekah at the well. Rebekah's father must have been happy to think that his daughter pleased such an important messenger for Abraham with her kindness.

> **what others say**
>
> **Patsy Clairmont**
>
> My personal history with the Lord is a dear reminder and a comforting agent in my life. When I think back on his loving kindness, my pulse begins to beat more evenly. Also, the ways that he secured his people in the Bible help to anchor my sometimes wavering heart. Recalling your history and the history of God's people can calm your unsettled mind.[4]

Just as Eliezer told the family about God's faithfulness in leading him to Rebekah, we should recall the ways God has worked in our lives and share these stories with others. Such "testimonies" build our own faith and the faith of our listeners. These testimonies also help us, not only to recall what God has done previously, but to remind us that asking for God's help is just as effective with our new problems as it was with our old ones. The apostle Paul wrote that the stories in the Bible are as valuable now as they were two thousand years ago, because they provide us with <u>instruction</u> and benefit. The Bible is basically a "testimony" of God's work in his children's lives and a revelation of who he is.

On Your Way

> **GENESIS 24:50–53** *Then Laban and Bethuel answered and said, "The thing comes from the LORD; we cannot speak to you either bad or good. Here is Rebekah before you; take her and go, and let her be your master's son's wife, as the LORD has spoken."*
>
> *And it came to pass, when Abraham's servant heard their words, that he worshiped the LORD, bowing himself to the earth. Then the servant brought out jewelry of silver, jewelry of gold, and clothing, and gave them to Rebekah. He also gave precious things to her brother and to her mother.* (NKJV)

Whether or not this family actually believes in the God of Abraham, we do not know. But we do know the family calls upon the Lord for guidance. The family realized how advantageous a marriage into a rich family could be and how pleasant it would be to receive a lot of money and gifts, the bride price for Rebekah. In return for the bride price, the bride's family traditionally gave a dowry to the husband's family. Perhaps because Eliezer wants Rebekah for Isaac immediately, even without a dowry, nothing is

courage
Joshua 1:8

mentioned about a dowry. In this culture, the young woman's brother arranged his sister's marriage, and that's why her brother, Laban, begins the negotiation.

Stick Around Awhile

> GENESIS 24:54–58 *And he and the men who were with him ate and drank and stayed all night. Then they arose in the morning, and he said, "Send me away to my master."*
>
> *But her brother and her mother said, "Let the young woman stay with us a few days, at least ten; after that she may go."*
>
> *And he said to them, "Do not hinder me, since the LORD has prospered my way; send me away so that I may go to my master."*
>
> *So they said, "We will call the young woman and ask her personally." Then they called Rebekah and said to her, "Will you go with this man?" And she said, "I will go."* (NKJV)

Eliezer, after spending the night, wants to begin the trip home. Perhaps he fears that his elderly master, Abraham, will die before he gets home with Rebekah. But Laban wants the rich stranger to stay longer, because a longer stay increases the chance that the family will receive more gifts. Eliezer, however, only wants to fulfill his master's wishes and return home as quickly as possible.

Although we don't know for sure, Laban probably thought asking Rebekah to decide when to leave for her new husband would lengthen Eliezer's visit. After all, how can this young woman suddenly leave her home for a strange place, at a moment's notice? To his surprise, Rebekah, the adventurous one, agrees to leave right away. Laban's plan backfires.

Bible experts disagree on whether or not the brides in this ancient society were usually consulted about the marriage plans. Some say no; others say the marriage contracts required it. In this instance, though, we do know the bride-to-be is asked her opinion. Rebekah answers that she is ready to leave immediately, even though she may never see her family again.

God often calls us to do things suddenly or unexpectedly. He challenges us to have <u>courage</u> and trust him. Rebekah shows us her courage.

We're Out of Here

GENESIS 24:59–61 *So they sent away Rebekah their sister and her nurse, and Abraham's servant and his men. And they blessed Rebekah and said to her:*

> *"Our sister, may you become*
> *The mother of thousands of ten thousands;*
> *And may your descendants possess*
> *The gates of those who hate them."*

Then Rebekah and her maids arose, and they rode on the camels and followed the man. So the servant took Rebekah and departed. (NKJV)

God's promise
Genesis 12:1–3

After Rebekah's agreement, her family sends her away with a blessing, a traditional part of a bride going away to her new husband and new family. The family says, "May you become the mother of thousands of ten thousands" (Genesis 24:60 NKJV). Her family doesn't realize how much this blessing resembles <u>God's promise</u> to Abraham, nor do they know that this blessing will come true. Rebekah will be the ancestor of many people including the Messiah, Jesus.

what others say

Gary Smalley and John Trent

One way we can see the unique spiritual side of the family blessing is to look at how God used this concept to identify his line of blessing through one family until the coming of Christ.[5]

We Meet at Last

GENESIS 24:62–65 *Now Isaac came from the way of Beer Lahai Roi, for he dwelt in the South. And Isaac went out to meditate in the field in the evening; and he lifted his eyes and looked, and there, the camels were coming. Then Rebekah lifted her eyes, and when she saw Isaac she dismounted from her camel; for she had said to the servant, "Who is this man walking in the field to meet us?" The servant said, "It is my master." So she took a veil and covered herself.* (NKJV)

After a long trip, Eliezer brings Rebekah safely to Isaac. A contemplative person, Isaac is meditating in a field when he sees the

praying
Luke 5:16

Bride of Christ
John 3:29;
Revelation 19:7

Bride of Christ
believers in heaven,
believers in Jesus
(the Bride of Christ)

camel procession approach. Rebekah also sees Isaac in the distance. After learning that this man is her future bridegroom, she puts on her veil to indicate her betrothal and upcoming wedding. Later when she is married, she will not wear the veil.

> ### what others say
>
> **Marie Chapian**
>
> Solitude means withdrawal into God in the depths of your being. In silence and solitude, your individuality is affirmed.[6]
>
> **Cynthia Heald**
>
> If I am abiding—spending time alone with God and his Word—then my heart is being trained to ask for the eternal things of God. My heart becomes set on "things above, not on the things that are on earth." As I ask for that which is eternal, I begin to pray in the Spirit, according to the will of God and on the strong foundation of Scripture.[7]

To grow in the Christian walk without spending time with God is almost impossible. Even Jesus, who was God himself, spent much time <u>praying</u> and conversing with God.

Here at Just the Right Time

> GENESIS 24:66–67 *And the servant told Isaac all the things that he had done. Then Isaac brought her into his mother Sarah's tent; and he took Rebekah and she became his wife, and he loved her. So Isaac was comforted after his mother's death.* (NKJV)

Eliezer tells Isaac everything that happened and how, thanks to God, he found Rebekah. Obviously approving of the success of the trip, Isaac receives his new bride into his mother's tent. The marriage ceremony takes place, and Isaac and Rebekah find love in their marriage. Isaac loves Rebekah, and Rebekah comforts him, for Isaac is mourning the death of his beloved mother, Sarah.

A spiritual analogy can be drawn from Eliezer's trip to find a wife for Isaac. Abraham could represent God, the Father. Isaac could represent Jesus, the Bridegroom. Eliezer could represent the Holy Spirit, who seeks believers for the Son, and Rebekah could represent believers in Jesus who become the **Bride of Christ**.

Abraham's Death

go to

encountered God
Genesis 16:8–13

twenty years
Genesis 25:26

Second Coming
1 Thessalonians
4:16–17

Second Coming
when Jesus returns
to earth

> **the big picture**
>
> **Genesis 25:1–18**
>
> In Abraham's old age, he marries Keturah, and they have six sons. Abraham dies at the age of 175. He is buried by his two sons, Isaac and Ishmael, in Machpelah.

After Sarah's death, Abraham takes a new wife, Keturah, and they have more children. Finally, at the age of 175, Abraham dies. Isaac and Ishmael bury him in the cave of Machpelah, the same cave where Sarah was buried.

These same verses also note that Isaac was blessed by God and that Isaac lived by Beer Lahai Roi—the place where Hagar, Sarah's maid, encountered God years earlier.

Another Barren Wife

GENESIS 25:19–21 *This is the genealogy of Isaac, Abraham's son. Abraham begot Isaac. Isaac was forty years old when he took Rebekah as wife, the daughter of Bethuel the Syrian of Padan Aram, the sister of Laban the Syrian. Now Isaac pleaded with the LORD for his wife, because she was barren; and the LORD granted his plea, and Rebekah his wife conceived.* (NKJV)

Isaac marries Rebekah when he is forty years old and Rebekah is twenty. But Rebekah suffers from the same difficulty as her mother-in-law, Sarah: barrenness. As a part of God's plan, Isaac prays for his wife and she becomes pregnant—but only after twenty years have passed. They have waited a long time for God to fulfill his plan for Abraham's line to be fruitful.

> **what others say**
>
> **Jan Johnson**
>
> This sort of waiting is not passive. It is alert, active, and receptive, full of energy and commitment. Just as we're reminded to stay awake and alert for the **Second Coming**, we need to stay awake and alert for God's presence in the events around us.[8]

Whether Isaac prayed for Rebekah the whole time or only at the end of the twenty years, we do not know. But, since the Hebrew verb used here for prayer means "to entreat" or "to pray as a supplicant," he probably prayed all those years until God answered.

Sarah's and Rebekah's barrenness seems to block God's plan. But God often allows obstacles to seem to block his will. Then when God fulfills his promise, his glory and power are demonstrated in great ways. Joseph, Samson, and Samuel were all "miracle" babies, prayed for and provided in God's own timing and purpose.

Infertility can upset any couple, bringing them disappointment and disharmony. God doesn't want infertility to separate a couple, but he wants this obstacle to draw the couple closer together as they each pray for each other and for God's will. God has his own timing for the fulfillment of his purposes.

for your marriage

go to

Joseph
Genesis 30:24

Samson
Judges 13:24

Samuel
1 Samuel 1:20

timing
Proverbs 16:9

purpose
Jeremiah 29:11;
Isaiah 55:8–9

worrying
Philippians 4:6–7

Moses
Exodus 2:10

Not One, but Two

> GENESIS 25:22–23 *But the children struggled together within her; and she said, "If all is well, why am I like this?" So she went to inquire of the LORD. And the LORD said to her:*
> *"Two nations are in your womb,*
> *Two peoples shall be separated from your body;*
> *One people shall be stronger than the other,*
> *And the older shall serve the younger." (NKJV)*

Rebekah's pregnancy is very difficult, and she is concerned. Her unborn child seems to be always agitated and active. Instead of worrying, she seeks God's perspective. God tells Rebekah that two babies are growing inside her womb, and that these two babies are fighting with each other. God determines, in opposition to the natural order, the younger child will dominate the other.

The writer of Genesis—believed to be Moses—is not concerned with how God communicates this message to Rebekah, but what God communicates. We don't know how God told Rebekah she was

---

what others say

Cynthia Heald

The eternal, sovereign, majestic God of the universe wants to be intimate with us! He wants us to call, to cry, to sing to him.

> He longs to love, to refresh, to encourage us. He wants to answer our call and to tell us great and <u>unsearchable</u> thoughts.[9]

go to

unsearchable
Romans 11:33

carrying twins, but we know, through Moses' account in Genesis, God tells her she will have twin boys.

Hearing God's Message

God could have revealed or communicated his message to Rebekah in several ways. He could have:

1. shown himself in a dream,

2. communicated through a priest,

3. spoken to her heart or mind with a quiet knowledge, or

4. spoken out loud.

This battle in Rebekah's womb is the beginning of a long war between the twins and then their descendants: the Jews and the Edomites, descendants of Esau, the firstborn son. Even today, these two groups of people fight over possession of the Middle East.

Every pregnant woman can worry about a million things and Rebekah is no exception. Rebekah did the right thing in seeking God's perspective. God says, "Be anxious for nothing" (Philippians 4:6 NKJV), but instead trust him. Don't worry, pray!

apply it

Born at Last, or Double Trouble

GENESIS 25:24–26 *So when her days were fulfilled for her to give birth, indeed there were twins in her womb. And the first came out red. He was like a hairy garment all over; so they called his name Esau. Afterward his brother came out, and his hand took hold of Esau's heel; so his name was called Jacob. Isaac was sixty years old when she bore them. (NKJV)*

True to God's prediction, Rebekah gives birth to twin boys. Red and hairy, Esau arrives first. The second boy is born holding on to Esau's heel. This action was so striking and so according to God's

choice
Romans 9:11–12

ways
Isaiah 55:9

prediction that they chose the name Jacob for this child. The word "Jacob" resembles the Hebrew noun for "heel."

God had chosen Jacob as the son who would carry the spiritual heritage, rather than Esau, who, as the older brother, usually is chosen for the birthright (the double portion of the inheritance). This is God's supernatural <u>choice</u>, and we may not understand his choice. But God's <u>ways</u> are not man's ways. God knows his plan benefits mankind. "For I know the thoughts that I think toward you, says the LORD, thoughts of peace and not of evil, to give you a future and a hope" (Jeremiah 29:11 NKJV).

In this ancient society, infants were named to describe the child or influence the child as he grew. Naming a child was a very significant act because it communicated the hopes and blessings of the parents or relatives. It still does! But these two names, "Esau" and "Jacob," are wordplays. For instance, the name "Jacob" doesn't mean "heel," but is similar to the word for "heel" or "may he be at the heels." His name is also similar to "to watch from behind." As the future will show, Jacob becomes a deceitful kind of person who is always looking out for himself, in a sense "watching his behind!"

> **the big picture**
>
> **Genesis 25:27–34**
>
> From their first breath, the twins exhibit two different personalities and desires. Esau, the older, loves the land and hunting. Jacob prefers to stay home and be quiet.

For the Love of Food

The twins, completely different in personality and interest, are even loved differently by their parents. Esau, a skillful hunter who loves red meat, is preferred by his father, Isaac, because Esau brings him wonderful meat. Jacob, preferred by Rebekah, stays at home with his mother. Since Esau is the firstborn son, he owns the birthright, the special inheritance rights of the firstborn son.

But Jacob and his mother Rebekah want the birthright for Jacob, so Jacob seizes control of Esau's birthright through deceit. He gets Esau to exchange his birthright for a pot of stew by asking Esau to make the exchange when Esau is ravenously hungry. Esau mistakenly thinks he'll die from starvation, so he agrees. "Look, I am about to die; so what is this birthright to me?" (Genesis 25:32 NKJV). Of course, Esau isn't about to die, but his great hunger, an earthly passion, overrules him.

go to

wants
1 Timothy 2:4

saved
Acts 10:34

represent the Lord
John 13:35

> what others say
>
> **Naomi Rhode**
>
> We can build a family like no other in the world. A family that reaches out with love, acceptance, and patience to each member and all those who come in contact with it. A family that encourages each member to grow, develop their God-given talents and abilities, and fulfill his or her own particular destiny.[10]
>
> **Beth Moore**
>
> A divided heart places our entire lives in jeopardy. Only God can be totally trusted with our hearts. He doesn't demand our complete devotion to feed his ego but to provide for our safety.[11]

Favoritism, a Big Mistake

Isaac and Rebekah showed favoritism toward their sons, and their favoritism brought tragedy to their family. The energetic Rebekah preferred her opposite son Jacob and delighted in Jacob's quietness. Isaac, always the introspective one, preferred the active Esau, who loved the outdoors. The couple tried to diminish their weaknesses through the strengths of their two sons, instead of seeking God. This led to their disappointment, the jealousy between the two brothers, and the tragedy of a broken family. Showing favoritism always divides siblings and brings heartache to families.

Showing favoritism to your own children, or any person, goes against God's perspective that every person has the same worth and value. God <u>wants</u> everyone <u>saved</u>. He doesn't play favorites. By showing unconditional love to everyone, we <u>represent the Lord</u>.

The Same Old Lie

> the big picture
>
> **Genesis 26:1–34**
>
> Isaac gives into the same temptation that his father did: not trusting God for his safety in a foreign land. Instead of telling King Abimelech the truth that Rebekah is his wife, he says Rebekah is his sister.

graciously
Ephesians 2:8;
Titus 3:7

God appears to Isaac and promises Isaac the same things he promised his father Abraham: blessings, descendants, and land. Such a wonderful assurance does not, however, convince Isaac to trust God with his life. When Isaac fears he will be killed so someone else can marry Rebekah, he does just what his father did. He lies to King Abimelech and says Rebekah is his sister. God causes the lie to be revealed and despite the lie, the king generously and <u>graciously</u> gives favor to Isaac, and God brings Isaac prosperity.

Then God again appears to Isaac, affirming his promise. Isaac and his family are blessed by God, but Isaac and Rebekah have one worry: they are troubled that Esau, through his unwise choices in marriage, demonstrates that he is not worthy of his birthright—something God knew long before Esau married the heathen women. God blesses Isaac because of his grace, not because he deserved it.

This King Abimelech is a different king than the one Abraham dealt with years earlier. The word "Abimelech" is often used as a title for royalty and identifies many different people.

Blessing and Deceit

> GENESIS 27:1–4 *Now it came to pass, when Isaac was old and his eyes were so dim that he could not see, that he called Esau his older son and said to him, "My son." And he answered him, "Here I am."*
>
> *Then he said, "Behold now, I am old. I do not know the day of my death. Now therefore, please take your weapons, your quiver and your bow, and go out to the field and hunt game for me. And make me savory food, such as I love, and bring it to me that I may eat, that my soul may bless you before I die." (NKJV)*

Old and weak—perhaps almost one hundred years old—Isaac wants to make sure his favored son gets the blessing, even though God has determined Esau will not be its owner. Because Isaac favors his senses instead of his spiritual life, he is blinded—both physically and spiritually—to God's plan. Because of that spiritual blindness, he has also never made any positive spiritual impact upon his favored son, Esau. As a result, Esau does not seek Jehovah. Isaac encourages Esau to bring his favorite food and receive the blessing. Esau knows he's already pledged his birthright to his brother in exchange for a bowl of stew, but he can, at least, get his father's blessing.

go to

deceit
1 Peter 2:1

sovereignty
Genesis 25:23

repay
Romans 12:21

trust
Psalm 13:5

It Never Ends

GENESIS 27:5–10 *Now Rebekah was listening when Isaac spoke to Esau his son. And Esau went to the field to hunt game and to bring it. So Rebekah spoke to Jacob her son, saying, "Indeed I heard your father speak to Esau your brother, saying, 'Bring me game and make savory food for me, that I may eat it and bless you in the presence of the LORD before my death.' Now therefore, my son, obey my voice according to what I command you. Go now to the flock and bring me from there two choice kids of the goats, and I will make savory food from them for your father, such as he loves. Then you shall take it to your father, that he may eat it, and that he may bless you before his death. (NKJV)*

Rebekah, motivated by her favoritism for her favorite son and worry that Jacob might be cheated, hears Isaac's directions to Esau and thinks of another plan. Unable to trust God to bring about his own plan, she devises one of her own through <u>deceit</u>. She knows God's <u>sovereignty</u> has already dictated that Jacob will get the birthright, but her fear causes her to believe she must make sure he also gets the blessing. She tells Jacob to bring two goats so that she can prepare a dish smelling and tasting like the wild game Esau hunts. She must have been a great cook to accomplish this transformation! But her efforts work against God's great law to <u>repay</u> good, or evil, with good, and let God take revenge.

A mother's love and concern for her child can easily motivate her to forsake her <u>trust</u> in God. But God loves our children even more than we do! He created each child for a specific purpose, and he is much more capable of fulfilling his plan than we are. We can best love our children by entrusting them into God's hands and cooperating with God's plan. Our efforts cannot have the same power as God's will.

But Mom!

> **GENESIS 27:11–13** *And Jacob said to Rebekah his mother, "Look, Esau my brother is a hairy man, and I am a smooth-skinned man. Perhaps my father will feel me, and I shall seem to be a deceiver to him; and I shall bring a curse on myself and not a blessing."*
>
> *But his mother said to him, "Let your curse be on me, my son; only obey my voice, and go, get them for me." (NKJV)*

Jacob doesn't mind cooperating with his mother's plan, but he fears being discovered. He realizes how great the physical differences are between himself and his brother. Can he possibly trick his father, even though his father is blind? Rebekah assures Jacob that if there are any unpleasant consequences from their scheme, she will absorb them. Little does she know that she will pay, and so will Jacob.

Only God is in charge of determining the consequences of sin, not us. God will discipline us if we manipulate things—our manipulation is the opposite of trusting him.

You Feel Hairy

> **GENESIS 27:14–17** *And he went and got them and brought them to his mother, and his mother made savory food, such as his father loved. Then Rebekah took the choice clothes of her elder son Esau, which were with her in the house, and put them on Jacob her younger son. And she put the skins of the kids of the goats on his hands and on the smooth part of his neck. Then she gave the savory food and the bread, which she had prepared, into the hand of her son Jacob. (NKJV)*

Rebekah has everything ready for her plan to succeed: tasty food, Esau's clothes, and goatskin for covering Jacob's hands and neck. She seems to have thought of everything, and she probably delighted in her ability to carry out the deception. Obviously, she is counting on Isaac's blindness to make her scheme succeed.

destruction
Matthew 7:13–14

Success at Last

the big picture

Genesis 27:18–29

Isaac's blindness makes it almost impossible for him to detect the trickery. Since he smells the food and touches Jacob's hairy body, he is deceived and blesses Jacob, who he thinks is Esau.

Rebekah's plan seems to work. Whatever doubts Isaac had, he puts them aside. His senses are satisfied by the smell of the food, the touch of the hairy hands and neck, and the taste of wine. Jacob must lie to carry off the scheme, but Jacob rationalizes the deception. He has already taken possession of Esau's birthright, so he feels he deserves the blessing. Isaac gives the blessing to his second son, Jacob, naming him as the one who will "lord" it over his brother.

Just like Isaac, we can get caught up in basing our decisions on our senses. Even Rebekah thought she was doing what was best for her son, but she couldn't trust God to carry out his best for him. Today, our culture says, "If it feels good, do it." There's no consideration for the consequences of sin or how God's commands are intended for our good. We can easily become blinded to God's best and settle for something that seems good but in the end brings <u>destruction</u>.

I'm Sorry, Son

the big picture

Genesis 27:30–41

When Esau finds he has been tricked by Jacob, he is furious at his brother and begs his father for any kind of blessing at all. But the one he receives is not very positive.

Herod
Luke 23:11

curse
Genesis 27:13

When Esau returns from his successful hunt, he is bitterly disappointed to discover Jacob has again taken something from him: this time, the blessing. Esau faults Jacob, even though Esau only valued the blessing for its benefits, not its connection to God. Esau begs his father for some kind of blessing, but Isaac can only predict unfortunate living conditions for his favored son and his descendants, the Edomites. Esau's descendants will serve Jacob's descendants.

To this day, the Edomites live in a land less fertile than Palestine. Esau's dislike for his brother solidifies into hate, and he consoles himself with a plan to kill Jacob after his father dies. That hate was expressed by an Edomite, <u>Herod</u>, who reviled Jesus, and unfortunately, the hatred continues today.

Run, Jacob, Run

GENESIS 27:42–45 *And the words of Esau her older son were told to Rebekah. So she sent and called Jacob her younger son, and said to him, "Surely your brother Esau comforts himself concerning you by intending to kill you. Now therefore, my son, obey my voice: arise, flee to my brother Laban in Haran. And stay with him a few days, until your brother's fury turns away, until your brother's anger turns away from you, and he forgets what you have done to him; then I will send and bring you from there. Why should I be bereaved also of you both in one day?"* (NKJV)

Never lacking a plan based in manipulation, Rebekah recognizes the dangerous position her beloved son is now in and thinks of a new plan. Instead of confessing her sin and trusting God to bring healing to this broken family, she tells Jacob to go to her brother Laban's house and stay there until he can safely return home. The <u>curse</u> she took upon herself now bears its bitter fruit: she will never see her beloved, favored son again.

Not These Women

GENESIS 27:46 *And Rebekah said to Isaac, "I am weary of my life because of the daughters of Heth; if Jacob takes a wife of the daughters of Heth, like these who are the daughters of the land, what good will my life be to me?"* (NKJV)

One unconfessed deception brings on another, so now Rebekah influences her husband through suggestion rather than honesty. She tells Isaac she doesn't want to risk Jacob taking a nearby heathen woman as a wife. Since they both agree on this, Isaac is willing to be a part of this plan, without knowing Rebekah's real motive.

Once deception is started, further deception will be needed. Lies require more lies to cover up the first lie. Honesty is far better.

go to

disciplined
Hebrews 12:5–13

Get Thee a Wife, Son

the big picture

Genesis 28:1–9

Isaac agrees with Rebekah and sends Jacob off to the land of Rebekah's family with another blessing, telling him to get a wife there. In further disobedience to his parents, Esau marries more heathen wives.

Rebekah's plan works and Isaac sends Jacob to relatives, back in Rebekah's hometown. He commands Jacob to take a wife from there and blesses him with the Abrahamic Blessing. Esau, learning of Jacob's escape, is even more bitter than before. In a misguided effort to win back favor, he marries a descendant of Abraham through Ishmael. He still doesn't understand, at a spiritual level, why he shouldn't marry those who don't know Jehovah.

what others say

Frances Vander Velde

Her beloved Jacob went out into the world with wrong ideas of right and justice, of how to get along with others, and with the mistaken notion that sin pays.[15]

Never Again

GENESIS 49:31 *There they buried Abraham and Sarah his wife, there they buried Isaac and Rebekah his wife, and there I buried Leah.* (NKJV)

Many years later, Jacob does return with an enlarged family, but his beloved mother, Rebekah, is dead, buried in the same cave with Abraham and Sarah. Rebekah hoped she would only be without her favorite son for a few years, but she dies never seeing him again. As a result of her favoritism and manipulation, Rebekah was disciplined by the Lord.

Trying to fulfill God's plan in a human way only brings pain and unhappiness.

Chapter Wrap-Up

- Eliezer, commanded by Abraham, goes to find a wife for Isaac. In answer to prayer, Eliezer finds a beautiful and energetic young woman for Isaac named Rebekah, the grandniece of Abraham. Rebekah and Isaac are married. (Genesis 24:1–67)

- When Rebekah becomes pregnant, she is troubled about the baby and inquires of God. He tells her she will have twins, and contrary to the custom, the younger (Jacob) will gain the birthright instead of the older (Esau). (Genesis 25:19–25)

- Exactly as God predicted, Jacob grasps Esau's heel as if he were trying to displace him, even while being born. (Genesis 25:26)

- The twin boys are opposite in temperament. Isaac favors Esau and Rebekah favors Jacob. (Genesis 25:27–28)

- Jacob manipulates Esau to sell his birthright when he is extremely hungry for a pot of stew. Because Esau doesn't value his birthright, he exchanges it for soup. (Genesis 25:29–34)

- When Rebekah overhears Isaac say he'll give Esau the blessing, she doesn't trust God to prevent it. Instead, she takes matters into her own hands with an elaborate scheme that makes sure Jacob gets the blessing. As a result, Esau hates Jacob and Jacob must run for his life. Sadly, his mother never sees Jacob again. (Genesis 27:1–28:9)

Study Questions

1. What does Eliezer pray and how is his prayer answered?

2. What was Isaac doing when Rebekah arrived?

3. What did God determine would happen to the twin boys?

4. How did Rebekah deceive Isaac in order to make him bless Jacob instead of Esau?

5. What penalty did Rebekah pay for her deception?

Let's Get Started

Relationships are one of the most difficult things in life. In this chapter, we will focus on two sisters, Rachel and Leah, whose sisterly relationship suffered because they had the same husband. The experience of Rachel and Leah is a demonstration of the reality that God does not give his blessing to polygamous relationships. When we operate outside God's will, we will experience the same heartaches as Rachel and Leah.

go to

shepherds
Genesis 29:3

encounter
Genesis 28:13–15

Get Thee a Wife

the big picture

Genesis 29:1–10

In obedience to his father, Isaac, and in flight from his brother, Esau, Jacob leaves his home to search for a wife. He travels to the home of Laban, his mother's brother, in Haran (see Illustration #4). Here he is introduced to Laban's daughter, Rachel.

Jacob is forced to leave his home in Canaan because his brother, Esau, is determined to kill him. Told to find a wife at the home of his wife's relatives, Jacob goes to Haran and meets Rachel at a well. She is the daughter of Laban, who is Rebekah's brother. Jacob realizes that Rachel is his cousin, the daughter of his mother's brother. He's so inspired by this beautiful woman that he rolls the stone away from the well—a feat that normally required the strength of many shepherds.

It is unusual for a woman to be a shepherdess, but in the case of Laban's family, there are no sons. Rachel, as an obedient daughter, helps her father with the flocks since she has no brothers to do it.

On his way to Haran, Jacob has an encounter with God that encourages and energizes him. He is assured that God is with him. Just like Jacob, we too can experience God's encouragement as we spend time with and get to know him.

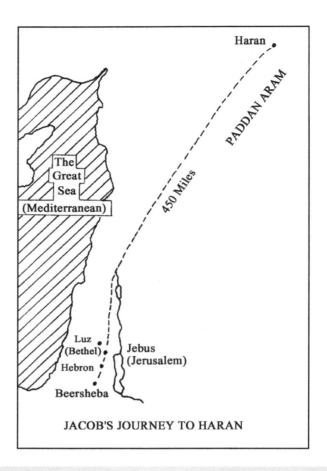

JACOB'S JOURNEY TO HARAN

A Kiss of Welcome

GENESIS 29:11 *Then Jacob kissed Rachel, and lifted up his
voice and wept. (NKJV)*

Jacob is so overcome with thanksgiving that he kisses his cousin
Rachel and cries out loud. He is thrilled to see God's hand in leading him right to the area of his relatives.

Many years earlier, <u>Eliezer</u>, Abraham's servant, had seen God's hand in leading him to Abraham's relatives to find a wife for Isaac, Abraham's son. Eliezer was also led by God to a well where he met Rebekah, who would later become Jacob's mother. Could this be the very same well? God continually proves himself faithful in leading this family, the descendants of Abraham.

go to

Eliezer
Genesis 15:2; 24:2

kissed
2 Samuel 20:9

holy kiss
Romans 16:16

> what others say
>
> ### Patsy Clairmont
>
> Not only will the Lord take up residence in our heart's home, but he will also lead and guide our decisions on which future doors we should enter. When opportunity knocks, it isn't necessarily in our best interest to step through every door. I'm grateful that the Lord offers to direct our steps.[2]

Because Jacob and Rachel are related, it is not inappropriate for him to kiss her. If they had been unrelated strangers, it would have been very inappropriate. When Jacob meets his uncle Laban, Laban kisses him in greeting. As soon as Laban heard the news about Jacob, his sister's son, he hurried to meet him. "[He] embraced him and kissed him, and brought him to his house. So he told Laban all these things" (Genesis 29:13 NKJV).

In the ancient world, people customarily used kissing as a way of greeting. Although men could not kiss women who were not their relatives, men often <u>kissed</u> men in greeting. Later in the Christian church, the Bible refers to giving a "<u>holy kiss</u>"—a kiss that is pure in motive and shows respect for the other person.

Kisses in the Bible

Purpose	Scripture
Greeting or Farewell	Genesis 33:4; Ruth 1:14; Romans 16:16
Sign of Respect	1 Samuel 10:1; 2 Samuel 15:5
Sign of Submission	1 Kings 19:18; Psalm 2:12
Family Love	Genesis 29:13; Luke 15:20
Romantic Love	Song of Solomon 1:2

I've Got You Now

GENESIS 29:12–15 *And Jacob told Rachel that he was her father's relative and that he was Rebekah's son. So she ran and told her father.*

> *Then it came to pass, when Laban heard the report about Jacob his sister's son, that he ran to meet him, and embraced him and kissed him, and brought him to his house. So he told Laban all these things. And Laban said to him, "Surely you are my bone and my flesh." And he stayed with him for a month.*
>
> *Then Laban said to Jacob, "Because you are my relative, should you therefore serve me for nothing? Tell me, what should your wages be?" (NKJV)*

Through his tears, Jacob explains he is Rachel's cousin, the son of her father's sister, Rebekah. In surprise and awe, Rachel runs to tell her father of this stranger's arrival, who is in turn just as excited. In Laban's home, Jacob shares stories about his family and Laban treats him as a son. Jacob stays there for a month before any further plans are required.

Evidently, Jacob isn't lying around that whole month. Jacob participates in the business of Laban's household: shepherding. No doubt, the fact that Laban's beautiful daughter Rachel is the chief shepherdess has something to do with his energy in helping out. Laban, who we will later find out has a strong personality with a greedy core, uncharacteristically shows concern about Jacob's working for nothing. He invites Jacob to name his wages. Because he probably could not have missed Jacob's loving gaze in Rachel's direction, Laban may have known what Jacob would say. Laban sees in this young man a possible son to make up for his lack of one. And if he becomes married to his daughter, Jacob would have to stay around for a while!

Laban will continue to trick and cheat Joseph, his son-in-law and his nephew, ten more times. Laban will break agreements with Jacob and will change his wages. Throughout his life, Laban will reveal his greed and deceitfulness.

Many years earlier, when Abraham's servant, Eliezer, had arrived to request Laban's sister Rebekah to be Isaac's wife, Laban first revealed his greedy core. As soon as [Laban] had seen the nose ring, and the bracelets on his sister's arms, and had heard Rebekah tell what the man said to her, he went out to the man and found him standing by the camels near the spring.

He said, "Come in, O blessed of the LORD! Why do you stand outside? For I have prepared the house, and a place for the camels" (Genesis 24:31 NKJV).

The Deal

GENESIS 29:16–18 *Now Laban had two daughters: the name of the elder was Leah, and the name of the younger was Rachel. Leah's eyes were delicate, but Rachel was beautiful of form and appearance. Now Jacob loved Rachel; so he said, "I will serve you seven years for Rachel your younger daughter." (NKJV)*

mohar
Genesis 34:12;
Exodus 22:16;
1 Samuel 18:25

mohar
reverse dowry

Leah, the older daughter of Laban, is described as having "delicate" eyes. Whether this refers to having poor eyesight, a scarred face, or lacking a delightful twinkle in the eyes, we do not know, but in contrast to Rachel's beauty, it doesn't matter. Jacob has already fallen in love with Rachel and in his naïveté and enthusiasm, he offers to work seven years in exchange for Rachel's hand in marriage. Not wanting his offer turned down, he gave more generously of himself than needed, but his star-filled eyes considered any length of work appropriate for becoming the husband of the beautiful and shapely Rachel. Interestingly, Rachel is never identified as loving her soon-to-be husband.

The exchange of a man's service for a wife was a normal part of the "**mohar**." The mohar was usually around thirty or forty shekels of silver. Since ten shekels of silver was a shepherd's expected wage for a year, Jacob was paying a high price for a wife.

The mohar is the reverse of a dowry, because instead of the bride's father giving money to his future son-in-law, the son-in-law gives money to his future father-in-law.

In ancient days, a father had complete control over his children, even to the point of having the freedom to sell his daughters as concubines or mistresses. The reasoning behind the mohar was that because the daughter helped her mother around the house, the bridegroom was replacing her service with money.

Usually sons and daughters of different families were negotiated for in marriage at an early age. Evidently, Leah and Rachel were not already committed. Customarily, after the two fathers negotiated, the "betrothal" took place as an item of business.

The betrothal was considered more significant than the actual forthcoming wedding. Once the betrothal was begun, it would be very unusual and difficult for the two parties to withdraw from their marriage agreement.

Mary and Joseph
Matthew 1:19;
Luke 1:27

waiting
Psalm 27:14;
James 1:3

Mary and Joseph were in the betrothal stage when Mary became pregnant with Jesus through the will of the Holy Spirit. Because she had already been determined to be his wife, he was in charge of taking care of the situation. In Scripture, he is referred to as her "husband" even though the wedding hadn't taken place.

Time Is a-Flyin'

GENESIS 29:19–21 *And Laban said, "It is better that I give her to you than that I should give her to another man. Stay with me." So Jacob served seven years for Rachel, and they seemed only a few days to him because of the love he had for her.*

Then Jacob said to Laban, "Give me my wife, for my days are fulfilled, that I may go in to her." (NKJV)

As if accepting an offer like Jacob's were a common occurrence, Laban consents, and because Jacob loves Rachel so much, seven years seems like a few days. Anticipation of joy and fulfillment can make the time go either quickly or slowly, but fortunately for Jacob, the years go by quickly. Once he has served his time, he eagerly reminds Laban of the promise. He has counted the days, and his part of the deal is finally complete.

what others say

Shirley Rose

How much of God's blessing do we miss by doubting him? If trusting God is hard for you, start small; learn to trust God for small things. As we are willing to act on our seedling faith, God will give us ever-increasing tests to allow that faith to grow.[3]

Cynthia Heald

Once when I was diligently interceding by asking, seeking, and knocking, what I was given was peace, what I found was the ability to persevere and to trust, and what was opened was a deepened intimacy with the Lord. My request has yet to be fully granted, but my prayer has been fully answered.[4]

We aren't told of Rachel's response during this time. Was she anxious to become Jacob's wife? If so, then her character was being developed through waiting. As we learn later, she was not a very spiritual woman, but God still worked in the lives of all Rachel's children. Waiting for something we want is a hard lesson, but it can bear much fruit if we let it.

He Didn't Have a Clue

GENESIS 29:22–24 *And Laban gathered together all the men of the place and made a feast. Now it came to pass in the evening, that he took Leah his daughter and brought her to Jacob; and he went in to her. And Laban gave his maid Zilpah to his daughter Leah as a maid.* (NKJV)

A feast is prepared at both the betrothal and the wedding ceremony. Unknown to Jacob, Laban substitutes Leah for Rachel on the wedding night. Since it is a dark night and the custom was to heavily <u>veil</u> the bride, hiding her appearance throughout the ceremony and into the bridal tent is easy. Jacob has no clue that he has been deceived. The text clarifies that Zilpah, a servant girl for Leah, is a part of this new family from the beginning. She will be important later in the story.

go to

veil
Song of Solomon 5:7

wedding ceremony
John 2:1–11

what others say

Jill Briscoe

However sorry we feel for Leah, we have to realize that she was apparently willing to go along with her father's deception—and an incredible deception it turned out to be.[5]

Stormie Omartian

All of us are planting something in our lives every single day, whether we realize it or not. And we are also reaping whatever we have planted in the past.[6]

Neither Rachel nor Leah seem to object to this transaction. Why should they? Leah is getting a husband, and Rachel most likely isn't in love with Jacob to the extent that Jacob is in love with her.

Or perhaps their objections weren't voiced. Even if they did not like their father's plan, they could not go against him. In that culture, a daughter couldn't object to her father's plans because of his authority over her.

Although this didn't happen with Leah and Rachel, the bride is usually picked up in a procession from her home and delivered to the groom's home for the <u>wedding ceremony</u> and feast. She remains

Jacob
Genesis 27:1–29

sow
Galatians 6:7

discipline
Hebrews 12:5–13

there to become the wife and daughter-in-law, now serving her mother-in-law instead of her own mother.

Sisters often have similar voices and if Jacob's senses had been dulled by the wine at the feast, we can understand why in the dark Jacob didn't realize Leah, not Rachel, was in bed with him. Or she may have realized it was best to say nothing.

Deception always bears distasteful fruit. Jacob had deceived his father, Isaac, in order to get Esau's birthright, and now Jacob is being deceived by a person who seems to be the ultimate deceiver. Whatever we sow we will also reap! God wants to discipline us for our own good, so that we'll make right choices in the future.

Wedding Morning Blues

> GENESIS 29:25–30 *So it came to pass in the morning, that behold, it was Leah. And he said to Laban, "What is this you have done to me? Was it not for Rachel that I served you? Why then have you deceived me?"*
>
> *And Laban said, "It must not be done so in our country, to give the younger before the firstborn. Fulfill her week, and we will give you this one also for the service which you will serve with me still another seven years."*
>
> *Then Jacob did so and fulfilled her week. So he gave him his daughter Rachel as wife also. And Laban gave his maid Bilhah to his daughter Rachel as a maid. Then Jacob also went in to Rachel, and he also loved Rachel more than Leah. And he served with Laban still another seven years.* (NKJV)

Jacob awakes on the morning after his wedding night and in the daylight he is shocked to discover he has been deceived. Laban doesn't admit to doing anything wrong; he rationalizes his deceit by saying customs dictate that a younger sister cannot be married before an older one. Laban quickly offers a new deal: finish this bridal week, and work another seven years for Rachel.

Leah probably wished that she could be Jacob's only wife. She may have dreamed that she would overwhelm Jacob with so much of her love that he would give up wanting Rachel. She must have cringed to hear her father offer Rachel in exchange for another seven years of Jacob's service.

pretended
Genesis 27:19

change
Philippians 3:15

Jacob is so in love that he is willing to go to great lengths to secure Rachel as his wife. Some Bible experts believe Jacob had to work a second set of seven years before Rachel became his wife, but others say Rachel became his second wife at the end of the required wedding week with Leah.

As was customary, Laban gives Jacob the servant girls of Leah and Rachel as part of the wedding gift. These servant girls will bear children for Jacob later in the story. In the Near East, it is still the custom for the older daughter to be married before the younger.

God is using Laban to refine Jacob's character. Jacob must have remembered how he had <u>pretended</u> to be his older brother in order to steal his father's blessing. When we have wrong ideas in our lives, God wants to <u>change</u> them. That's how he refines us and draws us closer to him.

what others say

Max Lucado

Find a place that will offer you an hour's worth of uninterrupted thinking. Then sit down. Take your pen in your hand and—are you ready?—write down what you believe. Not what you think or hope or speculate but what you believe.[8]

Jacob's Family

GENESIS 29:31–35 *When the LORD saw that Leah was unloved, He opened her womb; but Rachel was barren. So Leah conceived and bore a son, and she called his name Reuben; for she said, "The LORD has surely looked on my affliction. Now therefore, my husband will love me." Then she conceived again and bore a son, and said, "Because the LORD has heard that I am unloved, He has therefore given me this son also." And she called his name Simeon. She conceived again and bore a son, and said, "Now this time my husband will become attached to me, because I have borne him three sons." Therefore his name was called Levi. And she conceived again and bore a son, and said, "Now I will praise the LORD." Therefore she called his name Judah. Then she stopped bearing. (NKJV)*

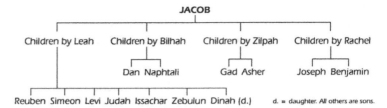

Jacob's Family

JACOB

Children by Leah | Children by Bilhah | Children by Zilpah | Children by Rachel

Dan Naphtali   Gad Asher   Joseph Benjamin

Reuben Simeon Levi Judah Issachar Zebulun Dinah (d.)   d. = daughter. All others are sons.

A Family at Last

The tension in Jacob's family (see chart) must be incredible. Two wives are trying to get their needs met: Leah through being loved and Rachel through having children. One wife can't do anything wrong, and one wife can't do anything right. God mercifully gives Leah some pleasure in life by allowing her to become pregnant. Rachel remains barren.

Leah never gives up hope that her husband will love her. As indicated by the names given to her children, Leah has a deep-seated faith in God. She credits God for her blessed children and is able to move from deep heartache to deep thanksgiving, while she still desperately wants Jacob to love her. Although not perfectly content, Leah seeks God in her predicament. She seems to realize that she cannot force Jacob to love her, but she certainly wouldn't mind if God forced him to do so.

We can learn from Leah, who made herself feel miserable by comparing herself to her beautiful sister Rachel. She must have felt bad at becoming Jacob's wife through deception. Certainly her father wasn't thinking about Leah or Rachel when he arranged the substitution to get seven more years of free labor from Jacob. When Rachel and Jacob finally do marry, Leah certainly knew, as the Bible states, Jacob "loved Rachel more than Leah" (Genesis 29:30 NKJV). Leah hoped her sons would earn her Jacob's love, but in time, she began to find joy in the children God had given her. Through Leah's story, we are warned not to compare ourselves to others and to look to God, not this world, for our happiness. Happiness is emotionally fickle, but joy comes from a choice to trust God and to look to him for our happiness. Happiness is something that happens to you, but contentment is something you choose.

contentment
Philippians 4:11–13

joy
1 Thessalonians 5:16

When we focus on getting our own needs met, not on the needs of others, disharmony and emotional pain are the result. In order to have harmony, we must trust God to meet our own needs and then reach out with his love to others.

Just as Leah could not force Jacob to love her, we can't force anyone to do or believe anything. Only God can change a heart.

Our character and spiritual life are fed by our choices. <u>Contentment</u> and <u>joy</u> are attitudes about life that do not require everything to go our way. Praising God, regardless of the situation, helps our minds and souls to focus on the blessings we do have, rather than being miserable about the ones we don't have.

A Desperate Rachel

> **GENESIS 30:1** *Now when Rachel saw that she bore Jacob no children, Rachel envied her sister, and said to Jacob, "Give me children, or else I die!"* (NKJV)

Whereas Leah's focus is on getting Jacob to love her, Rachel's focus is more on a competition with Leah. Of course, the cultural stigma of being barren contributes to her pain, especially since barren wives could easily be divorced or given lower status in ancient Eastern cultures. Because she doesn't fear being forced out of the home, for she knows Jacob loves her, Rachel is primarily jealous of Leah's children. It is also possible that over time Rachel would feel insecure about Jacob's love. Remember, Jacob had initially loved her for her beauty, but as she gets older and the beauty fades, will Jacob's devotion wane? Will Leah's children draw him to love her instead of Rachel? After all, in Eastern society, sons are highly valued. In her shallow thinking, Rachel is desperate to compete with her sister.

what others say

Barbara Johnson

Winners turn stress into something good; losers let stress turn life into something bad. Winners see an answer for every

go to

jealousy
Proverbs 27:4

envy
Proverbs 14:30

gossip
Proverbs 11:13;
16:28

problem; losers see a problem for every answer. The difference between winning and losing is how we choose to react to disappointments.[10]

Jan Frank

We must take time to plant the seeds of contentment in our heart's garden. We must pause and take notice of things in life for which we are thankful. We must learn to savor those precious moments when we are at peace with God, in spite of the circumstances around us.[11]

Jacob's family all share the same tent or groupings of tents, so the tension and anger between the two women and Jacob must have been obvious and felt by them all. Rachel is so desperate that she says she'll die if she can't conceive.

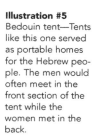

Competitive spirits always wreak havoc in relationships. Jealousy and envy, which often fuel gossip, tear down love and commitment between friends and family. The antidote is trusting that God is in control of our lives. He will provide what we truly need. Ultimately, no person can meet our needs, only God can. If we are focusing on others to hold the key to our happiness and contentment, we will be disappointed.

Substitute Mothers

> GENESIS 30:2–3 *And Jacob's anger was aroused against Rachel, and he said, "Am I in the place of God, who has withheld from you the fruit of the womb?" So she said, "Here is my maid Bilhah; go in to her, and she will bear a child on my knees, that I also may have children by her."* (NKJV)

Illustration #5
Bedouin tent—Tents like this one served as portable homes for the Hebrew people. The men would often meet in the front section of the tent while the women met in the back.

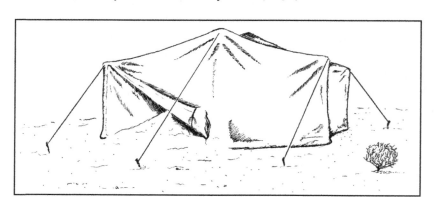

Normally quiet and peaceful, Jacob must have felt the full weight of his beloved wife's frustration. He reminds her he isn't God. Because Jacob cannot solve her problem, she creates a solution that is acceptable to their culture, but not to God. In that culture, children who are born to a wife's servant are considered the wife's children. Rachel tells Jacob to have a child through her maid, Bilhah.

second wife
Genesis 16:2

How history repeats itself! Many years earlier (see chapter 2), Jacob's grandmother Sarah couldn't bear children for her husband, Abraham. Sarah also hatched a plan to force the fulfillment of God's will through her own manipulation instead of trusting God's timing. Sarah gave her servant girl, Hagar, to Abraham as a <u>second wife</u>, and Hagar had his child. But like Rachel's plan, Sarah's plan only brings strife.

> **what others say**
>
> **Jill Briscoe**
>
> Yes, the beautiful and loved Rachel was struggling with rejection, too. And what rejection! The thought that God had bypassed her for another had to feel like total rejection. The fear that she was not good enough for God, or not fit to be trusted with children, must have haunted and taunted Rachel.[12]

Rachel seems to blame God instead of trusting him. Just like Sarah before her, efforts to override God's plan usually bring more heartache than the original pain. Blaming God only forces us to be angry and bitter toward him, thus separating us from his love. If we trust him, we will accept his will rather than blame him for our unhappiness. When we look to others to meet our needs, they become our substitute for God.

A Son at Last

GENESIS 30:4–13 *Then she gave him Bilhah her maid as wife, and Jacob went in to her. And Bilhah conceived and bore Jacob a son. Then Rachel said, "God has judged my case; and He has also heard my voice and given me a son." Therefore she called his name Dan. And Rachel's maid Bilhah conceived again and bore Jacob a second son. Then Rachel said, "With great wrestlings I have wrestled with my sister, and indeed I have prevailed." So she called his name Naphtali.*

When Leah saw that she had stopped bearing, she took Zilpah her maid and gave her to Jacob as wife. And Leah's maid Zilpah bore Jacob a son. Then Leah said, "A troop comes!" So she called his name Gad. And Leah's maid Zilpah bore Jacob a second son. Then Leah said, "I am happy, for the daughters will call me blessed." So she called his name Asher. (NKJV)

First Dan is born; then Naphtali. Rachel feels she is vindicated and has won the competition against her sister. Her focus is wrong; her trust is in human effort, and she won't be completely fulfilled through these children either.

Unfortunately, the competitive spirit rubs off onto Leah and she gives her maid, Zilpah, to Jacob so that she can continue to have children. Leah's faith in God seems to disintegrate as she focuses on the competition instead of on trusting God. Gad (which means "good fortune") and Asher ("happy") are the result.

Rachel and Leah are in competition with each other and constantly make comparisons about each other's families. Such cutthroat attitudes will only bring pain and emotional distance.

> **what others say**
>
> **Naomi Rhode**
>
> Don't compare your family relationships to ours or to others and devalue what you have. Often the family tree spreads its roots deeper into the soil and grows into an unusual shape. Enjoy your family regardless of the shape of your family tree.[13]

Happiness is not found in Jacob's household because the relationships are based in selfishness, not selflessness. Although we may think that trying to get our own needs met will bring happiness, it actually doesn't. God's spiritual perspective says that we receive more in giving. The apostle Paul quoted Jesus as saying, "It is more blessed to give than to receive" (Acts 20:35 NKJV).

Illustration #6
The Mandrake—In the Middle East, the mandrake is believed to stimulate fruitfulness in women. Note the root's humanlike form.

Give Me Those Mandrakes

GENESIS 30:14–16 *Now Reuben went in the days of wheat harvest and found mandrakes in the field, and brought them to his mother Leah. Then Rachel said to Leah, "Please give me some of your son's mandrakes."*

But she said to her, "Is it a small matter that you have taken away my husband? Would you take away my son's mandrakes also?" And Rachel said, "Therefore he will lie with you tonight for your son's mandrakes."

When Jacob came out of the field in the evening, Leah went out to meet him and said, "You must come in to me, for I have surely hired you with my son's mandrakes." And he lay with her that night. (NKJV)

forgive
Ephesians 4:32

Reuben finds some mandrake plants, which are considered aphrodisiacs, and Rachel wants them, believing they will help her to conceive. In bitterness, Leah accuses her sister of stealing her husband, which isn't true. And then as if Jacob is some "thing" that can be bargained for, Rachel gives Leah permission to sleep with their husband. What manipulation!

A mandrake is a stemless root that continually grows and is a part of the potato family. It has narcotic, habit-forming properties and can also be used as a laxative. Native to the Mediterranean region, the mandrake's root resembles a human figure and has a very strong fragrance that may be the origin of its use as an aphrodisiac (see Illustration #6). The mandrake plant is sometimes called by the name "love apple."

Jacob must be surprised when he returns from working with the flocks to find that he has been hired for the night! As for what he thinks of all this, the record is silent. But he must not have enjoyed the tension in the family, as indeed his wives didn't either. When relationships are not centered on wanting God's will, all sorts of difficult possibilities are created. If we want peace in our relationships, we need to <u>forgive</u>, knowing that God has forgiven us even more.

You've Had It All Wrong, Leah

GENESIS 30:17–21 *And God listened to Leah, and she conceived and bore Jacob a fifth son. Leah said, "God has given me my wages, because I have given my maid to my husband." So she*

Dinah
Genesis 34:1–31

Joseph
Genesis 37–50

assistant
Genesis 41:41

called his name Issachar. Then Leah conceived again and bore Jacob a sixth son. And Leah said, "God has endowed me with a good endowment; now my husband will dwell with me, because I have borne him six sons." So she called his name Zebulun. Afterward she bore a daughter, and called her name Dinah. (NKJV)

God gives Leah another opportunity to conceive, but he may not have agreed with her conclusion that she is being rewarded with a fifth son because she gave her maidservant to Jacob. In any case, Issachar ("reward") is born to Leah.

Somehow Jacob is with Leah again, and Leah bears a sixth son, Zebulun ("honor"). She still believes that giving Jacob children, which was indeed valued in that day, will buy his love. Her contentment in the Lord seems to be faltering rather than growing. Finally, Leah gives birth to the only daughter who is mentioned: <u>Dinah</u>.

Rachel, who finally uses the mandrakes, does not find them to be effective. And of course they're not, because it is not in God's will for a plant to get the glory which only he deserves. Whenever we try to use something as a substitute for God's work, we'll find it ineffective.

Joseph Is Born

GENESIS 30:22–24 *Then God remembered Rachel, and God listened to her and opened her womb. And she conceived and bore a son, and said, "God has taken away my reproach." So she called his name Joseph, and said, "The LORD shall add to me another son."* (NKJV)

Finally, for whatever reason in his holy plan, God allows Rachel to become pregnant. In view of how this child, <u>Joseph</u>, will be greatly used of God, we can understand why God opened Rachel's womb. Joseph's name can be identified as the Hebrew word for "add"; Rachel is expressing her belief that God will give her another son. But before he does, the family relocates.

In God's sovereign power, will, and plan, nothing that he wants can be prevented from happening, and nothing he prevents can be forced to happen. God wanted Joseph born after all of Jacob's other children were born, so that the plan to make him Pharaoh's <u>assistant</u> and savior of the Hebrews many years later would be fulfilled.

Women of the Bible

Home at Last

the big picture

Genesis 30:25–35:15

Jacob, Leah, and Rachel leave without telling Laban. He follows them and they work out their differences, before Jacob and his family return to Jacob's homeland.

After Jacob has been used by Laban for twenty years, Jacob devises a way to break free and to prosper his own flocks at Laban's expense; Jacob and his family quietly flee, afraid Laban will pursue and hurt them. Rachel again demonstrates her lack of dependence upon God because she steals Laban's family idols. When Laban catches up with them, he has been warned by God in a dream not to harm Jacob and the family. After working through the troubled family relationship, Laban finally blesses them and lets them go. But now Jacob, who has been told by God to return to his homeland, must face his brother, Esau. God ensures their meeting will be peaceful, and Esau is no longer angry. He welcomes Jacob and his family back to Canaan.

Beth Moore

what others say

You may be going through a confusing time right now. You may not know how God is going to use a situation in your life or why certain things have happened to you. But you can be encouraged and strengthened by recalling what you know about God in the midst of uncertainties.[15]

Rachel is depending on those useless little gods—about the size of miniature dolls—to bring protection. It is amazing what we think will bring us security or protection sometimes. The truth is that only God has the power to protect us.

You Had It All Wrong, Rachel

go to

name
Genesis 32:28–30

> **GENESIS 35:16–20** *Then they journeyed from Bethel. And when there was but a little distance to go to Ephrath, Rachel labored in childbirth, and she had hard labor. Now it came to pass, when she was in hard labor, that the midwife said to her, "Do not fear; you will have this son also." And so it was, as her soul was departing (for she died), that she called his name Ben-Oni; but his father called him Benjamin. So Rachel died and was buried on the way to Ephrath (that is, Bethlehem). And Jacob set a pillar on her grave, which is the pillar of Rachel's grave to this day. (NKJV)*

Rachel, who has become pregnant a second time, dies in childbirth. Her last words describe the son she will not raise: Ben-Oni, meaning "son of my trouble." Jacob doesn't want that constant reminder and renames him Benjamin, meaning "son of my right hand." On the family's journey to Bethlehem, Rachel is buried by the road. Jacob's beloved wife finally sees her greatest desires met in this second son—but it cost her life.

When we don't trust God, we can get focused on the wrong things as sources for our happiness. Rachel thought having children would bring her happiness, but she had the best thing all along: the love of a husband and the opportunity to trust God.

A Just Reward

> **GENESIS 49:31** *There they buried Abraham and Sarah his wife, there they buried Isaac and Rebekah his wife, and there I buried Leah. (NKJV)*

We are not told when Leah died, but we are told that she was buried in the cave in Machpelah where Abraham, Sarah, Rebekah, and Isaac had been buried. Jacob, whose <u>name</u> God later changes to "Israel," says that he will be buried beside her. The wife who was never given what she really wanted to be—the love of her husband, Jacob—did get the honor of being buried by his side. In the end, her unconditional, faithful, persevering love brought her more peace and contentment than Rachel ever knew, even though Rachel was greatly loved. Jacob's twelve sons will later lead the "Twelve Tribes of Israel."

Loving relationships are made through wise, selfless decisions, not through fickle feelings that can easily disappear.

Chapter Wrap-Up

- Rachel meets her cousin Jacob at the well. (Genesis 29:1–12)

- Laban tells Jacob that in exchange for seven years' work he may have Rachel for his wife. But seven years later on the wedding day, Laban deceives Jacob and gives him Leah instead of Rachel. (Genesis 29:21–25)

- Both Rachel and Leah are Jacob's wives. Jacob loves Rachel, but she does not bear children. Leah, however, gives birth to many children, which makes Rachel jealous. (Genesis 29:30–30:1)

- Rachel gives her maid to Jacob and eventually Leah does the same. In time, Rachel does give birth to two sons, and as a result, Jacob has twelve children—the future "Twelve Tribes of Israel." (Genesis 35:23–26)

- Leah always wanted to be loved by Jacob, and she is the one who is buried by his side in the cave at Machpelah. (Genesis 49:31)

Study Questions

1. Why did the seven years Jacob served Laban seem like only a few days?

2. What reason did Laban give for substituting Leah for Rachel on the wedding night?

3. Why is having children so important to Leah?

4. How did Rachel devise a plan to have children before God wanted her to conceive?

5. Why were mandrakes important to Rachel?

Chapter 5 Mary, Mother of Jesus

Chapter Highlights:
- Gabriel's Message
- The Messiah Is Born
- Mary's Heartaches
- A Son's Death and Resurrection

Let's Get Started

The name and image of Mary, the mother of Jesus, is revered by the large majority of people who have heard about Jesus. She is the epitome of surrender, sacrifice, and selflessness. God chose her for a very special role, yet she never asked for it. She was a common teenager who loved God and was willing to cooperate with God's plan to bring the Savior and Messiah into the world—even though it would require a high cost. We have much to learn from her.

go to

Messiah
John 1:4

Gabriel and Daniel
Daniel 8:16; 9:21

Zacharias and Elizabeth
Luke 1:5–25

Sermon on the Mount
Matthew 5:1–7:29

O Little Town of Bethlehem

LUKE 1:26 *Now in the sixth month the angel Gabriel was sent by God to a city of Galilee named Nazareth,* (NKJV)

The angel Gabriel's name means "strength of God" or "man or hero of God." In the Scriptures, Gabriel is frequently mentioned as a messenger bringing God's words to people. He appeared four times, and each appearance brought news about the coming Messiah.

Gabriel also brought messages from God to Daniel in the Old Testament and Zacharias (the husband of Elizabeth. When the text refers to "the sixth month," it means Elizabeth's sixth month of pregnancy.

Nazareth (see Illustration #7) is a small town in the area of Galilee. In a sense, Galilee is the county or province and Nazareth is the country. There were three provinces in Palestine at that time: Judea, Samaria, and Galilee. Galilee was in the upper section of Palestine—the northwest corner.

Jesus would have much of his ministry in Galilee. Nineteen of his thirty-two parables were spoken there, and twenty-five of his thirty-three miracles were performed there. Jesus also gave his great Sermon on the Mount there. Galilee is also known for the Sea of

Galilee—another area mentioned frequently in relation to Jesus' ministry. That body of water is given three other names in Scripture: <u>Sea of Chinnereth</u>, <u>Lake of Gennesaret</u>, and <u>Sea of Tiberias</u>.

Nazareth was considered an insignificant town, yet God used it in significant ways. The things that people of the world consider insignificant are the very things God loves to use—because then he gets the credit and glory. There is nothing and there is no one who is unable to be used by God.

Sea of Chinnereth
Numbers 34:11;
Joshua 12:3; 13:27

Lake of Gennesaret
Luke 5:1

Sea of Tiberias
John 6:1; 21:1

Illustration #7
Palestine—The Romans gave this land lying along the southeastern Mediterranean the name Palestine.

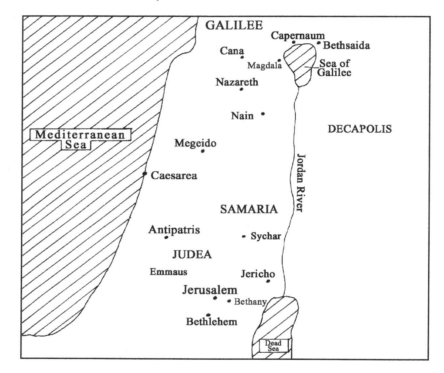

<u>A Virgin? No Way!</u>

LUKE 1:27 *to a virgin betrothed to a man whose name was Joseph, of the house of David. The virgin's name was Mary.* (*NKJV*)

The Jewish custom of marriage included an engagement followed by the actual wedding ceremony like our Western custom today, except that the engagement was much more binding and important than in our culture. The engagement or "espousal" began as soon as negotiations were completed between the groom's and the bride's respective parents or representatives (see chapter 4). After this negotiation process, even though the wedding ceremony had not taken place, the bride was considered legally married to the bridegroom. If the bridegroom died during the engagement, the bride was considered a widow.

grace
Ephesians 1:6

During the engagement, the bride could be claimed from her parents' home at any time for the wedding ceremony. The engaged couple did not live together during the espousal time, and they refrained from sexual relations—even though they were considered husband and wife. That is why Mary "belonged" to Joseph, even though they were not yet married, were not living together, and Mary was still a virgin. You can read more about Mary's betrothal to Joseph, her pregnancy through the Holy Spirit, and Joseph's desire to spare her public disgrace in Matthew 1:18–25.

Although we don't know for sure, most Bible experts consider Joseph an established, slightly older man. He is described in Matthew as "righteous." Mary was younger than Joseph, most likely in her late teenage years or possibly twenty but no older.

Two different genealogies for Jesus are given in the Bible: Matthew 1:1–17 and Luke 3:23–38. Most Bible experts say that the Matthew account tells of Joseph's ancestral line and the Luke account gives Mary's. Both Mary and Joseph came from the tribe of Judah but were descended from different families.

God Picks Mary

> LUKE 1:28 *And having come in, the angel said to her, "Rejoice, highly favored one, the Lord is with you; blessed are you among women!" (NKJV)*

Without warning, the angel Gabriel suddenly appears to Mary. Some wonder whether Mary was praying at the time. Of course, she could have been doing household chores or anything else. In the Jewish culture of that time, every young woman desired and prayed to be the mother of the Messiah. The time was ripe, according to the Scriptures. For a young woman, to be chosen to be the mother of the Messiah was the highest honor possible.

Gabriel's description, "highly favored," can also be translated "full of grace." Just as we often define grace as "God's riches at Christ's expense" and describe how we are favored by God with his unconditional love, Gabriel's greeting refers to her being noticed, chosen,

go to

Naomi
Ruth 1:20

humility
Acts 20:19

and favored by God over every other woman in history—dead, living, or yet to live.

what others say

Harold J. Ocknega

God looked down on the human race and chose the one lone, demure Jewish maiden from the town of Nazareth, and we ask why. The answer can only be, if we exclude the sovereign grace of God, that God looks upon the heart.[1]

Max Lucado

Only heaven knows how long Gabriel fluttered unseen above Mary before he took a breath and broke the news. But he did. He told her the name. He told her the plan. He told her not to be afraid. And when he announced, "With God nothing is impossible!" he said it as much for himself as for her. For even though he couldn't answer the questions, he knew who could, and that was enough.[2]

Gabriel also acknowledges that God is with Mary. In other words, she is aware of God, she worships him, and she knows him well. God is close to Mary.

Mary's name means "bitterness." Naomi, in the book of Ruth, asked people to call her "Mara" or "bitter." That is the root word for the names of Mary, Miriam, Marie, etc. Thankfully, Mary didn't live "down" to her name, and when you and I live in God's power, we do not have to succumb to the negative expectations of others.

What a Surprise!

LUKE 1:29 *But when she saw him, she was troubled at his saying, and considered what manner of greeting this was.* (NKJV)

We can only imagine Mary's surprise. What must have gone through her mind! This must have been the first time she'd had such an unexpected experience, and yet she handled it very well.

Evidently, she isn't afraid of Gabriel's appearance, and most important, she is taken aback to learn that God found special favor with her. Her surprise at God's selection shows her humility. Even though she knew she was an unworthy candidate for this honor because she certainly had done things that weren't godly, she also surrendered to God's choice.

As a young woman who prays and seeks God, Mary focuses on him, not herself. She doesn't expect to receive anything special from God. She most likely enjoys God just for the delight of it, rather than to receive something in return. Now she is being acknowledged by God, and it astounds her.

People who are humble are not aware of their own goodness or favor with God. Most often they think little of themselves—if at all. Yet true humility doesn't make a person feel bad about themselves. There's a balance between feeling valued by God as his creation and depending upon him for his power. Humility is crediting God for whatever he does through you. And it also involves receiving forgiveness for sinful choices in the past and moving on in Christ.

fear
2 Timothy 1:7

> **what others say**
>
> **Beth Moore**
>
> Satan hopes our horrible experiences will cause us to live in the past. *No way*—this pilgrim is moving forward, but I keep my experience tucked in my backpack. It serves to warn me along my way and to be of any help to another sojourner.[3]

Fear Not, Mary

LUKE 1:30 Then the angel said to her, "Do not be afraid, Mary, for you have found favor with God. (NKJV)

Gabriel gently assures Mary that she has nothing to <u>fear</u>. She's not in trouble with God. Instead, she has a special place in his plan for the world.

The angel doesn't scold Mary for her feelings. God understands that humans will have instant reactions to the circumstances they face. But he also expects us to readjust our thinking to trust in him. If we are in a relationship with God, we need never fear God or his hand upon our lives. We are favored as his sons and daughters—princes and princesses in his kingdom.

> **what others say**
>
> **Virginia Stem Owens**
>
> Did the angel Gabriel appear in a blinding light, beating wings that spanned the room? Probably not, since Luke says the girl was troubled by the angel Gabriel's words, not his appearance.[4]

Zacharias
Luke 1:11–14

Joseph
Matthew 1:20–21

Son
Psalm 89:22

Jehovah
the English version
of the Hebrew word
for God, Yahweh

Mary doesn't know that Gabriel recently appeared to her blood cousin Zacharias. Zacharias was also afraid when the angel visited him. How wonderful it is that God looks at our hearts, knows us, and doesn't withhold his plan because of our fear. He works with us, walking us through his plan. His desire is that we learn to trust him more and more. As we do, our fears diminish.

Gabriel Drops the Bombshell!

> LUKE 1:31 *And behold, you will conceive in your womb and bring forth a Son, and shall call His name JESUS. (NKJV)*

Mary learns that she will become pregnant and give birth to a child named Jesus. The Jewish custom was that the father or his close relatives named the child. Mary may have wondered whether she would actually have the power to name her son, but God is taking care of the details by appearing to her betrothed, Joseph.

Jesus, our interpretation of the Hebrew name "Jeshua" or "Joshua" means "**Jehovah** is Salvation." From the very beginning, Jesus' destiny and purpose are determined by God.

He's Got What It Takes

> LUKE 1:32–33 *He will be great, and will be called the Son of the Highest; and the Lord God will give Him the throne of His father David. And He will reign over the house of Jacob forever, and of His kingdom there will be no end." (NKJV)*

Mary's mind must have been in shock, yet the angel's words burn themselves into her consciousness, never to be forgotten. Gabriel describes her future son in five significant ways:

1. He is "great," meaning he is mighty and powerful.

2. He is called the Son of the Highest, referring to his equality with Jehovah God himself. In the Scriptures that Mary knew so well, only Jehovah God is called the "Highest." Yet, the angel says her son will also be called the "Highest." In addition, the significance of the word "Son" is major. In Semitic thought, "son" meant "carbon copy," in the sense that a son displayed the same charac-

teristics as his father; therefore, Gabriel is saying this child will have the nature of God himself.

3. God will give her son the throne of their ancestor King David. Mary knows that the angel is referring to the unbroken reign of Jewish kings from the establishment of the **United Kingdom** with Saul through the Exile. Gabriel tells her that her son will be the next king who will sit on the throne.

4. As a part of sitting on the throne, Mary's son Jesus will rule as a king over the **house of Jacob** forever. Jesus will rule both temporally on earth and spiritually forever. Jesus is the King and in charge of everything. He is in control.

5. All that God the Father is giving to his Son, Jesus, Mary's child, will never stop and cannot be taken away.

Surely all these <u>promises</u> about Jesus would have reminded Mary of God's promises to David. Because Mary knows the Scriptures, she would recall what God said about his temporal throne through <u>Solomon</u> and his future, spiritual throne through the Messiah. Mary would also know that this messenger of God is referring to the promised Messiah.

King David is the baby's "father" in the sense that Scripture often bypasses the name grandfather and calls any ancestor "father."

How Can This Be?

LUKE 1:34 *Then Mary said to the angel, "How can this be, since I do not know a man?"* (NKJV)

Mary doesn't doubt the Messiah is coming, nor does she refute the credentials of this future spiritual King. Mary knows the angel is telling her that her son will be the Messiah. But she does ask an intelligent question: "How can this be?" In spite of her incredible experience, she wants to know how she can conceive a child while a virgin.

Mary's question isn't one of doubt in God's ability or plan, only one of curiosity about how God intends to carry out his plan. Her mind knew she could not conceive, so how would God do the impossible?

promises
2 Samuel 7:13–16

Solomon
1 Kings 1:38–50

United Kingdom
the Israelites are
united into one
nation

house of Jacob
through this family
of Jacob, God
revealed his plans to
bring the Messiah

doubts
Luke 1:18

John the Baptist
Matthew 3:1–12

know more
Luke 12:48

faithful
Isaiah 25:1

provide
Romans 12:3

In contrast to Mary, her cousin Zacharias <u>doubts</u> Gabriel's message: Elizabeth, his wife, will have a child. The angel must have expected greater faith of Zacharias, a priest supposed to know God intimately. Besides, Elizabeth's pregnancy was not nearly as inconceivable since the couple had a sexual relationship. Zacharias's questions and lack of faith result in his loss of speech until his promised child, who will become <u>John the Baptist</u>, is born.

Mary was told she would become pregnant while a virgin. Her news was a much harder thing to grasp, yet Mary did not doubt. Her innocent question about how conception was possible did not disturb God.

God is reasonable in his expectations of us. From those who <u>know more</u>, he expects more. To those who are not as knowledgeable, he is gracious and merciful in response to questions. With such a loving God, we can be assured that he knows our hearts and only expects that which is reasonable from us. And if it requires more faith, he is <u>faithful</u> to <u>provide</u> it.

what others say

Eugenia Price

If the Lord God was going to bring it about, she could relax and rest, knowing that whatever he did, would be good and right. Mary knew this because she knew God himself. Surely she was filled with awe and wonder, but now she knew there would be no stranger involved. It would be her Lord, himself, and her reply came naturally and quietly.[5]

Could Mary be thinking that Joseph would become the father? Yet that would only make the child another human being like themselves. Something very unique and special must occur for the angel's ideas to take place.

<u>Here's the Way It Is, Mary</u>

LUKE 1:35 *And the angel answered and said to her, "The Holy Spirit will come upon you, and the power of the Highest will overshadow you; therefore, also, that Holy One who is to be born will be called the Son of God. (NKJV)*

Although we might not feel that this response offers much explanation, evidently it is enough for Mary. She doesn't question it or ask for more information. We can only accept by faith the creative contact that the Holy Spirit made within Mary's body at some point, either within seconds or within days of Gabriel's message. Whether Mary actually felt something in her body we do not know.

After Christ was conceived within her by the Holy Spirit, her pregnancy was like any other's pregnancy. Yet this supernaturally formed child was the essence of Jehovah God and a woman. He would be both **divine** and human: something that had never happened before and would never happen again. Mary's womb was chosen to carry Jesus, but he already existed in eternity.

provides
1 Thessalonians 5:24

divine
of God

See What God Has Already Done!

LUKE 1:36–37 *Now indeed, Elizabeth your relative has also conceived a son in her old age; and this is now the sixth month for her who was called barren. For with God nothing will be impossible." (NKJV)*

Knowing her need for reassurance, God helps Mary in a way that is particularly relevant to her. Mary's cousin, Elizabeth, who has been barren for many years, is now pregnant. Even though Elizabeth lives some distance away, Mary has most likely heard of Elizabeth's struggle to conceive over the years. They may have even talked at the festival days. Perhaps Mary looked up to Elizabeth as a godly woman or as a kind of mentor.

The angel's words about Elizabeth are of great importance and joy to Mary. God is saying, "You can depend on me! See what I've already done! The impossible!" The angel's seven words speak of the powerful, majestic, mighty, and magnificent God, who can do anything he wishes. Elizabeth, without aid of surgery or fertility drugs, has become pregnant according to God's plan. Mary might think, "If God can do that, then I can certainly trust him with his plan for me."

God says the same thing to us when he challenges us to step out in faith toward a new venture, project, or relationship. God always provides us with the strength necessary to do the work he has planned for us.

Here I Am, Lord

LUKE 1:38 *Then Mary said, "Behold the maidservant of the Lord! Let it be to me according to your word." And the angel departed from her.* (NKJV)

Mary responds with trusting cooperation and submission. She tells the truth about who she is—a servant who is willing to allow God to use her in whatever way he sees fit. She knows the consequences of becoming an unwed mother: What will people think of her? Who can she trust to tell? What will Joseph think? What will her relatives and friends think of her? Will Joseph divorce her? The Scriptures say he should. So many fears could have stifled her ability to cooperate with God, but instead she chooses to respond based on her great faith in God, her knowledge of his nature, and the assurance God has given her.

The word "maidservant" that Mary uses is really "slave." Some translations also use the word "handmaiden," a female slave. In our modern times we don't like the word "slave." To think of ourselves as a slave to God seems crude. But whether we call ourselves slave or servant, we are pledging ourselves to obey God in whatever he wants us to do.

> **what others say**
>
> **Herbert Lockyer**
>
> The Holy Spirit, by his gentle operation, took Deity and humanity and fused them together and formed the love-knot between our Lord's two natures within Mary's being.[6]

Faith is taking one step at a time, according to God's will. Mary might have wanted to ask more questions and know the future, but if so, she resists. She is content to know that God has taken her this far and rests in the additional knowledge that he'll take her the rest of the way. Faith says, "God will tell me more in time," and Mary courageously accepts God's mission for her.

Wait Until You Hear This

LUKE 1:39–40 *Now Mary arose in those days and went into the hill country with haste, to a city of Judah, and entered the house of Zacharias and greeted Elizabeth.* (NKJV)

Hearing about Elizabeth's pregnancy makes Mary want to see her. Perhaps Mary is thinking, "If Elizabeth has experienced God's miraculous work, maybe she'll understand what's happening to me!"

Perhaps Mary's mother is dead, and so Elizabeth is the first person she wants to tell. We know from later verses that Mary does have a sister named Salome. Assuming Salome is younger, Mary probably wouldn't feel comfortable sharing the news with her. In any case, Mary seeks out her cousin Elizabeth.

To visit her cousin, Mary made the long trip, a journey of several hundred miles, by herself. Some Bible experts believe Mary began the journey after she told Joseph about her pregnancy. Initially, Joseph made plans to divorce Mary, albeit secretly. If Mary knew of Joseph's plans, she must have gone to visit Elizabeth with a doubly heavy heart. Only after an angel assured Joseph that Mary's pregnancy was God's work did he go through with his plans to wed her.

Salome
Mark 15:40

divorce
Matthew 1:19

strength
Philippians 4:13

> ## what others say
>
> ### Harold J. Ocknega
>
> Her fears were keen because of the shame which would come to her in the world, and yet there was always the reassuring message of the angel that had been given to her and the confidence of her faith that the God who now was fulfilling his prophecies would care also for her.[7]
>
> ### Pam Farrel
>
> God doesn't point to his place for us and say, Good luck, hope you can pull it off! No, God leads us to be usable by living the calling through us by his spirit, and that pulls the pieces together.[8]

Sometimes we too need to make a great effort, with God's strength, to obtain the encouragement we need. For example, we might make an appointment with a Christian counselor to help our faltering marriage or do away with inappropriate habits. Sometimes God calls us to take great pains to represent him. He might call us to leave our homes and do missions work. At his direction we may change or give up our jobs to stay home with the children. Sometimes we might take a job at lower pay in ministry, trusting that he'll provide for finances. In all things, if he calls someone to do something, he promises to provide everything that person needs:

time, energy, finances, encouragement, approval . . . you name it, he'll provide it.

Elizabeth's Song

> LUKE 1:41–45 *And it happened, when Elizabeth heard the greeting of Mary, that the babe leaped in her womb; and Elizabeth was filled with the Holy Spirit. Then she spoke out with a loud voice and said, "Blessed are you among women, and blessed is the fruit of your womb! But why is this granted to me, that the mother of my Lord should come to me? For indeed, as soon as the voice of your greeting sounded in my ears, the babe leaped in my womb for joy. Blessed is she who believed, for there will be a fulfillment of those things which were told her from the Lord." (NKJV)*

Mary enters the home of Zacharias and Elizabeth, greets her cousin with a kiss on the cheek, and immediately receives the encouragement she needs. Elizabeth's baby responds within her because the Messiah is in his presence. Elizabeth, instantly given supernatural wisdom and insight through the Spirit, knows that standing before her is the mother of the Messiah. Unable to tone down her joy, Elizabeth loudly acknowledges this young woman as blessed or "well spoken of." Mary, she says, is the most honored of all women because of the child within her. The word "Lord" means both the Greek word "Messiah" and the Hebrew word "Yahweh." By using the word "Lord," Luke communicates to both Jewish and Greek readers that Jesus is actually God.

what others say

Shirley Rose

If we could only learn to keep our secret. We must quietly keep God's message in our hearts and give ourselves time to understand and grow into the challenge. As privileged as Mary's position was, she did not reveal her private knowledge before the proper time. She was patient. We must also learn to wait for God's timing.[9]

intercession
Romans 8:27

Elizabeth tells Mary that her baby has moved within her. Elizabeth is six months pregnant and probably has been able to feel her unborn baby's movements for months. This particular movement, however, was special enough that she had to tell Mary about it.

Some Bible experts suggest Elizabeth did not feel her baby move until Mary arrived. If so, Elizabeth must have worried about her unborn baby. When the baby finally moved, Elizabeth probably felt relieved as well as thrilled.

Elizabeth's exclamations boosted Mary's faith and determination. Can you imagine how negative thinking might have begun to overwhelm Mary during her long trip to Elizabeth's house? Once God's assurance becomes an event of the past, we often wonder if we really did experience his leading or just imagined it. We can begin to doubt whether God really has the power or is in control of what he's asking us to do.

If Mary, in her humanness, had begun to allow doubts to cripple her faith or to make her stumble, she must have been bolstered by Elizabeth's joy. Certainly, Elizabeth's words gave Mary a treasure for future times, when people misunderstood God's mission for her or gossiped behind her back. The angel had indeed come to Mary. Fortunately, Elizabeth knew the truth, even though Mary hadn't told anyone. Mary knew God would prove himself faithful, no matter what.

Elizabeth greeted Mary personally and called Mary's baby "my" Lord. Elizabeth has already accepted Jesus as her Messiah, her Savior and Lord. Many people report that they came to know Christ with little influence from others or even knowledge of the evidence for Jesus' life. Elizabeth was one of those people. For everyone who believes, whether after deep reflection or through quick acceptance, the credit should go to God's Holy Spirit, who prompts us to have faith even in a faithless world. And who knows how many people had been praying for them without their knowledge.

Hannah
1 Samuel 2:1

The apostle Paul said, "For this reason we also thank God without ceasing, because when you received the word of God which you heard from us, you welcomed it not as the word of men, but as it is in truth, the word of God, which also effectively works in you who believe" (1 Thessalonians 2:13 NKJV).

Mary's Song

> LUKE 1:46–48 *And Mary said:*
> *"My soul magnifies the Lord,*
> *And my spirit has rejoiced in God my Savior.*
> *For He has regarded the lowly state of His maidservant;*
> *For behold, henceforth all generations will call*
> *me blessed. (NKJV)*

Although the text indicates that Mary "said" these words, we believe that this was actually a song, Mary's spontaneous and joy-filled praise song to God. Note the word "magnifies." Luke 1:46–55 is often called "The Magnificat," referring to the Latin word for "magnify."

Mary is so overwhelmed with joy that she can't keep from praising God. She calls him her Savior, demonstrating her knowledge of sin and her need to be restored to fellowship with God. By calling him her Savior, we can see that she has a close, personal relationship with the Lord rather than a distant one.

God has allowed Mary to know that, in the future, people will know her as a woman who received God's special favor, not because she deserved it, but because of his choice.

what others say

Stormie Omartian

When I praised and worshiped God, it was like being hooked up to a spiritual IV. As long as I had my heart and eyes lifted to God in worship and praise, the joy of the Lord poured into my body, mind, soul, and spirit and crowded out the darkness and depression. It worked every time.[11]

Virginia Stem Owens

Like Hannah's, Mary's song is highly political, stressing the way God will vindicate and elevate the lowly and powerless, while subjugating the high and mighty. Neither Mary nor her listen-

listeners would have made distinctions between spiritual and political realms, however. She is, in fact, echoing Gabriel's message that her son will be the king who restores Israel, affirming publicly what she has been told privately.[12]

rehearsing
Psalm 150

The Prayers and Songs in the Bible

Scripture	Description
1 Samuel 2:1–10	Hannah praises God after he enables her to finally become pregnant. She focuses on how he helps the weak.
Luke 1:68–79	Zacharias prophesies about the ministry of his son, John the Baptist.
Luke 2:29–32	Simeon praises God for revealing the Messiah.
The Psalms	David and others offer a variety of songs and prayers dealing with many different emotions, struggles and victories.

Praise and thanksgiving are different. While giving thanks focuses on what God does, praise focuses on who God is and brings us closer to him. Because disbelief, doubt, and distrust of God are often fueled by wrong ideas about him, praising him and <u>rehearsing</u> his wonderful nature shatter wrong ideas and replace them with faith and trust. Praise causes our hearts and minds to focus on the truth about God.

A Promise Fulfilled

LUKE 1:49–55
For He who is mighty has done great things for me,
And holy is His name.
And His mercy is on those who fear Him
From generation to generation.
He has shown strength with His arm;
He has scattered the proud in the imagination of
their hearts.
He has put down the mighty from their thrones,
And exalted the lowly.
He has filled the hungry with good things,
And the rich He has sent away empty.
He has helped His servant Israel,
In remembrance of His mercy,
As He spoke to our fathers,
To Abraham and to his seed forever." (NKJV)

Israel
Genesis 32:22–32

Mary mentions many of the attributes of God as her song continues in Luke 1:49–55.

He is:

1. mighty and powerful (verses 49 and 51)

2. holy (verse 49)

3. merciful to those who turn to him (verse 50)

4. disciplining those who are proud (verses 51–52)

5. aware of people's thoughts and motives (verse 51)

6. able to set up or remove those in authority (verse 52)

7. able to honor the humble (verse 52)

8. capable of fulfilling the needs of people who seek him (verse 53)

9. never forgetful about his chosen people, the Israelites (verses 54 and 55).

what others say

Harold J. Ocknega

Thus in the very first promise given in the Garden of Eden, we have the implication of a Virgin Birth, for it does not say the seed of the man, but the seed of a woman, which would be absurd and a manifest impossibility were it not by the direct creative power of God.[13]

Mary refers to her son's birth as the fulfillment of God's promise many years earlier—through the covenant given to Abraham and continued through his promises to Abraham's descendant, originally named Jacob and now called <u>Israel</u>.

Mary's experience fulfills God's promise of redemption in Genesis 3:15, where he tells Satan that the seed of the woman will bruise him on the head. That is significant because physically only the man has a "seed" and the woman is the receptor of the man's seed. When God refers to the woman's seed, he foretells the Virgin Birth.

Let Me Learn from You

LUKE 1:56 *And Mary remained with her about three months, and returned to her house. (NKJV)*

works
Ephesians 2:10

Mary lives with Elizabeth for three months—until Elizabeth's baby John (John the Baptist) is born. Evidently, she returns to her own home and not to Joseph's home.

> ## what others say
>
> **Beth Moore**
>
> God promised his plans are to prosper us, to give us hope and a future (Jeremiah 29:11). The Word of God and Christ's indwelling Spirit equip us to fulfill the <u>works</u> preordained for us in God's perfect plan. As my mom would say, Get busy![14]

Just as Mary is prepared for her future by spending time with Elizabeth, God promises to provide everything we need to serve him and fulfill his plan for our lives. Mary needs encouragement and someone to believe her, and God provides both in a miraculous way. God always supplies the knowledge, tools, and ability to carry out his purposes—although they may not be supplied until the last minute!

Joseph Agrees to God's Plan

> ## the big picture
>
> **Matthew 1:18–25**
>
> While Mary is visiting Elizabeth, an angel appears to Joseph, her legal husband, and the angel explains to Joseph what God is doing through Mary. When Joseph understands God's plan, he decides not to divorce Mary.

After Mary becomes pregnant, she tells Joseph what happened. At first he doesn't believe her and plans to divorce her quietly, without exposing her to public scrutiny and humiliation. But God intervenes by sending an angel to assure Joseph in a dream that Mary has conceived through the Holy Spirit. The angel also tells Joseph to name the baby Jesus and identifies him as the Savior. Joseph risks his own embarrassment by obeying God and taking Mary into his home as his wife, though he and Mary do not have sexual relations.

infidelity
Leviticus 20:10

prophecy
Isaiah 7:14–16;
9:6–7;
Micah 5:2–3

Bethlehem
Micah 5:2

ancestral line
Matthew 1:1–17

Law
the law of Moses;
the Ten
Commandments
and other Old
Testament laws God
gave the Israelites

Roman Empire
land under Roman
rule decree: imperial
order

According to the **Law**, the punishment for <u>infidelity</u> is death. At the very least, Mary and Joseph risk humiliation and gossip, for everyone will realize that Mary became pregnant before joining Joseph in his home. Many will conclude the couple had sexual relations before the wedding ceremony.

God Uses a Decree

the big picture

Luke 2:1–4

Caesar Augustus calls for a census. To obey this decree, Mary and Joseph must go to Bethlehem at the time of the baby's birth.

Caesar Augustus rules the **Roman Empire** from 27 BC to AD 14. Augustus doesn't realize it, of course, but God uses his decree to bring about just the right conditions for Jesus' birth to fulfill a <u>prophecy</u> given many years earlier—that the Messiah would be born in <u>Bethlehem</u>.

The purpose behind Caesar Augustus's census is to tax everyone. Bible experts believe the decree was issued about 8 BC, but the decree may not have taken effect for several years.

On to Bethlehem

Because Joseph's <u>ancestral line</u> originates with King David, Joseph must register in Bethlehem, seventy miles away. Joseph and Mary surely see God's hand in this, because they know what Scripture says: the Messiah will be born in Bethlehem. Because Mary is far along in her pregnancy, she and Joseph probably travel more slowly than others who must make the same journey, so that by the time they arrive in Bethlehem, there are no accommodations left.

God can use anything and everything for his purposes. He controls everything that happens in our world, though we are often unaware of exactly how he is working. The Jews of that time were probably very unhappy about the census. Had they known how this census would fulfill prophecy, they might not have been so upset.

When Joseph and Mary come to Bethlehem (see Illustration #7), the small but important town has a population of about three hundred people. Most live in boxy, whitewashed homes located on top of a low but rather steep ridge. Caravans come through Bethlehem on their way to Egypt. King David was born here, and the tomb of Ruth, from the Old Testament book of Ruth, is here.

swaddling
Ezekiel 16:4

> **what others say**
>
> **Carol Kent**
>
> I know that in the midst of my personal circumstances, which at times have felt hopeless and pointless, God is intimately involved in shaping the core of me because he loves me. I also know that I have an eternal purpose, and I want to radically and thoroughly release my will to his will.[15]

A King in a Manger

LUKE 2:5–7 *[Joseph went there] to be registered with Mary, his betrothed wife, who was with child. So it was, that while they were there, the days were completed for her to be delivered. And she brought forth her firstborn Son, and wrapped Him in swaddling cloths, and laid Him in a manger, because there was no room for them in the inn. (NKJV)*

The wonderful event finally happens! In God's perfect timing and provision, the Messiah is born exactly where God had predicted four hundred years earlier. You can find a prophecy about the place of Jesus' birth in Micah 5:2, about the time of his birth in Daniel 9:25, and about the unusual conception in Isaiah 7:14. We do not know whether Joseph finds the local midwife to help or if the poor couple handles the birth all by themselves, but Mary gives birth just like any other mother.

Two thousand years ago, parents wrapped their newborns in long cloth strips, believing this wrapping ensured straight limbs and prevented broken bones (see Illustration #8). This practice, called "swaddling," is significant, because the shepherds are told that they will find the baby in swaddling clothes lying in a manger. The Bible says Jesus was born in "a manger." In those days, animals were often sheltered in caves, and the mangers, or feeding troughs, were carved into the cave walls. It is very likely that Jesus was born in such a cave—a dingy, foul-smelling, and unsanitary setting (see Illustration #9). But most likely, Mary and Joseph did their best to make it habitable for their new baby.

sympathize
Hebrews 4:14–15

other children
Mark 3:31–32

God allowed his Son, Jesus, to be born in such unpleasant surroundings, so his Son would identify with the struggles facing ordinary men and women. Of course, God could have planned for Jesus to be born into a royal family, but God wanted Jesus to be part of a common family. That's how Jesus knows what it feels like to be human. Even though he is God and does not sin, he is able to sympathize with human weaknesses.

what others say

Joyce Meyer

If you and I are going to enjoy the fullness of God in our lives, we must go through periods in which we have to stand alone. Sometimes that is good for us because we get too caught up with people. Sometimes we must be left with nobody so we will learn to depend solely upon the Lord.[16]

Max Lucado

Tell God what hurts. Talk to him. He won't turn you away. He won't think it's silly. If it matters to you, it matters to him.[17]

Because the Bible specifically notes that Jesus was Mary's firstborn son, as opposed to her only son, we know she had other children later. Her other sons are mentioned later in Scripture, and most of them become believers in Jesus the Messiah.

Illustration #8
Swaddling—Babies were wrapped tightly in cloth strips because the parents thought the cloth bands encouraged the development of healthy limbs.

The events in Jesus' life, both big and small, were predicted in the Old Testament.

Jesus' Life Predicted in Old Testament

Prophecy	Subject	Fulfillment
Isaiah 7:14	Born of a virgin	Matthew 1:18–23
Micah 5:2	Place of birth	Matthew 2:1–6
Hosea 11:1	Escape into Egypt	Matthew 2:14–15
Jeremiah 31:15	Slaughter of infants	Matthew 2:16–18
Isaiah 9:1–2	Ministry in Galilee	Matthew 4:12–16
Isaiah 53:4	Healing the sick	Matthew 8:16–17
Psalm 78:2	Teaching parables	Matthew 13:34–35
Zechariah 9:9	Riding a donkey	Matthew 21:1–9
Zechariah 11:13	Potter's field	Matthew 27:6–7

prophecy

While Shepherds Watched Their Flock

the big picture

Luke 2:8–20

Angels appear to some shepherds out in their field as they watch over their sheep. In a brilliant display of God's power, the angels tell them about the baby Jesus' birth, and the shepherds want to go visit the baby Messiah.

go to

Moses
Exodus 16:10;
20:18; 40:34

presence
2 Chronicles 7:1;
Ezekiel 1:27–28

The birth of Jesus brings many wonderful and extraordinary things. God sends angels to announce the incredible news that the Messiah has been born. The visible glory of God appears to these humble shepherds. They are terrified at first, but once they hear the specific instructions of where to find him, they are willing to leave their sheep and find the baby Jesus. After seeing the fulfillment of what they've been told, they are eager to tell others. And the shepherds attribute the wondrous things they experience to God, not to coincidence.

God's glory, when he manifests himself personally, is referred to many times in Scripture. Moses requested to see God in person, but God had to shield Moses from fully seeing him. No person can actually see God and live. His glorious presence is not only too amazing to view, but his holiness makes any sinful person completely unworthy to see him.

The shepherds long to find the baby Messiah. Unlike many people through the ages who have been offered the truth about Jesus as

ambassadors
2 Corinthians
5:20–21

God's Savior and don't want to find out more, the shepherds want to find out more and are willing to risk the loss of their livelihood—their sheep—in order to seek God. Refusing Jesus from entering your life is a very serious decision, with unfortunate consequences. God gives mercy and grace to those who are willing to leave behind the things that block them from making God the Lord and Savior of their lives.

The lowly shepherds are given the privilege of being the first "evangelists" for Jesus. Instead of choosing people whom the world might consider more worthy for such a privilege, God shows us that anyone can tell others about Jesus. In fact, God calls us his "<u>ambassadors</u>."

Amazing!

LUKE 2:19 *But Mary kept all these things and pondered them in her heart. (NKJV)*

Mary is amazed by all these things. Although she knows her son is God and the Messiah, she still must marvel at being at the center of such a marvelous work of God. Her initial knowledge of God becomes the foundation for her faith, so she can trust God in spite of all these amazing things. Mary's life gives us one of the Bible's best examples of courageous submission to God.

Illustration #9
Manger—Many ancient animal feed boxes or mangers can be seen today in this part of the world, often in natural caves where the animals were kept. Jesus was probably born in a cave and placed in a stone manger.

Mary's Future Ponderings and Heartaches

Mary would continue to ponder over many things during the life of Jesus. At times, those "ponderings" would become full-fledged heartaches. Here are some of them.

- Luke 2:41–50: Jesus teaching in the temple. Mary and Joseph find 12-year-old Jesus (whom they thought was lost) in the temple teaching grown men. Jesus tells them, "I must be about my Father's business." We can only imagine Mary's confusion since most sons grow up doing the same business as their fathers. Mary knew Jesus had a special calling, but she couldn't have understood all it entailed.

- John 2:1–11: Jesus' response to Mary at the wedding in Cana. It would seem that Mary is eager and maybe even a little impatient for Jesus to get started on his ministry. Or maybe her compassion for the ill-planned wedding overrides her trust in her son and she makes a request that he gently rebukes. Although she had faith enough to tell the servants to prepare, her heart may have wondered why Jesus responded as he did.

- Matthew 12:46–50: Jesus calls other people who follow him his mothers and brothers. Talk about rejection! Did she take it that way? We don't know, but most mothers would feel rejected. She had faith in him from his birth, but even his "own people" thought he was "out of His mind" (Mark 3:21 NKJV). Mary isn't identified specifically in that group, but she must have been torn wondering how she could convince even her own relatives to believe in Jesus' ministry.

- John 19:25–27: Jesus dies on the cross. Mary's heart must have broken to see her own flesh and blood dying a cruel and torturous death, especially since he was totally innocent of the charges. When she agreed to become the mother of the Messiah, she didn't know all she signed up for, and this had to be the biggest heartbreak of all.

- Acts 1:14: Mary must have been astonished to know Jesus had risen from the dead (we don't know if he appeared to her specifically or not). And then she must have been overjoyed to be involved in the expanding group of believers. Mary's heartache and confusion about Jesus' mission must have been replaced by a confidence in knowing God had fulfilled his plan.

go to

meditate
Philippians 4:8

roots
Colossians 2:6–7

circumcised
Genesis 17:12–13;
Leviticus 12:3

present
Exodus 13:2, 12;
34:20

what others say

Harold J. Ocknega

One's beliefs and one's thoughts always lead to one's actions.[18]

Steve Farrar

We need both the right diet and the right exercise. Prayer and Scripture go together, and we are most effective when we have a good balance of the two. The man who studies the Bible without praying will develop a good mind with a cold heart. The man who prays without knowing Scripture will consistently pray outside the will of God, for that is where his will is revealed.[19]

The way for us to grow spiritually is to "ponder" and meditate upon God's Word, God's work in our lives, and the truth about him. Without thinking about those things, we will stay dormant in our faith and ability to trust God. But the more we meditate on God, the more our spiritual roots will sink deeply into faith in him.

A Young Man Moves On

the big picture

Luke 2:21–24

As the Jewish law dictates, Mary and Joseph take baby Jesus to be presented in the temple. Like every couple who dedicate their baby to God, they also offer a sacrifice.

Joseph names the baby "Jesus" as God instructed him. "Jesus" is the Greek form of the Hebrew name "Joshua," meaning "Yahweh is salvation."

According to God's instruction, Jesus is circumcised eight days after he is born. Then thirty-three days after his birth, Mary and Joseph travel the short distance from Bethlehem to Jerusalem to present their first son to God, in accordance with the Old Testament. They are also required to give a sacrifice indicating Mary is no longer "unclean" because of giving birth.

what others say

Frances Vander Velde

How exciting it was to be in the Temple with her special child! In the court of the women she met other mothers, with their babies and offerings. Mary was poor and had little to bring—just two doves which the priest took from her, after perhaps, reading aloud from Leviticus twelve.[20]

twelve
Leviticus 12:3

According to the Law of Moses, a woman who gives birth to a son is considered unclean for seven days (Leviticus 12:2); then on the eighth day, the male child is circumcised (Leviticus 12:3); for an additional thirty-three days, she remains unclean (Leviticus 12:4); and then she sacrifices an offering to be ceremonially **purified** (Leviticus 12:6–8). A woman who gives birth to a daughter is considered unclean for fourteen days (Leviticus 12:5); then for an additional sixty-six days, she remains unclean (Leviticus 12:5); and finally she sacrifices an offering in order to be ceremonially purified (Leviticus 12:6–8).

purified
anything unclean or polluted has been removed

Simeon: "Look! He's the One!"

the big picture

Luke 2:25–39

While Mary, Joseph, and baby Jesus are in the temple, two people identify Jesus as the Messiah. They are Simeon and Anna, and they have been waiting a long time to see God's provision of salvation.

While Mary and Joseph are in the temple fulfilling the requirements of Jesus' circumcision, Simeon, a godly man who doesn't know them, suddenly takes the baby Jesus in his arms and prophesies that Jesus is indeed the Messiah.

Mary and Joseph are amazed again. Simeon says Jesus has come both for the Jews and the Gentiles. Although they may have anticipated Jesus' ministry to his own people, they might have been shocked to think he would also minister to non-Jews.

Simeon says that those who accept Jesus as the Messiah will "rise" because of their salvation. Those who refuse Jesus' offer will "fall" spiritually. He also indicates that Jesus will face much opposition.

Simeon then predicts the great distress and pain Mary will experience in the future. She cannot imagine the deep hurt she will experience. Later in her life, Simeon's words probably provide comfort to Mary. Perhaps remembering his words helps her understand that her role as Jesus' mother requires her to experience much grief.

Anna: "Yes! He's the One!"

go to

mentor
Titus 2:3

expected
1 Corinthians 10:13

Jesus
John 16:33

share
1 Peter 4:12–13

As if Simeon's prediction isn't enough, eighty-four-year-old Anna, who serves God in the temple, suddenly comes up to Mary and Joseph. Anna also acknowledges that their baby is the future Redeemer of the Jews. The heads of these new parents must have been swimming as they left Jerusalem.

Perhaps many years later, when Mary is a widow, she remembers Anna and how she accepted her widowhood without bitterness. Anna only enjoyed seven years with her husband, and perhaps Anna inspires and encourages Mary to be accepting of God's plan. Maybe Anna becomes a kind of <u>mentor</u>.

When we need help in facing difficulties, God often provides mentors and encouragers, as he did for Mary. The Bible says to find help in counselors and those who offer their expertise, opinions, and encouragement. Seeking help is not a sign of weakness but of wisdom. "Without counsel, plans go awry, but in the multitude of counselors they are established" (Proverbs 15:22 NKJV).

When we experience struggles, we need to understand that what we're experiencing is typical and should be <u>expected</u>. Being Christians doesn't mean we won't face difficulties and temptations. In fact, the apostle Paul said we should expect it. So did <u>Jesus</u>. If we know we should expect temptations and difficulties, we can prepare to face them in God's power. As Christians, our suffering for Jesus' sake will bring him glory. We'll eventually <u>share</u> that glory in heaven.

Wow, Visitors

> ### the big picture
>
> ### Matthew 2:1–12
>
> Several wise men from the East contact King Herod about what they've learned through astrology: a king has been born recently in his area. King Herod sends them to find this "King of the Jews" in Bethlehem. They find Jesus and worship him with their gifts. Fortunately, an angel tells them not to report their discovery to King Herod, so they do not give away the child's location.

Not only is Mary amazed at God's work through the shepherds, through Simeon, and through Anna, she is equally amazed when Magi from the East come to visit. They bring gold, frankincense, and myrrh for the child. The wise men have already alerted King Herod (also known as Herod the Great) that they know the Messiah has been born. The king says he wants to worship the Messiah and sends the wise men to find him. But in a dream, the Magi are warned not to report back to Herod.

Although our traditional Christmas songs speak of three Magi from the East, Scripture does not actually tell us how many there were. Because of the three different gifts, many people have assumed that there were three men, but we don't know. What do you think?

God might have had the Magi bring gifts, so that Mary, Joseph, and Jesus would have the means to protect Jesus by traveling to Egypt (see Illustration #10). When God provides financially for his people, he may not mean it for their comfort or extravagant living, but for purposes he chooses.

Out of Here

the big picture

Matthew 2:13-21

Warned in a dream that Jesus' life is in danger, Mary and Joseph travel to Egypt and stay there until the danger is past.

Herod sees Jesus as a threat to his reign. He thinks Jesus is going to become a king over his land rather than a spiritual king. Herod's horrible cruelty in other situations is well known, so to no one's surprise, Herod plans to kill all children two years and younger who are located in Bethlehem and its surrounding areas. In a dream, an angel tells Joseph to escape to Egypt.

Illustration #10
Mary's Journey—
Mary and Joseph
fled with their two-
year-old Jesus to
Egypt. Two or three
years later, the fam-
ily returned and set-
tled in Nazareth in
Galilee.

go to

prophecy
Hosea 11:1

Nazareth
Judges 13:5

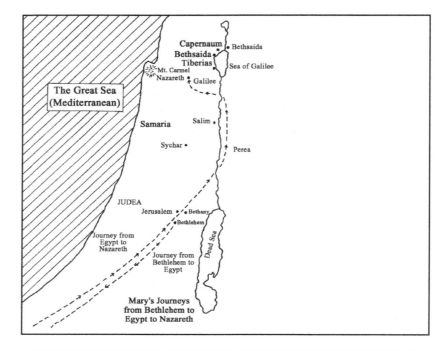

The Great Sea
(Mediterranean)

Capernaum
Bethsaida • Bethsaida
Bethsaida •
Tiberias • Sea of Galilee
Mt. Carmel
Nazareth • Galilee

Samaria
Salim •

Sychar • Perea

JUDEA
Jerusalem • • Bethany
• Bethlehem

Dead Sea

Journey from
Egypt to
Nazareth

Journey from
Bethlehem to
Egypt

**Mary's Journeys
from Bethlehem to
Egypt to Nazareth**

what others say

Eugenia Price

Mary depended upon her Son because of what she had
learned about him through their years together. We can do
this, too. True faith is the natural result of knowing what God
is like. It is never dependent on our being able to understand
all that he may be trying to say to us.[21]

Mary and Joseph's trip to Egypt is also in accordance with scriptural <u>prophecy</u>. Eventually Herod dies, and an angel tells Joseph in
a dream that they can return to Israel. But he is further directed to
go to <u>Nazareth</u>. This also fulfills a prophecy.

What a Fright!

the big picture

Luke 2:41-50

Jesus and his parents go to Jerusalem for the yearly feast, and
his parents think Jesus is lost. But he's not lost; he's doing his
heavenly Father's work. They find Jesus teaching the religious
teachers as well as listening to them and asking them questions.

On the way back from a yearly feast in Jerusalem, Mary and Joseph can't find Jesus. In these traveling bands, the youth often travel with others their age. So at first, Mary doesn't miss Jesus. This can be taken to indicate that Jesus is a responsible boy whom his parents trust.

know
John 5:19

By the end of the first day of traveling, Jesus' parents can't find their twelve-year-old son. After searching, they decide to return to Jerusalem, and the return takes the entire second day. On the third day, they find him in the temple. They are amazed that Jesus is actually teaching the religious teachers. He responds, "Why did you seek Me? Did you not know that I must be about My Father's business?" (Luke 2:49 NKJV). Of course, Mary gently rebukes him, but Jesus isn't offended. He must have understood their concern. But he has more important things to do. Regardless, according to God's will, Jesus returns to his parents, all the while growing physically, mentally, and emotionally. Jesus knows fully who he is by the age of twelve.

> ### what others say
>
> #### Frances Vander Velde
>
> Mary's child had perfect, uninterrupted fellowship with the Father, and gradually developed to the full consciousness of His mission.[22]

Mary remembers everything that happens, but her heart and mind still cannot fully comprehend Jesus' purpose. Although Mary and Joseph are at a loss for completely understanding Jesus' mission, the boy Jesus knows full well.

When God calls you to a specific purpose, you can be confident in it and not swerve from it, even though others may not understand. Just as Jesus keeps to his purpose, all of God's children have something important to accomplish for him. Nothing need prevent them from doing it.

Just as Jesus knows his purpose, he knows his heavenly Father intimately. Out of that intimacy, he is able to <u>know</u> and do the Father's will. You and I can't really know what God wants us to do, without knowing God.

Where's the Wine?

the big picture

John 2:1-11

Mary realizes that the wine is running out at a wedding in Cana. She tells Jesus, and he responds by providing the wine that the bridegroom needs so that he won't be embarrassed by his huge mistake.

As a woman, Mary spots the problem facing a newly married couple in the town of Cana. Because wedding feasts usually last seven days, knowing how much food and wine to provide is difficult. At this wedding, the groom hasn't planned well or perhaps many people show up unexpectedly. Regardless, being without enough food or wine is a major disgrace in this culture. Mary is not simply being courteous. She wants to save the groom great embarrassment, even humiliation.

Jesus hasn't yet done any miracle, so whether Mary is expecting one is uncertain. But for sure, she believes in Jesus' power to do something about the situation—otherwise she wouldn't have asked.

After Mary calls Jesus' attention to the problem, Jesus calls her "woman." Although Jesus' response to his mother may seem disrespectful, the word "woman," as he gently spoke it, conveys respect. Jesus is also indicating that from now on, he is severing his closest ties with her. Never again do we hear him call her "mother." As his ministry is about to start, he must have a new relationship with her. He is her Lord and Savior, and she is his spiritual daughter, just like any other woman or man.

Some mothers might not have appreciated Jesus' gentle rebuke, but Mary doesn't resist his comments. Over many years of learning to trust God, she is now able to trust him for this new phase of their relationship.

At his mother's request, Jesus comes through and rescues the wedding. He not only creates wine but the very best-tasting wine.

Mary must have been very pleased with Jesus' sensitivity to her request and the needs of others. As a mother, she must have felt proud of her son, even though only a few people learned what actually happened.

go to

pruning
John 15:1–2

Perhaps Mary has been waiting these thirty years for Jesus to reveal himself as the Messiah, and she feels this wedding is the perfect opportunity. In those thirty years Jesus had been responsible for the carpentry work that supported his mother and brothers (and possibly his sisters) after Joseph's death. We do not know when Joseph died, but since he is not mentioned in these later accounts, we can conclude that he is not alive.

Whatever God does, he does well. Just as Jesus created an exceptional wine, he creates wonderful things in our lives. In the midst of difficulties, we may not see his work or be able to acknowledge it, but even problems and disappointments are God's way of pruning his children and creating something good.

Depending on God and looking to him for everything in our lives—not just the big things—makes us feel close to him. As we remember who he is and know he's big and powerful enough to handle any situation we face, we deepen our friendship with him.

Drawing closer to God requires a faith and trust that says, "Whatever you do, God, I'll cooperate. You know best. I trust you. Do your perfect will." Without such dependence, we feel like we're observing God at a distance. But surrendering ourselves to his loving care makes us feel comfortable and secure in his presence. If we are afraid, we won't be able to relax and trust him to do the best thing. Prayer is asking God to intervene and reveal himself.

apply it

Mary Is Left Out

JOHN 2:12–13 *After this He went down to Capernaum, He, His mother, His brothers, and His disciples; and they did not stay there many days.*

brothers
John 2:12

Now the Passover of the Jews was at hand, and Jesus went up to Jerusalem. (NKJV)

By the beginning of Jesus' ministry, Mary is no longer actively involved in her son's life. After a few days with her and her other sons, Jesus leaves them behind. When he left, Mary might have remembered Simeon's prediction that her heart would be pierced. This is one of those times. Once she had been intimately involved in his life, but no more.

Is He Crazy?

MARK 3:20–21 *Then the multitude came together again, so that they could not so much as eat bread. But when His own people heard about this, they went out to lay hold of Him, for they said, "He is out of His mind." (NKJV)*

Whether Mary is concerned we don't know for sure, but she probably is. Understandably, Jesus' family is concerned for his health. He's not eating properly, and most likely not resting as they think best. They intend to "lay hold" of him. In other words, they plan to "make an arrest." Obviously, their attempt is not successful, for Jesus continues his ministry. Mary must have been anxious as she dealt with the disbelief of Jesus' <u>brothers</u> and her own misgivings about his work. Though she believes in his calling, she certainly could not like his long, strenuous days and his missed meals.

> **what others say**
>
> **Max Lucado**
> When Jesus' brothers didn't share his convictions, he didn't try to force them. He recognized that his spiritual family could provide what his physical family didn't. If Jesus himself couldn't force his family to share his convictions, what makes you think you can force yours?[24]

Mary may also be concerned that her son seems so alone at times. Although the disciples surround Jesus, maybe she worries that no one understands or supports him like family. Yet every mother must remember that God wants our children to be needy, so that they will need him. If we are somehow able to meet all their needs—and we can't—they will have no need to seek and depend on God. Even

Jesus has to depend on his heavenly Father. Mary could not meet all his needs, even if she wanted to. Only God can do that.

More Heartburn

go to

come
Revelation 3:20

leaves
Hebrews 13:5

MATTHEW 12:46–50 *While He was still talking to the multitudes, behold, His mother and brothers stood outside, seeking to speak with Him.*

Then one said to Him, "Look, Your mother and Your brothers are standing outside, seeking to speak with You."

But He answered and said to the one who told Him, "Who is My mother and who are My brothers?" And He stretched out His hand toward His disciples and said, "Here are My mother and My brothers! For whoever does the will of My Father in heaven is My brother and sister and mother." (NKJV)

Mary's heart must be troubled and hurt again as Jesus distances himself from her in yet another incident. Yet she knows he speaks the truth. She doesn't pursue her need to speak with him, which demonstrates yet again her trust in God. You can also read about this incident in Mark 3:31–35 and in Luke 8:19–21.

what others say

Virginia Stem Owens

Now Mary, so willing in her youth, so confident at the Cana wedding, begins to have doubts about this touring miracle business. Realizing that her boy can't attract large crowds without also attracting the notice of the officials, she wonders if her son has lost his mind.[25]

Mary may begin to wonder about the validity of Jesus' ministry. At times, every Christian wonders about her own calling as a child of God. Did it really happen? Did Jesus really <u>come</u> into my life? Is he really still here or has he left? Yet remembering that special point when she invited Jesus into her heart and life, along with reviewing—even memorizing—scriptural promises will bring an assurance that Jesus never <u>leaves</u> us nor forsakes us.

Heartache of a Son's Death

JOHN 19:25–27 *Now there stood by the cross of Jesus His mother, and His mother's sister, Mary the wife of Clopas, and Mary Magdalene.*

When Jesus therefore saw His mother, and the disciple whom He loved standing by, He said to His mother, "Woman, behold your son!" Then He said to the disciple, "Behold your mother!" And from that hour that disciple took her to his own home. (NKJV)

After three years of ministering to people and revealing God's love, Mary's son, Jesus, is tried in court, found guilty based on lies, and then crucified on a cross. After thirty-three years of loving and trusting Jesus, Mary's heart must break to see him hang on the cross. She certainly did not anticipate this horrible scenario when she told the angel more than thirty years earlier, "Behold the maid-servant of the Lord! Let it be to me according to your word" (Luke 1:38 NKJV).

Would she want to take it back now? Regardless of her distress, she is there for her son. The fact that she is standing, not sitting in dejection or without strength, shows her commitment to God's final plan. In many ways, all that has happened over the years, all those "piercings" of her heart, has prepared and strengthened her to deal with this ultimate challenge.

As Mary stands by her son, she hears him ask his Father to forgive those who are crucifying him. That must have been important for Mary to hear because his words probably kept her from bitterness toward those who killed her son and from losing her trust in God. If Jesus wants them to be forgiven, shouldn't she also forgive them? Once again, Mary shows her courage by standing by her son at the cross.

Then, moments later, in concern for his mother, Jesus directs the disciple John to take her into his home. She must have been touched by this act of love for her.

We don't know why her other sons aren't designated by Jesus to be her caretakers. Maybe because they still do not believe in him, Mary would have no one to share her beliefs. John believes the same way as Mary. Being with John provides great comfort for her during the next three days.

Just as Mary's heart and faith were strengthened over time to cope with the devastation of seeing her son sacrificed for the sins of the world, so each one of us is strengthened—through God—for the things we face now and in the future. God promises to walk with us and to strengthen us. If we refuse to cooperate with his pruning and strengthening process, we could find ourselves unable to cope when more difficulties come.

He Is Risen!

ACTS 1:12–14 *Then they returned to Jerusalem from the mount called Olivet, which is near Jerusalem, a Sabbath day's journey. And when they had entered, they went up into the upper room where they were staying: Peter, James, John, and Andrew; Philip and Thomas; Bartholomew and Matthew; James the son of Alphaeus and Simon the Zealot; and Judas the son of James. These all continued with one accord in prayer and supplication, with the women and Mary the mother of Jesus, and with His brothers.* (NKJV)

Our last view of Mary, along with Jesus' brothers, who finally believe in him, is one of joy and peace. Jesus has been raised from the dead and has ascended into heaven. Now she knows all is well for her son, and she is most likely an important part of the new Christian community.

That Mary is mentioned along with all the disciples points to the fact that she was one of Jesus' close followers. She was with him when he was born, as he grew up, and when he died. Mary serves as a great inspiration to women who yearn to follow Christ without wavering.

Chapter Wrap-Up

- The angel Gabriel suddenly appears to a young Jewish woman named Mary and tells her she will become the mother of the Messiah. Although she asks an intelligent question, she doesn't ask it out of doubt. She gives her heartfelt and verbal assent to God's plan. (Luke 1:26–38)

- In fulfillment of all God's prophecies about the birth of the Messiah, Mary gives birth to Jesus in Bethlehem, even though she doesn't live there. (Luke 2:1–7)

- At times Mary's heart is pierced with pain and possibly doubt as she sees her son go through many difficult times, including living without a home and seemingly rejecting her and her family. (Matthew 12:46–50)

- The ultimate piercing of her heart occurs when she sees Jesus hanging on the cross for the sins of the whole world—including hers. But three days later, she rejoices over his resurrection. (John 19:25–27)

Study Questions

1. Who tells Mary she will give birth to the Messiah and how does he address her?

2. How does the angel's announcement that Mary's relative Elizabeth is pregnant help to build Mary's trust in God's plan for her?

3. How does Mary's song of rejoicing build and reveal her faith in God?

4. What indicates that Mary and Joseph were poor at the time of Jesus' birth?

5. Why were Mary and her other sons concerned about Jesus' health?

Part Two
Women of the
Old Testament

Chapter Highlights:
- **Jochebed, Puah, and Shiphrah**
- **Rahab**
- **Deborah**
- **Manoah's Wife**
- **Hannah**

Chapter 6 Women of Strong Faith

Let's Get Started

Women of the Bible practice their faith in both big and small ways. Some risk their lives for their faith, while others bring God's words to their communities. Many women wisely turn their difficulties over to God, trusting that he will provide. No matter how they express their faith, God is pleased and responds to them. Today these women provide us with role models of women whose faith overcame their individual struggles. These women of the Bible turned to God, and so should we.

You Told a Lie?
(Jochebed, Puah, and Shiphrah)

> ### the big picture
> ### Exodus 1:15–2:10
> The population of the people of Israel grows in Egypt, and a new pharaoh, who doesn't honor the memory of the beloved Joseph, fears the potential power of so many people. He commands that all Jewish male babies be killed, but three women—Jochebed, Puah, and Shiphrah—risk their lives to disobey his command.

In the first and second chapters of Exodus, Jochebed, Puah, and Shiphrah are singled out for their bravery and their efforts to save the Hebrew children. In Egypt, the population of the Israelites has grown to the point where their large numbers threaten the Egyptians, even though the Egyptians hold the Hebrews captive as slaves. The Egyptian pharaoh commands that all Hebrew male children be killed so that the population of the Israelite community can't expand any further. In particular, he commands the two midwives of the Hebrew community, Shiphrah and Puah, to kill all the male Hebrew babies.

Despite the possible danger to their own lives, Shiphrah and Puah disobey the order. They lie to Pharaoh, telling him that Hebrew

other Scripture
Numbers 26:59

Miriam
Exodus 2:4

sovereign
Isaiah 25:1

hates lying
Proverbs 6:16–17

Peter and John
Acts 4:19–20

women give birth so fast that the babies arrive before the midwives can get there. Even though the women tell a lie to the pharaoh, God blesses them and their own families and brings them prosperity.

At this same time, an Israelite woman named Jochebed (she is not named in this passage, but we know this from <u>other Scripture</u>) gives birth to a beautiful son and hides him for three months. Then she risks everything by putting him in a wicker basket and instructing his sister, <u>Miriam</u>, to place the basket in the river. Through God's <u>sovereign</u> control, God causes Pharaoh's daughter to find the basket with its crying baby. God causes Pharaoh's daughter to feel compassion for the baby, even though she identifies him as a Hebrew child who should be killed. Instead of death, he is taken into the household of Pharaoh as this woman's son. That child will be, of course, the future deliverer of the Hebrews—Moses!

> **what others say**
>
> **Marjorie L. Kimbrough**
>
> Once Jochebed was convinced that Miriam knew exactly what to do, she was able to let go of her beloved child and let God and her daughter do what she knew they would.[1]

Although God doesn't want us to lie, perhaps in rare situations, such as the one the midwives experienced, we must lie to others in order to obey God's higher authority and rules. God says he <u>hates lying</u>, but obeying him may require it. This certainly doesn't happen often. But God is always our foremost person to please.

<u>Peter and John</u> refused when commanded by the Jerusalem authorities to stop preaching about Jesus. They didn't lie, but they refused to obey the ruling. At times, civil disobedience, possibly including lying, might be necessary to obey God.

Lying should never be done lightly. Lying, under the direction of God, is a very rare situation and probably will not happen in our lifetimes.

Come On In! (Rahab)

> **the big picture**
>
> **Joshua 2:1–24**
>
> While the Israelites explore the land God has promised them, they send spies into the town of Jericho. These two men find

When Joshua and the large group of Israelites arrive at the Jordan River to move into their inherited land in Canaan, they wait for their two spies to return with information about Jericho. The two men enter Jericho and encounter Rahab, a harlot (prostitute) in that city, and they lodge at her home. Because Rahab has heard of their God, she believes the Israelites will be successful in conquering the land.

The same day the king of Jericho learns that the two spies are staying in Rahab's house, and he tells her to bring the men to him. Fortunately, she has already hidden the two men on her roof under stalks of flax. When night comes, Rahab goes to her roof, tells the men of her faith in God, and asks them to spare her and her family when the Israelites attack. They agree, and Rahab lets them down from her roof by a scarlet rope. The men tell her to protect herself and her family by hanging the same scarlet rope in her window, and she does.

When the Israelites attack, God causes the walls of Jericho to fall down in a great victory for the Israelites. Rahab and her family are <u>saved</u>. Rahab leaves prostitution, marries <u>Salmon</u>, and becomes the mother of <u>Boaz</u>, who will marry Ruth. Both Rahab and Ruth are named in the lineage of <u>Jesus</u>.

Rahab's life reminds us that God never excludes anyone, and nor should we. No one is unable or unworthy to receive God's redemptive power. No sin is beyond God's ability and desire to forgive. Perhaps Rahab's scarlet rope foretells the shedding of the blood of Jesus.

go to

saved
Joshua 6:22–25

Salmon and Boaz
Matthew 1:5

Boaz
Ruth 2:1

Jesus
Matthew 1:5;
Ruth 4:18–22

Hall of Fame
Hebrews 11:31

what others say

J.I. Packer and Carolyn Nystrom

The Bible gives us life stories of many persons whom God chose and called to his service. Again and again it takes time out to tell us of the weaknesses, moral lapses and spriitual failures in their lives. God's way with these folk is to change them as he uses them.[2]

Even though Rahab is described as a harlot, she is listed in the Hebrews "<u>Hall of Fame</u>" of faithful believers and is named in the

action
James 2:22–26

kings
Judges 17:6

Barak
Judges 4:6

song
Judges 5

book of James as someone whose faith takes <u>action</u>. Because she believed in the Hebrew God, she is accepted as faithful. Regardless of our past, God wants to include us in his "Faithful Hall of Fame Believers."

the big picture

Judges 4, 5

Deborah, a judge and prophetess during the time of the judges, did many mighty things for God and was highly respected as a woman of God. Not only did she hear God's voice and give directions to the Israelites, she composed praise music that celebrated God's glorious works.

Victory's Coming! (Deborah)

Deborah lived in the land of Israel during the time when judges ruled the land, before God allowed Israel to have <u>kings</u> to rule them. She predicts Israel's deliverance. At one point, Deborah brings this message from God to the people: "Has not the LORD God of Israel commanded, 'Go and deploy troops at Mount Tabor; take with you ten thousand men of the sons of Naphtali and of the sons of Zebulun; and against you I will deploy Sisera, the commander of Jabin's army, with his chariots and his multitude at the River Kishon; and I will deliver him into your hand'?" (Judges 4:6–7 NKJV).

Their current oppressor is Jabin, king of Canaan. Deborah tells an Israelite warrior, <u>Barak</u>, that he should lead ten thousand men in battle, but he replies by saying he won't go without her. She agrees, and her presence comforts him and gives him confidence. Israel is delivered from its oppressor as Deborah predicted (see Illustration #11). Later, Deborah and Barak write a beautiful <u>song</u> giving glory to God for the victory he gave them. In the song, they review all the wonderful things God had done for them.

what others say

Marjorie L. Kimbrough

Barak was smart enough to realize that all of the instructions for the victory were being given to Deborah, so he did not want to venture out without her.[3]

God gives both women and men messages for guiding people and representing God's will. Many years after the days of Deborah, the apostle Paul taught the believers in Galatia that there is no <u>gender difference</u> within the body of Christ. Only for practical daily living does Paul give instructions specifically for women and men, wives and husbands. But in our relationship with Christ, God does not make a distinction between male and female.

gender difference
Galatians 3:28

Nazirites
Numbers 6:2–6

Illustration #11
The Attack of Judges—This map shows where Deborah and Barak fought the attack of the Canaanites.

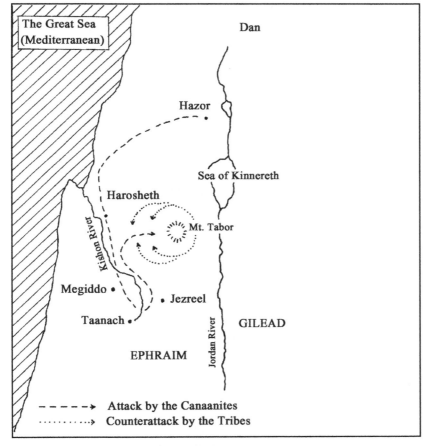

The Great Sea (Mediterranean)

Dan

Hazor

Sea of Kinnereth

Harosheth

Kishon River

Mt. Tabor

Megiddo

Jezreel

Taanach

Jordan River

GILEAD

EPHRAIM

– – – – ➤ **Attack by the Canaanites**
· · · · · · · ➤ **Counterattack by the Tribes**

It's a Boy! (The Mother of Samson)

the big picture

Judges 13–14:4

An angel brings the wonderful news to a childless Hebrew woman that she will have a son who will have a special purpose. But to fulfill this purpose, he must become a member of a special group called the <u>Nazirites</u>. The mother believes God's message, and just as God said, her son Samson becomes God's mighty deliverer for the Israelites.

Delilah
Judges 16:4

A barren woman and her husband, Manoah, live in Israel during the time of the judges. The Philistines, the Israelites' enemies, are being used by God to discipline his disobedient people, the Israelites. Suddenly this unnamed woman is visited by an angel of the Lord (see Judges 13:3). The angel tells this wife of Manoah that she will finally conceive and give birth. The angel instructs her to follow the rules of the Nazirites, a special religious group, and to have her son follow the Nazirite rules as well.

When the angel appears again, he speaks to the husband as well as the wife, so both can hear the angel's instructions. After the angel leaves, the couple realizes they were in God's presence. Manoah fearfully believes that they will be killed, because in the past, no one could be in God's presence and live. But his wife, wisely and with great faith in the goodness of God, says, "If the LORD had desired to kill us, He would not have accepted a burnt offering and a grain offering from our hands, nor would He have shown us all these things, nor would He have told us such things as these at this time" (Judges 13:23 NKJV).

This mother-to-be realizes that all the wonderful things experienced in the angel's presence would not have happened if God planned to kill them. She's right, and the angel's words come true. Samson is born. His parents try to be a godly influence, and while he is not perfect, as we know from his affair with <u>Delilah</u>, in time, he becomes a mighty deliverer of the Israelites.

what others say

Marjorie L. Kimbrough

The person who needed the instructions had already gotten them. Manoah would have to trust his wife. He would have to learn that God speaks to women as well as to men.[4]

Naomi Rhode

If I have the gift of being a great planner of the future, a cum laude graduate, a positive thinker with abundant faith in God, but lack the daily encouragement and interest in my children's current goals and hurts, I am missing my highest calling.[5]

Nazirites were set apart to live godly lives. They were to abstain from fermented drink, from cutting their hair and from contact with dead bodies. Usually, such a vow to be a Nazirite was for a limited period of time, but God called Samson to it for his entire life—although he didn't always follow its rules.

Manoah asks the angel, "Now let Your words come to pass! What will be the boy's rule of life, and his work?" (Judges 13:12 NKJV). Isn't that the question all parents have about their children? We think that if we can know what our children should grow up to become, we can be more successful in directing our children in God's will. But just as the angel doesn't fully answer Manoah's question, God does not answer similar questions from us. As in other parts of our lives, God wants us to walk by faith, and faith is, of course, particularly important when we're parents. He also wants us to understand that we cannot force our children to walk in the way we think they should. We can only be faithful in influencing them to grow closer to God. Faith believes that God is in control of our children's lives.

Eli
1 Samuel 1:3

It's Another Boy! (Hannah)

the big picture

1 Samuel 1–2:21

Hannah is one of her husband's two wives, but she, unlike the other wife, has no children. The other wife teases her unmercifully about her infertility, so Hannah feels hurt and sad. She prays to God, and he answers her prayers by giving her a son. That son is Samuel, who will be a faithful judge of Israel.

A godly woman, Hannah is ridiculed relentlessly for her infertility by the other, fertile wife of her husband. Hannah wants a child desperately, and she frets about all the painful humiliation she endures. In time, she takes her deep longing to God, praying for a child and vowing to dedicate her child to service in God's temple. As she prays at that temple, her murmured petition is misinterpreted by Eli, the priest, as the mutterings of a drunk. More humiliation! Hannah explains to Eli that she is actually petitioning God. Eli, without knowing her request, tells her that her prayer will be granted. By faith, she believes him and returns home rejoicing. God answers her prayer and gives her a son, Samuel, who will become a godly judge in Israel.

prayer
1 Samuel 2:1–10

pray
1 John 5:14

Certainly most mothers would regret promising to give their young child to someone else to raise. No matter what Hannah feels, she keeps her promise. She feels gratitude for God's gift of Samuel, and she composes a beautiful <u>prayer</u> to God, rejoicing in his faithfulness. After Samuel is weaned, she delivers him to the temple. From then on, she can only visit him once a year. Perhaps as reward for her faithfulness, Hannah has more children.

what others say

Marjorie L. Kimbrough

With her prayer and her promise, Hannah exceeded the three barren biblical women, Sarah, Rebekah, and Rachel, who preceded her. All had grieved because of their barrenness, yet Hannah was the only one who engaged in fervent prayer and made a solemn vow of expectation for the life of her child.[6]

Jan Johnson

At times, our conversation with God may imitate the way Samuel's mother, Hannah, poured out her soul to God because of her infertility. She was so intense that the priest Eli assumed she was drunk.[7]

Jill Briscoe

Surely Hannah must have been tempted to renege on her promises once Samuel was born. To keep the little one until he was three or even four and then give him up must have been sheer torture. Yet Hannah had promised God the child should serve him, and she kept her word.[8]

Hannah immediately believed Eli's promise that her prayer was answered. She changed from a sad, weeping woman to a joyful one. When we believe God has heard our prayer, we too change our countenance from sad to happy. If we <u>pray</u> according to God's will, we know that he'll hear us and answer. That's where our joy comes from.

The vows or commitments we make to God must be taken seriously. Hannah surely wept at leaving her beloved first son at the temple. But because she had made that commitment with God and because it was God's will for the deliverance of Israel, she kept her promise. As a result, God rewarded her with more children.

Although we can't always count on great blessings when we obey God or keep our <u>commitments</u> to him, we know that we win his favor and his pleasure.

commitments
Numbers 30:2

Make Me a Cake! (Widow of Zarephath)

> ### the big picture
>
> ### 1 Kings 17:8–24
>
> Because of a drought, a Gentile widow and her son expect to die from lack of food. But God causes Elijah, an Israelite prophet, to come to the widow's door. She obeys what Elijah says, and God provides both food and healing.

Totally discouraged, a Gentile woman stops trying to solve her problems, which include a drought and the resulting famine. Instead, she prepares a last meal for herself and her son before they die from starvation. At that moment, the Jewish prophet Elijah shows up at her door in the village (see Illustration #12) and tells her, "Do not fear; go and do as you have said, but make me a small cake from it first, and bring it to me; and afterward make some for yourself and your son" (1 Kings 17:13 NKJV).

Elijah challenges her faith by requiring the widow to use the last of her food and prepare him a meal. He promises her that she won't run out of food. Her faith in "his" God strengthens her. She follows Elijah's directions and his promise comes true. The widow learns to turn a few resources into abundance with God's help. Generosity often requires giving out of scarcity, not just abundance.

But once again, the widow's faith is challenged when her son dies. She blames Elijah, and he brings her son back to life. As a result, she acknowledges him as a man of God and puts her trust in his God.

> ### what others say
>
> **Barbara Johnson**
>
> There is no way around suffering. We have to go through it to get to the other side. Many folks deny their pain. They try to bury themselves by escaping everyone and everything. If you don't face your grief and work it through, it will eat you alive.[9]

Jesus
Luke 4:26

Illustration #12
Israelite Village—
Today in Israel, you
can find the remains
of hundreds of typi-
cal Hebrew villages,
with their character-
istic cluster of low,
flat-roofed buildings.

While on earth, <u>Jesus</u> uses the example of the widow of Zarephath to show how gracious God is to both the Jews and the Gentiles. God has no prejudice toward certain groups of people. He loves everyone and wants everyone to know his great love for them.

The widow of Zarephath must make a very difficult choice.

Will she risk having nothing for her last meal or trust that Elijah's God will provide for her and her son? Each of us faces a similar choice: Can we trust God when we are most needy? But a little faith goes a long way. God might challenge us to give our all, but he always gives back in abundance. The more we commit to God, the more he can bless us.

Oil, Oil, and More Oil! (The Widow and a Pot of Oil)

the big picture

2 Kings 4:1–7

A prophet's widow complains to another prophet, Elisha, that her sons will be sold as slaves because she doesn't have any money. Elisha tells her to do something really strange. When she obeys, God works a miracle that gives her the income she needs to keep her sons.

After a prophet's widow complains to Elisha that her sons will soon be sold as slaves, he challenges her faith by telling her, "Go, borrow vessels from everywhere, from all your neighbors—empty vessels; do not gather just a few. And when you have come in, you shall shut the door behind you and your sons; then pour it into all those vessels, and set aside the full ones" (2 Kings 4:3–4 NKJV). Amazingly, the original oil in her jar never runs out, because God reproduces the little oil she has. She keeps pouring and pouring until she fills up all the jars she and her sons have collected. She sells the surplus oil to pay her debt, and the money saves her sons from slavery.

parable
Matthew 25:14–30

faithful service
3 John 5

> ## what others say
>
> ### Marilyn Willett Heavilin
>
> The Lord gave us all of our creative ability and he didn't expect us to ignore it; he just asks that we employ it in righteous directions.[10]

When Elisha first asks the widow what she has available, she replies, "Your maidservant has nothing in the house but a jar of oil" (2 Kings 4:2 NKJV). Her eyes are blinded to the possibilities she possesses. When God asks us how we are going to serve him, we don't want to answer "Nothing." Are we going to focus on the "nothing" or on the talents God has given us?

In Jesus' parable about the talents, he doesn't focus on how much we're given or how much we produce for him, but whether we offer faithful service with whatever we have.

Would You Believe...a Boy! (Woman of Shunem)

> ## the big picture
>
> ### 2 Kings 4:8–37
>
> A barren woman who lives in Shunem blesses the prophet Elisha by feeding and sheltering him. To bless her, Elisha prays she can have a child. She miraculously conceives and gives birth. That beloved son dies but is raised to life by Elisha.

An infertile woman gives food to the prophet Elisha. Then the woman convinces her husband to build a little room for Elisha, so he can rest when he passes through their country. She does all this unselfishly without being asked and without expecting anything in

burden
Matthew 11:28–30

return. Elisha's servant, Gehazi, suggests to Elisha that the woman would like a child. Elisha predicts she'll have a child the following year. At first, she can't believe the news, but one year later, she gives birth to a son who is very loved.

Tragedy strikes when the child dies, but she knows to turn to Elisha. Before she leaves to get Elisha, she tells her husband, "Everything will be all right." She rides to the prophet and pleads for her son's life. Elisha returns and raises the child back to life.

> ### what others say
>
> **Max Lucado**
>
> Learn from each thump. Face up to the fact that you are not "thump-proof." You are going to be tested from now on. You might as well learn from the thumps—you can't avoid them. Look upon each inconvenience as an opportunity to develop patience and persistence.[11]

When you experience tragedy or unhappiness, to whom do you run? This woman knew to go to someone who represented the Lord. Because we can have a personal relationship with God himself, we can, unlike the grieved mother of Shunem, run to God directly. He is always available and sensitive to our pleas for help and direction. He says, "Come to me if you have a <u>burden</u>."

Chapter Wrap-Up

- Even though Pharaoh has commanded the midwives and the mothers of the Hebrews to kill all male children, Jochebed, Puah, and Shiphrah disobey and God rewards them. (Exodus 1:15–2:10)

- Rahab provides protection for the Israelite spies and, as a result, she and her household are saved when God hands Jericho over to his people. (Joshua 2:1–24)

- A prophetess during the time of the judges, Deborah speaks God's words to the people. She predicts a great victory for Israel and, after the victory, she composes a song giving glory to God. (Judges 4–5)

- A barren Hebrew woman believes God's message for a son. Her son Samson becomes God's mighty deliverer for the Israelites. (Judges 13–14:4)

- Hannah, her husband's second wife, is barren, unlike the other wife. God answers her prayers for a son—Samuel, a faithful judge of Israel. (1 Samuel 1–2:21)

- A widow and her son are prepared to die during a drought, but God provides both food and healing. (1 Kings 17:8–24)

- A prophet's widow receives help from Elisha through a miracle. God reproduces oil in vessels. Her abundance is determined by how many vessels she borrowed from neighbors. (2 Kings 4:1–7)

- A barren woman miraculously gives birth. Her beloved son dies but is raised to life by Elisha. (2 Kings 4:8–37)

Study Questions

1. Why did Pharaoh want the male Hebrew babies killed, and what ingenious method did Jochebed use for saving her son?

2. Why did Rahab believe that God would allow his people, the Israelites, to conquer her city?

3. Why did judges rule the land of the Israelites during the time of Deborah the prophetess?

4. What did the Nazirites stay away from?

5. What challenge does Elijah give the widow of Zarephath?

6. What did Elisha tell the prophet's widow to do to save her sons from slavery?

7. What does the woman of Shunem do for Elisha that prompts him to reward her by predicting she'll have a child?

Chapter 7 Esther

Chapter Highlights:
- A New Queen Is Chosen
- Haman's Plan
- God's Intervention
- Deliverance!

Let's Get Started

Can you imagine a book of the Bible that doesn't mention God? In the book of Esther, God's name is not mentioned, yet his handiwork and fingerprints are all over this amazing story of Esther. A courageous young woman named Esther saves the Jewish people at a dangerous point in their history. Perhaps the author doesn't name God, because God's presence is so obvious in the story. We don't know who wrote the book of Esther, but many Bible scholars believe the book's author lived at the time of Esther.

Esther provides an inspiring example for us. Her story shows that each of us has been chosen by God for a purpose, just as Esther was chosen for a purpose. While we probably will not save a whole group of people as Esther did, we have missions from God just as important. Let's see how God, without being named, does his work through Esther.

He Is a Party Animal

Esther 1:1–8

the big picture

King Xerxes, king of the Persian Empire, reigns over a large empire. To show off his wealth, power, and possessions, he throws a huge party in his impressive and lavish palace.

King Ahasuerus, who is also called Xerxes in the Hebrew text and some biblical translations, ruled the Persian Empire for twenty-one years, from 485 to 465 BC. His vast domain included 127 provinces from India, in the part known today as West Pakistan, to Ethiopia (see Illustration #13). These land holdings differentiate his reign from the reign of his grandfather, also King Ahasuerus. Between his reign and his grandfather's reign, his father, King Darius, led the Persian Empire.

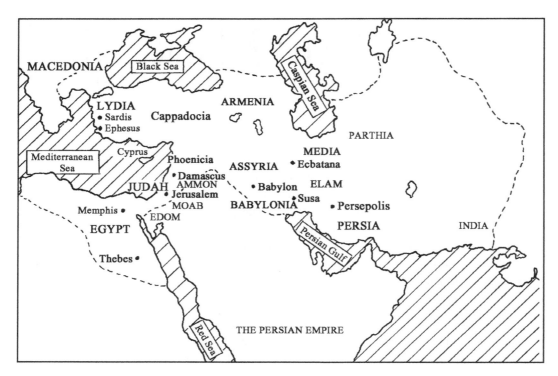

Illustration #13
Persian Empire—The Persian Empire dominated the ancient world at the time of Esther.

In the third year of his reign, this King Ahasuerus plans to wage war against Greece, probably because he seeks revenge for his father's defeat in Greece. To win everyone to his side and to build confidence in his war plans, King Ahasuerus throws a party at Shushan or Susa, one of his three main capitals. His party lasts an incredible 180 days.

Some Bible experts believe that the same people did not party for 180 days but that different people attended at different times. In this way, the king could entertain all the important people, the people he wanted to impress. During the party, the king displays his wealth and power for his army officers, the princes from surrounding provinces, and other officials. Of course, the guests also drink, feast, and perhaps help the king plan the war.

After this incredible 180-day party, the king holds a seven-day feast for all the citizens of Shushan. Again, he provides free food and drink for his guests. Not surprisingly, the feast becomes a drunken party.

At this time in Jewish history, many of the Jews who were exiled from Persia have returned to Jerusalem. The Jews in Jerusalem are rebuilding what was started earlier, and these Jews in Jerusalem consider the Jews who voluntarily remain in Persia to be disobedient to God's purposes. Perhaps some Jews have stayed in Persia because they have established themselves and enjoy prosperity and good treatment from the Persians.

No matter why some Jews chose to disobey by remaining in Persia, the book of Esther shows God's mercy and grace. God works for the safety and protection of the Jews in Persia, despite their disobedience. Specifically, the book of Esther takes place during the long interval between the sixth and seventh chapters of the book of Ezra. The biblical books of Ezra and Nehemiah relate the stories of those who returned to Jerusalem to rebuild.

We're told that King Ahasuerus's throne room resembles a Grecian temple, and the hall alone covers between two and three acres (see Illustration #14). The archaeological site of Susa or Shushan has been discovered between the rivers Shapur and Dizful.

Don't Make a King Mad!

the big picture

Esther 1:9–22

The king wants to show his guests the beauty of his wife, Queen Vashti, so he calls for her to attend his party. But she is giving her own party for the women, and she refuses to appear in front of King Ahasuerus and his drunken mob. Furious, the king puts out an edict looking for a new queen to replace her.

During King Ahasuerus's party, Queen Vashti is putting on her own banquet for the women, when she is called by an official—at the king's summons—to wear her crown and make an appearance to show off her beauty before the drunken officials and citizenry. She refuses. Her refusal is not editorialized in the Bible text—we are not told if what she did was right or wrong. According to the account in the Bible, Vashti isn't asked to do anything immoral or lewd, so we can't know why she refuses.

The drunken king becomes furious, especially after his officials point out how the queen's refusal could undermine the power of husbands all over the country. Soon the king feels compelled to use his queen as an object lesson to show that all wives must obey their husbands, and Queen Vashti is deposed from her position. In a further attempt to solidify the position of the men of the empire, an edict is sent throughout the kingdom saying that women will give honor to their husbands, no matter who they are—great or small.

In the time of Esther, women were not considered equals with men. Whenever Christianity influences a country or culture, Christianity brings respect and value to women and children.

Vashti is thought to be the same person called Amestris. Amestris is attributed by the Greeks to be King Ahasuerus's wife and the mother of their son; this son will later become the next king.

Illustration #14
King Ahasuerus's Palace—King Ahasuerus, remembered for his failed invasions of Greece in the 480s BC, lived and worked in palaces with this floor plan.

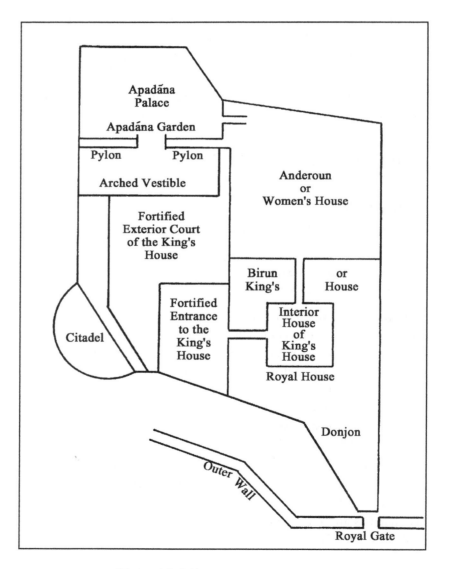

Apadána Palace

Apadána Garden

Pylon   Pylon

Arched Vestible

Anderoun or Women's House

Fortified Exterior Court of the King's House

Citadel

Fortified Entrance to the King's House

Birun King's

or House

Interior House of King's House

Royal House

Donjon

Outer Wall

Royal Gate

mutual submission
Ephesians 5:21

counsel
Proverbs 12:4–5

his Word
Psalm 119:9, 11

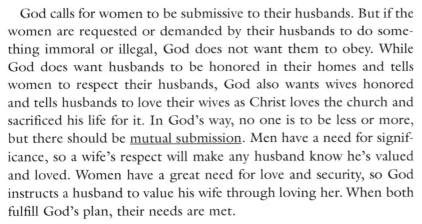

what others say

Shirley Rose

Vashti was not just being arbitrary when she refused his request. Her status demanded more respect than this. On the other hand, no one dared stand up to the king. But this number-one wife refused to be a spectacle for his drunken friends.[1]

Pam and Bill Farrel

The goal in intimate conversation with your spouse is not to analyze emotions and come up with some kind of solution that will make your spouse never feel this way again. The goal is simply to grow a little closer and reaffirm your love.[2]

God calls for women to be submissive to their husbands. But if the women are requested or demanded by their husbands to do something immoral or illegal, God does not want them to obey. While God does want husbands to be honored in their homes and tells women to respect their husbands, God also wants wives honored and tells husbands to love their wives as Christ loves the church and sacrificed his life for it. In God's way, no one is to be less or more, but there should be mutual submission. Men have a need for significance, so a wife's respect will make any husband know he's valued and loved. Women have a great need for love and security, so God instructs a husband to value his wife through loving her. When both fulfill God's plan, their needs are met.

King Ahasuerus seems to be easily swayed by his officials, even though he regrets following their advice. He provides an example of how we should not be swayed by the messages that the world gives. The world's messages are often completely opposite to God's right ideas and help. We can be influenced by TV, movies, music, marketing campaigns, official studies, polls, and ungodly friends' advice. To find godly means for overcoming our struggles and temptations, we must seek God's counsel through godly people and through his Word.

Mordecai
Esther 2:5

exiled Jews
2 Kings 24:14–15

So, You Want to Be Queen

the big picture

Esther 2:1-20

King Xerxes gets lonely for a queen, so an official edict is sent out requesting women to apply for a new queen's position. Many women apply, but the king will select Esther, a young Jewish woman, to be queen. But Esther does not reveal her Hebrew nationality, because her cousin, Mordecai, who raised her, tells her not to.

Four years later, after King Ahasuerus returns from his disastrous war in Greece, he regrets deposing his queen. Now he has a large harem, so he didn't miss women in general, but Queen Vashti in particular. Maybe his defeat in Greece bruised his ego, and he wants to be with a woman he loves.

His officials, fearful he'll reinstate Vashti as queen and she will punish the officials for their treachery to her, suggest a way to find a new queen. The king agrees and, through an edict, he asks maidens from the land to "try out" for the position of queen.

Now a Jew named <u>Mordecai</u> is introduced into the story: Mordecai, one of the <u>exiled Jews</u> from Jerusalem. Mordecai, who is about forty years old, lives in Shushan, and he has raised his orphaned cousin, Esther, to young adulthood.

Wisely, Mordecai tells Esther to keep her Jewish heritage a secret, and she obeys him. Esther, whose Hebrew name "Hadassah" means "myrtle" and whose name "Esther" comes from the Persian word for "star," is very beautiful. She is taken into the palace—maybe by force or maybe at Mordecai's suggestion—as one of the potential candidates for queen. We don't know Esther's feelings about her candidacy or even her feelings about the king.

For a year, all the candidates for the position of queen receive beauty treatments, while they stay at the palace. Then each young woman spends one night with the king in the hope of gaining his favor. Hegai, the official in charge of the women, likes Esther and gives her preferential treatment. Finally, Esther gets her turn to please the king. While she prepares for her night with the king, her worried cousin Mordecai paces outside the palace walls.

At this time, Esther is believed to be about twenty years old. She goes to the king and pleases him so much that she is chosen to be

Women of the Bible

the next queen. Although God's name is not mentioned, God is orchestrating everything that is happening. So Esther is now the queen.

Esther spends the night with the king and pleases him. Such a situation goes against God's directives for his people to remain sexually pure and live godly lives. The book of Esther does not explain why God has Esther sleep with the king as part of his plan for saving the Jews. But we do know that God causes Esther to have favor with Hegai and the king in order to fulfill his purposes.

Mordecai's great-grandfather <u>Kish</u> had been exiled from Jerusalem into the land of Persia or Babylon along with <u>Jehoiachin</u>. His captivity is one of several captivities named by historians.

Kish
Esther 2:5

Jehoiachin
2 Kings 24:8

overthrown
Daniel 1:1–2

Zedekiah
2 Kings 24:17

seek peace of captive land
Jeremiah 29:7

Israelites' Other Exiles and Captivities

When	Where
740/741 BC	Mordecai's ancestors exiled in Persia
720 BC	Ten tribes carried away by kings of Assyria
605 BC	Tribes of Judah <u>overthrown</u> by rulers of Babylon
598/597 BC	Jehoiachin and other nobles taken away
582 BC	<u>Zedekiah</u> led away and Jerusalem laid to waste

In most instances, when the Hebrews were exiled, they were treated fairly and often became merged into the society of their captors. The prophet Jeremiah even told the captives they should <u>seek the peace of their captive land</u>.

A Plot Is Exposed

ESTHER 2:21–23 *In those days, while Mordecai sat within the king's gate, two of the king's eunuchs, Bigthan and Teresh, doorkeepers, became furious and sought to lay hands on King Ahasuerus. So the matter became known to Mordecai, who told Queen Esther, and Esther informed the king in Mordecai's name. And when an inquiry was made into the matter, it was confirmed, and both were hanged on a gallows; and it was written in the book of the chronicles in the presence of the king.* (NKJV)

After Esther is queen, her cousin Mordecai is sitting as an official at the gate. The city gate is like "city hall" and at the gate, much business takes place. Somehow, through God's provision, Mordecai hears a plot against the king's life. He gives the information to Esther, and she passes it along, giving credit to Mordecai. The rebels are hanged, but Mordecai isn't given any reward for his service to the king.

In those days, a king gave extravagant rewards for those who were loyal or who served the king well. Mordecai must have been disappointed, but God's plan will be revealed later, and Mordecai's sacrifice will be rewarded in even greater ways later. While this story of a thwarted assassination seems like an aside now, later in Esther's story, God will use this event in his sovereignty to bring about the fulfillment of his plan to protect his people.

Many years later, King Ahasuerus is killed in an assassination plot. But for now, God protects him, so that God's own purposes can be fulfilled.

Mordecai isn't rewarded immediately, just like Christians know that they must wait to be rewarded in heaven for their right choices.

God will reward us in heaven, and one of the ways he does that is with crowns. Here is a listing of the crowns we will receive.

God Rewards in Heaven

Crown	Scripture
Crown of Life	James 1:12; Revelation 2:10
Crown of Righteousness	2 Timothy 4:8
Imperishable Crown	1 Corinthians 9:25
Crown of Rejoicing	1 Thessalonians 2:19
Crown of Glory	1 Peter 5:2–4

Just like Mordecai, we may deserve credit, appreciation, or reward for something we've done or accomplished. Maybe we weren't acknowledged publicly for our efforts in completing a project and others were. Or, maybe our boss took credit for the contract we got. We can't expect to receive all the credit we deserve, but God knows everything we do. Even if we don't get credit now—even in our lifetime—God will generously reward us in heaven. Some of those rewards will be the crowns we'll wear in heaven.

Haman's Plan

the big picture

Esther 3:1-15

King Ahasuerus promotes a man, Haman, to second in command over the kingdom. But Mordecai refuses to bow before Haman, because bowing goes against his Jewish faith. That's why Haman hates Mordecai, and to take revenge, Haman plots to kill all the Jews in the empire.

About four years after Esther becomes queen, King Ahasuerus promotes Haman to the position of second in command over all of his kingdom. In that position, people bow before him, but Mordecai, as a Jew, refuses. As a Jew, Mordecai must not worship anyone except God, and Mordecai feels bowing to Haman is like worshiping him.

Mordecai refuses to bow, and all the people at the gate notice. Haman, his pride stung by Mordecai's disrespect, becomes so angry and vengeful that he decides to kill all the Jews, just because one Jew refused to bow to him. Early in April, 474 BC, Haman seeks advice from the astrologers and magicians about when he should kill the Jews. To get an answer, they cast a lot, called "Pur," a Persian word. The Pur indicates that his diabolical plan should take place one year later. Of course, God's provision of a year before the slaughter of the Jews enables the Jews to take action against the plot.

Haman continues his plan by seeking the king's approval and cooperation. In a deceptive way, Haman tells the king, "There is a certain people scattered and dispersed among the people in all the provinces of your kingdom; their laws are different from all other people's, and they do not keep the king's laws. Therefore it is not fitting for the king to let them remain. If it pleases the king, let a decree be written that they be destroyed, and I will pay ten thousand talents of silver into the hands of those who do the work, to bring it into the king's treasuries" (Esther 3:8–9 NKJV).

What a contrast between King Ahasuerus and Almighty God. King Ahasuerus doesn't care that a whole group of his subjects are to be murdered. Easily influenced by those who have his attention, this king is erratic in his responses.

lots
Proverbs 16:33

jealous
Exodus 20:5

ashamed
Mark 8:38

signet
an official seal of
authority

lots
a way to get an
answer by throwing
stones

Haman sweetens his request by offering to pay ten thousand silver talents (750,000 pounds) to the king's treasury for the work to be done. It's a huge sum, equivalent to several tens of millions today. For example, the historian Herodotus notes that Darius I (King Ahasuerus's father) received almost fifteen thousand talents of silver in an entire year in revenue. Certainly, Haman didn't actually own that much money but planned to take it from slain Jews.

The king, without verifying the information or being concerned for his people, gives Haman permission to issue an edict in the king's name using the king's official seal on his **signet** ring. Letters are sent telling the people that they can destroy the Jews on the thirteenth day of the month of Adar twelve months later. This translates to March 7, 473 BC. Nothing, not even the king's desires, can change an official edict of the king.

> **what others say**
>
> **Kay Arthur**
> Although we have been given a free will, still God so rules and overrules that no person, angel, demon, or devil, nor any circumstance of life, can thwart his plan.[3]

The historian Herodotus writes about a "Pony Express" postal system first used more than two thousand years ago in the Persian Empire. Men on horseback passed the mail from one rider to the next. Herodotus wrote, "These men will not be hindered from accomplishing at their best speed the distance while they have to go either by snow, or rain, or heat, or by the darkness of night." Because of the vastness of the empire, a letter could take up to eight weeks to reach someone in the empire's outer boundaries.

Not by coincidence does the Pur indicate the Jews' annihilation should not take place until a year after the edict is sent. God is completely in charge of everything, even to the controlling of the throwing of <u>lots</u>. Haman may feel excited about the seeming success of his plan, but God has everything under his control the whole time, just as Scripture indicates.

God calls for us to represent him by not making any allegiance to or worshiping another created god or another person. Mordecai keeps his integrity by doing what he believes he should do. God is a <u>jealous</u> God and requires our loyalty. Jesus also said that he can't honor those who are <u>ashamed</u> of him.

The Bible mentions several instances of fasting for a variety of reasons.

Examples	Scripture
Personal or private struggles	1 Samuel 1:7
Repentance	1 Samuel 7:5
Public difficulties	1 Samuel 31:11–13
Grief	2 Samuel 12:16
Sadness	Nehemiah 1:4
Worry	Daniel 6:18
Preparation for ministry	Acts 13:3

Reasons	Scripture
Seeking guidance	Judges 20:26
Humility	Psalm 35:13–14
Confession of sin	Nehemiah 9:1
Seeking God	Joel 2:12
Victory over temptation	Matthew 4:1–11
Prayer	Luke 2:37

What a Bummer

the big picture

Esther 4:1–17

Mordecai tells Esther about Haman's plan and encourages her to intercede before the king. But at this time, Esther doesn't feel as if she has the king's favor. Nevertheless, she decides to approach the king, even though her action could put her in danger.

Mordecai learns of Haman's edict to destroy all the Jews and responds by grieving in sackcloth and ashes. Evidently, Esther is cut off from news outside the palace, because she doesn't know about the plan. So misunderstanding why Mordecai is in sackcloth, she sends him clothes to wear. Then Mordecai sends Esther a message explaining the edict and encouraging her to approach the king to get his help. Esther replies that the king hasn't sent for her for thirty days, so she doesn't know her status with him.

In those days, a king protected himself by not allowing anyone into his presence unsummoned. If anyone approached and the king didn't want the person in his presence, the king could order the per-

fast
Joel 1:14;
Luke 2:37

approach
Hebrews 4:16

son killed on the spot. Knowing the king is unreliable and easily swayed by other people's opinions, Esther realizes by approaching the king's inner chamber, unsummoned, she risks her life. If the king extends his golden scepter to the uninvited guest, the guest is welcome, but Esther can't know if the king will extend the scepter to her.

Mordecai tells Esther that he knows God's deliverance will come from somewhere for the Jewish people, but if any Jew dies, Esther will not be safe, even as royalty. And then he gives her the challenge, "Yet who knows whether you have come to the kingdom for such a time as this?" (Esther 4:14 NKJV).

Esther must have been deeply touched by this challenge, for she decides to risk all. While uninvited guests can request an audience with the king, Esther fears her request will be turned down. She decides to risk her position and her life and to approach the king's throne room without invitation. She implores for Mordecai to ask people to <u>fast</u>. Then she tells him, "And if I perish, I perish!" (Esther 4:16 NKJV). Esther speaks, not with bitterness, but with determination to act.

Esther felt fearful approaching the king, but God wants us to <u>approach</u> his throne room with confidence—not fear.

what others say

Marilyn Willett Heavilin

Generally when we think of prayer, we think of our talking to God because our prayers are often monologues rather than dialogues. We talk to God, but we seldom sit still long enough for Him to respond. Prayer should be a two-way interaction.[4]

Carol Kent

Esther was face-to-face with the biggest risk of her life. God had placed the potential in her to gain an audience with the king. It meant uncertainty, possible failure, and fear. Talk about "eagle" flight training! The rest is history. Because of her obedience and willingness to transcend the fear of failure, her Jewish people were saved from possible annihilation at this frightening time in their history.[5]

There are many in the Bible who fasted: Moses, Israelites, Samuel, David, Elijah, Ninevites, Nehemiah, Darius, Daniel, Anna, John's disciples, Pharisees, early Christians, apostles, and Paul. Even Jesus fasted. If he needed to fast, then how much more we should. The Bible recommends it as an important aspect of the spiritual life.

Protection Against Wrong Attitudes While Fasting

Wrong Attitude	Scripture
From other people's criticism	Psalm 69:10–13
From impure motives	Zechariah 7:5–6
Against ungodly living	Isaiah 58:1–14
From public display	Matthew 6:16–18

purposes
Ephesians 2:10

Perhaps Esther is worrying that the king and his officials will see her approach as disrespectful: the very reason Vashti was deposed as queen years earlier. If Vashti was deposed, even if she was the mother of King Xerxes' son, what might happen to Esther? Esther undoubtedly feels anxious for her life.

Although God's name is not mentioned in this book of the Bible, Esther and Mordecai do fast for God's will and the success of Esther's approach to the king. Although Bible experts differ on whether fasting also includes prayer, most biblical references to fasting include prayer. To get close to God, we must spend time with him in prayer, Bible study, and occasional fasting. In the Bible, fasting is an important spiritual discipline that draws us more fully and honestly into God's presence and helps us know God's will and his ways. Fasting not only includes refusing food, it also includes giving up an activity as a means of spending more time with God.

Mordecai suggests to Esther that she has become queen for such a time as this. God's children are always placed where he wants them for his <u>purposes</u>. Nothing that happens to the child of God is a coincidence, and when we look at every situation and encounter as God-directed, we will more easily fulfill his plan. This knowledge should also make each of us feel needed, valuable, and important: we are fulfilling God's purposes for his kingdom.

God's Intervention: Esther, You Rule

the big picture

Esther 5:1–14

Esther approaches the outer chamber of the king and is received by King Ahasuerus. After she has his attention, she invites him and Haman to a banquet. Haman's joy about being

God is in control
Proverbs 21:1

invited to a royal banquet is soured by Mordecai's continual refusal to bow. Haman plans to kill Mordecai even before the rest of the Jews are slaughtered.

On the third day of her fast, Esther appears in the inner court of the king. Thankfully the king extends his golden scepter, and she is received. What a relief! <u>God is in control</u> of the king's response. He says to her, "What do you wish, Queen Esther? What is your request? It shall be given to you—up to half the kingdom!" (Esther 5:3 NKJV).

When the king offers her up to half the kingdom, he means he will give her what she wants, not that he will literally give her half his kingdom. Esther has not only been fasting for three days, she has also been preparing a banquet. Now she invites the king and Haman to the banquet.

That same evening, the king and Haman attend her banquet. While we don't know why, Esther says nothing about Haman's plot. Maybe she feels the timing isn't right, or she senses the king is not fully receptive to her. Regardless, she asks the king and Haman to return the next day for another banquet. Evidently, the king loves this cat and mouse game and agrees—besides, he loves parties and banquets! Remember, he's given plenty of his own. Esther has prepared the bait successfully.

Haman, still unaware that Esther is one of the Jews he plans to kill, is thrilled to be invited to these exclusive banquets. Yet, Haman's joy is lost when he sees Mordecai's disrespect at the gate. Haman is so upset that he goes home. Instead of rejoicing at his good fortune and high position, Haman boasts about his accomplishments and complains about Mordecai. His family and friends respond by encouraging him to build a gallows, probably an impaling stake fifty cubits (seventy-two feet) high to kill Mordecai. Such a height guarantees that everyone in the city can see it, but, of course, Haman doesn't know God's plans for his change.

what others say

Eugenia Price

She did not fall into the trap tumbled into by so many women when they allow their emotions to rule the moment. Esther used her head, even though her heart was heavy with fear.[6]

what others say

Marilyn Willett Heavilin

As we wait on the Lord and listen for his voice, he <u>promises</u> that he will give us direction.[7]

Faith is exemplified by Esther, who besides seeking God in prayer and fasting, is also taking action by preparing banquets. Faith doesn't just sit back and do nothing; faith cooperates in whatever way God directs. Faith requires both dependence on God and <u>action</u>. Just as Esther gained the <u>strength</u> she needed through fasting, we can call upon God for the strength we need. God's delays are not necessarily his denials, but always turn into <u>deeds of goodness</u>.

Haman allows circumstances and people's responses to determine his emotions and attitudes. He can't enjoy the blessings of his life because he keeps focused on what displeases him. God wants us to base our emotions and attitudes upon his love for us. His love, unlike the favor or approval of others, <u>never changes</u> and is guaranteed to bring lasting joy and contentment. We <u>learn</u> about the joy and contentment God's love brings us, when we take time to meditate on <u>God's blessings</u>.

Just as Esther gives herself time before she asks the king to protect the Jews, we too should give ourselves time, so we do not jump ahead of God's plan. Sometimes we get impatient, because we think God has forgotten or doesn't know the best way. Waiting for God's will can be hard, but we need to wait. When we put our own plans into action, we put ourselves in danger.

Haman's wife unwisely feeds her husband's pride, and his excessive pride will result in her own downfall and the death of her sons. A wife should give wise <u>counsel</u> and build up her husband to consider the noble and honorable things of life.

promises
Psalm 32:8

action
James 2:17

strength
Philippians 4:13

deeds of goodness
Jeremiah 29:11

never changes
Ephesians 3:17–19

learn
Philippians 4:11

God's blessings
Philippians 4:8

counsel
Proverbs 20:18

<u>Can't Sleep</u>

the big picture

Esther 6:1–14

In an incredible example of great timing, King Ahasuerus is reminded of Mordecai's good deed five years past and asks Haman how to honor someone. Thinking he'll be honored, Haman suggests great things. Then Haman is devastated when Mordecai, not him, is the person being honored.

efforts
Proverbs 16:18

God furthers Queen Esther's efforts by keeping the king awake one night. Because he can't sleep, the king listens to his valet read him the court chronicles recording the events and deeds of his reign. He certainly knew boring reading would put him to sleep! He probably also wanted to hear about the wonderful things he had done so far during his twelve years as king.

God uses the reading of the chronicles to bring to light Mordecai's good deed five years before when Mordecai revealed the assassination plot against the king's life. Any part of the chronicles could have been read to the king, but God caused the section pertaining to Mordecai's good deed to be read.

When King Ahasuerus realizes Mordecai has never been honored, he wants to honor Mordecai's good deed immediately and remedy the delay. By now, the sun has risen, and Haman "just happens" to be seeking an early morning audience with the king—Haman intends to ask permission to hang Mordecai on the impaling stick. Haman is invited into the king's throne room and the king asks him, "'What shall be done for the man whom the king delights to honor?' Now Haman thought in his heart, 'Whom would the king delight to honor more than me?'" (Esther 6:6 NKJV).

Haman recommends these wonderful benefits for that person: a royal robe (Esther 6:8); a ride on a royal horse already ridden by the king (Esther 6:8); the service of a noble prince (Esther 6:9); and the accompaniment throughout the city by a prince who announces his arrival (Esther 6:9). Haman could have suggested money, but he craves peer respect and honor.

Haman's <u>efforts</u> at having himself elevated by the king come crashing down. When King Ahasuerus says to do that for Mordecai, Haman is devastated. He obeys the king and leads Mordecai on the king's horse in a procession through the city streets. His grief increases when he returns home to hear his wife and friends predict his downfall, based on their reading of Persian omens and signs. But before he can react, Haman is called to Esther's second banquet.

what others say

Virginia Stem Owens

Meanwhile, back at the palace, the king is having trouble sleeping. So he tells his valet to bring his favorite book, The Adventures of Ahasuerus, King of Persia, and read him a bedtime story. As it happens, the book falls open to the account of how Mordecai foiled the assassination plot against the king by his bodyguards.[8]

God says that the <u>humble</u> will be lifted up and the proud disgraced. Constantly needing recognition to feel significant, Haman never feels he can be honored enough or given enough wealth. But riches and awards rarely satisfy us for long, because these gifts are temporary. God wants us to seek spiritual wealth and approval from him, because God's love and approval bring us contentment, peace, and a sense of constant significance.

The Persians referred to omens and signs as a means of predicting the future. They looked to "fate," but God wants us to seek his will through the Bible and prayer. <u>Astrology</u> and witchcraft are **abominations** to God.

At the time of Esther, God used something as small as the king's insomnia to further his plans for the Jews. Today he uses both big and little things to help us overcome difficulties, resist temptation, and further God's plans for us. In God's eyes, everything, big or small, can bring him glory. Nothing or no one is too insignificant or unworthy to be used by him. God knows when even a <u>sparrow</u> falls.

Bad News, Haman

go to

humble
James 4:10

astrology
Deuteronomy 18:10

sparrow
Matthew 10:29

abominations
detested things

the big picture

Esther 7:1–10

At Esther's second banquet, she has an opportunity to plead for the lives of her people. When the king asks about the source of the danger, Esther points to Haman. Haman is exposed, found guilty, and hung at the king's command.

At Esther's second banquet, King Ahasuerus, Haman, and Esther are enjoying the wine when the king asks Esther for her request. She explains that according to the edict, she is one of the group of people who are to be exterminated. She continues, "For we have been sold, my people and I, to be destroyed, to be killed, and to be annihilated. Had we been sold as male and female slaves, I would have held my tongue, although the enemy could never compensate for the king's loss" (Esther 7:4 NKJV).

Esther tells him that selling them into slavery would, at least, bring

qualities
Psalm 103:8–10

the king money, but their deaths don't bring the king any benefits. The king seems unaware of the plan she is talking about. Or else, he has forgotten it. This poor leader does not even know what is going on in his kingdom. Esther, we guess, points to Haman and identifies him as the wicked one.

Haman must be filled with terror, and the king, who is now furious, exits into the garden. Some Bible experts believe the king is trying to regain his self-control, although kings didn't need to exercise self-control in those days. Bible experts aren't sure why the king would leave. He certainly hasn't tried to control his anger on previous occasions. Some believe he was trying to think of a way to legally condemn Haman, but in truth, the king can make any decision he wants without support for his choice. Other experts believe he is trying to figure out what to do with Haman. When the king returns, he sees Haman falling on Esther's couch, seeking her mercy. The king becomes even madder, for he views Haman's behavior as an attack upon his queen. As his family predicted, Haman's day now gets even worse. The king condemns Haman, and the palace servants cover Haman's face—a custom for those about to be executed.

Haman must have made enemies in the king's court, because one of the king's attendants, Harbonah, quickly suggests the gallows Haman built for Mordecai. The king agrees, and Haman is immediately impaled on the very pole he built for Mordecai. God has brought justice.

what others say

Patsy Clairmont

There is One who desires us to know his undeserved love and his security. He longs to be in an ongoing relationship with us. Scripture tells us he is the one who knocks at the door of our heart, seeking entry. He won't barge in, but if we open our heart's door, he promises to come in and partake of life with us.[9]

But the creator God of the universe is a God of wonderful <u>qualities</u>: unconditional love, always making wise and good choices for his people, fair, and angry only at unrighteousness. He is stable and consistent in his responses. No wonder people are afraid of King Ahasuerus, but they need not fear Jehovah God.

God is a <u>God of justice</u>. His full justice will not be executed on this earth, but every knee shall bow before him in the future, in acknowledgment of him as the only God. Every enemy of his will also receive the justice they are due. Until then, <u>God is patient</u>, so that as many of us as possible will turn to him.

Mordecai Wins

the big picture

Esther 8:1-17

Haman's property and position are given to Mordecai, but there's still the problem of the edict against the Jews. Since the edict can't be reversed, the king allows a second edict to be issued, giving permission to the Jews to defend themselves.

God of justice
Psalm 9:8;
Revelation 19:11

God is patient
2 Peter 3:9

God's intervention becomes even clearer as Mordecai receives everything Haman wanted: property, power, and position. Even the signet ring, previously used by Haman, is given to Mordecai. But even the king himself cannot change the previous edict, for a Persian king's edict was irreversible. Evidently, Queen Esther doesn't understand Persian laws because she pleads with the king to reverse the first edict. Of course, she does not mention the king's cooperation in Haman's plan.

King Ahasuerus explains that his edict can't be changed, but she and Mordecai can use his signet ring in whatever way they desire to help their situation. As a result, Queen Esther and Mordecai issue a new edict saying that when the Jews are attacked, they can defend themselves. This new edict is sent out eight months before the planned attack. Once again, the Persian pony express carries the message through the large Persian Empire.

When Mordecai leaves the king's presence, everyone rejoices, especially the Jews. Some people even become Jewish converts because of their respect for God's chosen people.

Mordecai's Edict (Esther 8:11)

- Jews had the right to assemble.

- Jews could defend themselves.

immutable
Malachi 3:6

- Jews could destroy any who attacked them.

- Jews could claim the possessions of their attackers.

what others say

Kay Arthur

Man can be right with God! Righteousness is more than goodness; it is a right standing with God.[10]

The Persian kings' edicts were <u>immutable</u> because the king was believed to be a god whose plan could not be changed. A change suggests a correction for a mistake and a divine king could not make a mistake! A king making an unwise choice was unacceptable to the Persians' belief system. In the biblical viewpoint, God is unchanging and his plans are also unchangeable. But God always reaches out with his mercy, so people will turn from evil ways and seek his forgiveness.

This important edict went out to empower the Jews to defend themselves, bringing the Jews hope and strength.

Deliverance!

the big picture

Esther 9:1–32

When the day of attack comes, the Jews defend themselves and win great victories. The Feast of Purim is instituted in celebration of God's deliverance.

On March 7, 473 BC, a date when the first edict could have wiped out the Jews, they are safe, thanks to the second edict. The Jews are protected by the many who fear Mordecai's new power with the king. In addition, the Jews protect themselves in Shushan and kill five hundred, including the ten sons of Haman. Esther secures a second day of protection for the Jews in the city of Shushan, and three hundred more enemies are killed. In the outlying areas, the Jews kill seventy-five thousand enemies.

Though the second edict gave the Jews power to seize their enemies' possessions, they refrain. They want to communicate the purity of their motives. Through all of this, Mordecai soars in popularity and power.

Because of their tremendous success, the Jews spontaneously celebrate their deliverance, and they call their celebration the Feast of Purim. The word "purim" comes from the Persian word "Pur" or "lot," because Haman used a Pur to determine a date for his planned murder of the Jews. Purim, then and now, celebrates God and his power to turn what is meant for evil into something good.

go to

festivals
Exodus 5:1

After the people spontaneously celebrate, they establish a specific holiday through Mordecai, who becomes a high official. He records the events and sends letters about it (9:20). Esther sends a second set of letters (9:29). These letters explain that the celebration should include fasting and prayers, along with celebrating God's deliverance.

what others say

Marilyn Willett Heavilin

If God is who he says he is, he can do anything he pleases. He has all the power in the world, so we can look to him to make the right decisions.[11]

God loves for his people to celebrate God's work and actions on the people's behalf. So many people have an image of God as a "spoilsport," too serious to have fun. But throughout Scripture, God instructs his people to plan <u>festivals</u> and celebrations, so that they will have time to both relax and remember God's great deeds.

Just as the Jews were empowered by the king's second edict to fight their enemies, Christians have God's power to fight their enemy, Satan. The Christian's weapons include prayer (Colossians 4:2); the armor of God (Ephesians 6:11); the power of the Holy Spirit (Romans 15:13); the fellowship of believers (1 John 1:9); and godly counsel (Titus 2:1–15).

apply it

Lasting Fame for Mordecai and Esther

ESTHER 10:1–3 *And King Ahasuerus imposed tribute on the land and on the islands of the sea. Now all the acts of his power and his might, and the account of the greatness of Mordecai, to which the king advanced him, are they not written in the book of the chronicles of the kings of Media and Persia? For Mordecai the Jew was second to King Ahasuerus, and was great among the Jews and well received by the multitude of his brethren, seeking the good of his people and speaking peace to all his countrymen.* (NKJV)

During the twentieth year of the king's reign, in 465 BC, King Ahasuerus is assassinated. Today, this king is mostly remembered for his queen, Esther, and the ways God worked through him to save the Jews, rather than for his power or wealth. Both Esther and Mordecai have lasting fame for the strength of their faith and conviction. From Esther's courage, we can draw strength, especially when we too must take a stand for God and do more than we think possible.

Without mentioning God's name, the writer of the book of Esther lets us know that God is at work through the story's incredible string of helpful coincidences. The Jews know that God will take care of them, even if his name isn't mentioned. God's great power can be exalted without direct reference to him. He is the master controller of all things and without his permission, nothing is done.

what others say

Jan Johnson

A journal is a place to talk to God, to pour out hurts, to write down questions for God, to sit and enjoy wasting time with him.[12]

God designs celebrations and holidays to bring joy and to remember his great deeds and faithfulness in the lives of his children. The Feast of Purim reminds Jews of God's sovereignty and power. Holidays, such as Christmas and Easter, remind Christians of God's work in the lives of his beloved people. Other kinds of celebrations of the devotional life, such as journaling, record God's work in individual lives and build faith when they are reviewed.

Events After the Exile in Babylon

Persian Kings	Dates of Their Reign	Biblical Events	Scripture	Dates
Cyrus	559–530 BC	• Edict of Cyrus for the return.	Ezra 1:1–4	538 BC
		• *First return* of 49,897 exiles, under Zerubbabel (to build the temple).	Ezra 2	538 BC
		• The altar and temple foundation built.	Ezra 3:1–13	536 BC
Cambyses	530–522 BC			
Smerdis	522 BC			
Darius I	521–486 BC	• Haggai prophesied.	Book of Haggai	520 BC
		• Zechariah prophesied.	Book of Zechariah	520–518 BC

Events After the Exile in Babylon (cont'd)

Persian Kings	Dates of Their Reign	Biblical Events	Scripture	Dates
Ahasuerus (Xerxes)	485–465 BC	• Accusation against Judah.	Ezra 4:6	486 BC
		• Esther became queen.	Esther 2:17	479 BC
Artaxerxes	464–424 BC	• Artaxerxes stopped the rebuilding of Jerusalem.	Ezra 4:7–23	ca. 464 BC –458 BC
		• *Second return* of 4,000–5,000 exiles, under Ezra (to beautify the temple and reform the people).	Ezra 7–10	458 BC
		• *Third return* of exiles, under Nehemiah (to build the walls of Jerusalem).	Book of Nehemiah	444 BC
		• Nehemiah's second return.	Nehemiah 13:6	ca. 430 BC
		• Malachi prophesied.	Book of Malachi	450–430 (?)

Signs of God

In the story of Esther, God shows his sovereignty through events that some might call "happenstance." But with God, there are no coincidences. The book of Esther records many incidents that God orchestrated to fulfill his plans. Here's a list of them.

Incidents That Fulfilled God's Plans

Verse(s)	Incident
Esther 1:12	Queen Vashti's refusal.
Esther 2:9	Esther found favor with Hegai.
Esther 2:17	King favored Esther.
Esther 2:21–23	Mordecai reveals plot.
Esther 3:7	A lot determines time.
Esther 5:2	Esther enters king's throne room.
Esther 5:14	Haman has gallows built.
Esther 6:1–3	King reviews Mordecai's deed.
Esther 6:4	Haman enters palace.

Chapter Wrap-Up

- After King Ahasuerus deposes Queen Vashti, Esther is chosen as the new queen. (Esther 1, 2)

- Second in command of King Ahasuerus's kingdom is Haman, who hates Mordecai and Jews. He hatches a plot to have them exterminated. (Esther 3:1–15)

- Through a series of divine interventions, God prevents Haman's plan from occurring. (Esther 6, 7)

- The Jews are given permission to defend and attack their enemies. As a result, none of them are destroyed. (Esther 8:11–9:32)

Study Questions

1. Why do the king's advisers want to have Queen Vashti deposed?

2. How does God show his sovereignty when Esther is first being prepared for the king?

3. How does God use the omission of Mordecai's reward?

4. How does Esther respond to Mordecai's challenge to talk to the king even though she's not currently favored by him?

5. How does the festival become known as the Feast of Purim?

Chapter 8 Women of Power

Chapter Highlights:
- Jezebel—Experiencing God's Discipline
- Athaliah—Sowing What We Reap
- Shulammite Woman— Power of Love

Let's Get Started

Power can reap goodness or evil, turn us toward or away from God, create a godly heart or a wicked one. In this chapter we examine the lives of three women who were given power. Two of them, Jezebel and Athaliah, used their powers to create evil and retreat from God. But the third, the woman loved by Solomon in the Song of Solomon (or the "Song of Songs") expressed her power through love, the most wonderful kind of power.

Each of us has more power than we realize. What we do with it is our choice, but God wants us to use it for godly purposes. Let us learn to do so by studying the lives of these three women.

Jeroboam
1 Kings 11:26

Baal
Numbers 25:3

Baal
name for any number of male gods

Get Away, Jezzie! (Jezebel)

1 KINGS 16:29–33 *In the thirty-eighth year of Asa king of Judah, Ahab the son of Omri became king over Israel; and Ahab the son of Omri reigned over Israel in Samaria twenty-two years. Now Ahab the son of Omri did evil in the sight of the LORD, more than all who were before him. And it came to pass, as though it had been a trivial thing for him to walk in the sins of Jeroboam the son of Nebat, that he took as wife Jezebel the daughter of Ethbaal, king of the Sidonians; and he went and served* **Baal** *and worshiped him. Then he set up an altar for Baal in the temple of Baal, which he had built in Samaria. And Ahab made a wooden image. Ahab did more to provoke the LORD God of Israel to anger than all the kings of Israel who were before him. (NKJV)*

When we first meet Jezebel, she is already an evil woman deeply steeped in the worship of Baal, the god of her own country. Jezebel quickly influences her new husband, Ahab, and together they begin to spread this false religion to all of Israel.

While Israel started as one country during the reigns of Saul, David, and Solomon, Solomon's two sons split the nation into Judah and Israel. These two countries have been influenced by the false

Ashtoreth
1 Kings 11:5

King Solomon
1 Kings 11:4–5

Ashtoreth/Astarte
Canaanite goddess
of fertility, known
also as Asherah

Asherah pole
object used by
Asherah followers

gods worshiped in nearby nations. Baal and Asherah are two of the false gods, but there are more, including a goddess named **Ashtoreth** or **Astarte**. <u>King Solomon</u> succumbed to this goddess during his reign.

> **what others say**
>
> **Herbert Lockyer**
>
> It may be that Ahab was more luxury-loving and sensual than cruel, but under the complete domination of a ruthless woman, he was forced to act against his finer feelings.[1]
>
> **Virginia Stem Owens**
>
> For obvious reasons, fertility deities most often came in pairs. Their worship included the physical reenactment of the gods' cosmic coupling, which supposedly brought fruitfulness to fields and flocks. Astarte's temples were stocked with priestesses who played the part of the goddess, receiving the seminal offering of male worshipers—who were expected to make cash donations as well. In special emergencies or community disasters, these gods required the sacrifice of children, often by burning.[2]

Ahab doesn't have to marry Jezebel, but he marries her because the marriage brings political benefits. The wickedness of Ahab—an already evil king, considered to be the worst in Israel up to that time—worsens by Jezebel's influence. She encourages him to worship Asherah, the mother goddess, and to practice ritual prostitution through the sexual images on an **Asherah pole**.

"Baal" is a Hebrew word for "lord" or "master" and refers to any number of gods worshiped by the countries surrounding Israel and Judah. An Asherah pole was carved with idols for the worship of Asherah, the mother goddess. The pole usually shows the goddess as a nude.

God's Prophets Killed by Jezebel

> **the big picture**
>
> **1 Kings 18:1–46**
>
> In a show of force, Jezebel kills many of God's true prophets. But God sends his brand of discipline upon her and Ahab by pre-

venting any rainfall. God's prophet Elijah predicts a <u>drought</u> and challenges the priests of Baal to have their gods send fire to burn a sacrifice on the altar. No matter how much the priests try to make fire consume the sacrifice, it fails. But when Elijah calls for Jehovah God to send fire, he succeeds. As a result, Elijah is able to kill many of Baal's priests and prophets.

drought
1 Kings 17:1

To solidify her power and evil religion, Jezebel kills many prophets of the Lord. The result is that everyone is scared of her—everyone except Elijah. Elijah tells her husband, Ahab, that God will bring a drought to the land, and God stops the rain. Elijah, because he represents the Lord, becomes the enemy of Jezebel and Ahab. Jezebel not only supports her evil religion by killing people, she also supports the priests of Baal by having them over for dinner every night. Elijah says, "Now therefore, send and gather all Israel to me on Mount Carmel, the four hundred and fifty prophets of Baal, and the four hundred prophets of Asherah, who eat at Jezebel's table" (1 Kings 18:19 NKJV).

Some time later, Elijah challenges Baal's priests and prophets to a kind of religious duel. He tells them to build an altar and to ask Baal to call down fire to burn the sacrifice. Though Baal is the god of fire, nothing happens, even though the priests cut themselves and call for their god's attention. Elijah taunts them by saying, "Cry aloud, for he is a god; either he is meditating, or he is busy, or he is on a journey, or perhaps he is sleeping and must be awakened" (1 Kings 18:27 NKJV).

Of course, nothing happens. But when Elijah calls upon God, Jehovah sends fire and burns the sacrifice and the altar. Empowered by God, Elijah kills the priests and prophets of Baal. Now he's really in trouble with Ahab and Jezebel.

what others say

Jill Briscoe

Believing Baal to be far more vigorous and powerful a god than El—the God of the Israelites—she told Ahab that his troubles stemmed from worshiping the wrong deity. Jezebel and her people believed Baal to be the god of rain and fire, and it wasn't long before the queen made her beliefs influence the land.[3]

go to

dining table
1 Kings 18:19

God brings a drought on the land to show he is the one in charge, not Jezebel's god, Baal. The priests of Baal must be very frustrated when they can't bring the rain to reverse God's drought. When Baal doesn't send fire from heaven, the frustrated priests "cut themselves, as was their custom, with knives and lances, until the blood gushed out on them" (1 Kings 18:28 NKJV).

When we represent the Lord as Elijah did, we too can be fearless. God has our lives in his hands, and nothing can harm us without his permission. We don't know why God allowed his own prophets to be killed, but what God does is always intended to bring him glory.

Elijah Gets Weak in the Knees

> 1 KINGS 19:1–4 *And Ahab told Jezebel all that Elijah had done, also how he had executed all the prophets with the sword. Then Jezebel sent a messenger to Elijah, saying, "So let the gods do to me, and more also, if I do not make your life as the life of one of them by tomorrow about this time." And when he saw that, he arose and ran for his life, and went to Beersheba, which belongs to Judah, and left his servant there.*
>
> *But he himself went a day's journey into the wilderness, and came and sat down under a broom tree. And he prayed that he might die, and said, "It is enough! Now, LORD, take my life, for I am no better than my fathers!" (NKJV)*

When Jezebel hears that Elijah killed Baal's priests and prophets, she takes it as a public insult because they sat at her <u>dining table</u>. They were her personal friends, representing her evil religion. Angered, she threatens Elijah's life. Elijah, who is usually the rock of Gibraltar with his faith in God, is suddenly stricken with terror and runs for his life.

We can see from Elijah's fear the power of Jezebel's evil hold over the land and the people. She does indeed have the power to kill Elijah, but God would never allow it. Unfortunately, Elijah loses his trust in God's power.

what others say

Joyce Meyer

There were people in the Bible called slingers who defeated their enemies by slinging stones and throwing dirt into their wells, contaminating their life source of water (see 2 Kings

In the book of Job, <u>God limits</u> Satan's evil activities in Job's life. Satan may not do anything beyond what God sets as boundaries. In fact, Satan has to ask God's permission to do anything to Job.

Satan can enter God's throne room and while he's there, Satan busily <u>accuses</u> Christians before God. But God always defends his children. In God's eyes, they are not condemned. They are forgiven and favored.

Although we may feel threatened at times by those who don't agree with our faith in God or by our spiritual enemy Satan, nothing can happen to us except what God allows. Even if someone is convinced they can harm us, we, like Elijah, are completely in God's loving care. God is in charge of everything that comes our way.

Remember, when we face trials that come from God, they do have a purpose. The apostle Paul wrote, "[We] rejoice in hope of the glory of God. And not only that, but we also glory in tribulations, knowing that tribulation produces perseverance; and perseverance, character; and character, hope. Now hope does not disappoint, because the love of God has been poured out in our hearts by the Holy Spirit who was given to us" (Romans 5:2–5 NKJV).

God limits
Job 1:10, 12; 2:6

accuses
Revelation 12:10

key point

Ahab Wants What He Wants!

the big picture

1 Kings 21:1–7

Naboth, who lived in Jezreel, owned a vineyard located close to the palace of Ahab and Jezebel. Ahab wanted to use Naboth's vineyard as a vegetable garden for the palace, and in exchange, Ahab offered him another vineyard or money. But Naboth refused. He had inherited his land, and he saw his land as belonging to God, with himself as the land's steward. To sell the land would violate the land laws (see Leviticus 25). Ahab became angry. Naboth accused Ahab of violating the covenant regarding land and also implied that he did not want any association with the royal house. Naboth said, "'The LORD forbid that I should give the inheritance of my fathers to you!' So Ahab went into his house sullen and displeased because of the word which

land
Leviticus 25:23–28;
Numbers 36:7

blaspheming God
Leviticus 24:16

> Naboth the Jezreelite had spoken to him; for he had said, 'I will not give you the inheritance of my fathers.' And he lay down on his bed, and turned away his face, and would eat no food" (1 Kings 21:3–4 NKJV).

Ahab is so stung by Naboth's refusal that he takes to his bed. His wife, Jezebel, asks him, "Why are you so sullen? Why won't you eat?" He tells her about Naboth's reply. Jezebel tells him to get up and eat, because she will get the vineyard for him.

Although Ahab had every right to offer to buy Naboth's land, he doesn't have the right to make Naboth sell. When Naboth refuses him, Ahab acts like a spoiled child. Jezebel sees his depression, hears the reason, and takes matters into her own hands.

From the Jewish perspective, the land of a man's ancestors should remain in the family. God commanded that they not sell their inheritance of <u>land</u>. That's why even an offer from the king would not convince Naboth to sell land that had been in his family's possession for many years. And why didn't Ahab want to keep God's Law? The answer is simple; Ahab was greedy. He would rather have a garden for his palace than obey God's commands. We should remember to be happy with what we have, and to obey God even if it means doing without something we really want.

To Ahab's credit, he doesn't take the land by force. Jezebel grew up in a country where the rights of individuals are not valued. God's wonderful laws value the rights of individuals, but from Jezebel's perspective, a king should have anything he wants.

Jezebel's Plan for Naboth's Death

the big picture

1 Kings 21:8–16

Jezebel causes people to lie about Naboth, to say Naboth blasphemed God and the king. In Israel's law, blaspheming God and the king is punishable by death, so Naboth is killed, and Ahab takes his land.

Jezebel influences elders and nobles to follow her instructions, even though her orders are in opposition to God's laws. <u>Blaspheming God</u> is a crime punishable by death, but God's Law requires <u>two witnesses</u> for condemning someone. Intended to encourage people to live righteous lives, God's laws were not to be misused by someone like Jezebel. Satan is obviously using Jezebel to promote his own plan for cruelty and hatred.

Like Jezebel, those who are evil are good at devising plans that twist God's righteousness. Though Jezebel has an evil heritage through her father, who was a priest of Baal, God holds her responsible for her own actions.

go to

two witnesses
Deuteronomy 17:6–7

convinced Eve
Genesis 3:1–6

Satan
John 8:44

good
Psalm 25:8

what others say

Max Lucado

This yellow-bellied father of lies doesn't dare meet you face-to-face. No sir. Don't expect this demon of demons to challenge you to a duel. Not this snake. He hasn't the integrity to tell you to turn around and put up your dukes. He fights dirty.[5]

Satan, the Christian's accuser and enemy, twists God's words and laws. Satan loves to make it seem like God doesn't want the best for his people. That's how Satan <u>convinced Eve</u> that God was withholding something good in the Garden of Eden. <u>Satan</u> always lies and twists the laws of God to make God look like the spoilsport.

Satan takes God's good things of the world and works to create evil from them. For instance, God designed sex for mankind's pleasure, but Satan turns it into destructive immorality. If God has said something is good for you, don't let Satan misuse and twist it into something unhealthy and sinful.

When God establishes a law, it is not meant to deprive his creation of something good but to protect it from something evil. God only has the good of his creation in mind. In fact, he is the very embodiment of <u>good</u>, with no element of evil in him. God does not want anything bad or evil for anyone or anything.

key point

God's Judgment on Ahab and Jezebel

the big picture

1 Kings 21:17–26

Because Jezebel twists God's law to get Naboth killed, God sends Elijah to tell Ahab that they will be judged and condemned by God. He says that both will die gruesome deaths, and Ahab's blood will be licked by dogs and Jezebel's flesh will be eaten by dogs.

go to

mocked
Galatians 6:7

just God
Zephaniah 3:5

married to unbelievers
2 Corinthians 6:14

stir up
2 Timothy 1:6;
2 Peter 1:13

God is never <u>mocked</u>. God will judge the sin of Jezebel and Ahab. Scripture says, "There was no one like Ahab who sold himself to do wickedness in the sight of the LORD, because Jezebel his wife stirred him up" (1 Kings 21:25 NKJV). Because God is a <u>just God</u>, he sends Elijah to tell Ahab that he and his wife will be killed. Then Elijah tells him that their bodies will not be given the respect due to a king and queen. Instead, Ahab's blood will be licked up by dogs and Jezebel's body will be eaten by dogs.

> **what others say**
>
> **Max Lucado**
> What matters most in life is not what ladders we climb or what ownings we accumulate. What matters most is a relationship.[6]

When Elijah predicts such a gruesome death, he is predicting the worst possible end in his culture. In Israel, dogs are always wild in the streets, eating out of the trash and never treated as pets. Therefore, to be eaten by one is the most disgraceful kind of death possible in Israel.

Although Jezebel plotted Naboth's death, God holds Ahab responsible as well, because he doesn't do anything to correct the injustice and because his heart is basically evil. Ahab deserves a death as horrible as his wife's.

Ahab and Jezebel form an evil team. Because of the close bond of marriage, spouses are influenced by each other. That is why God doesn't want believers to be <u>married to unbelievers</u>. Such a union will produce different agendas and goals in life, rather than both being dedicated and committed to serving God and bringing him glory. When a husband and wife are both dedicated to the Lord, they "<u>stir up</u>" and encourage each other to serve the Lord, rather than to do evil. Unfortunately, Jezebel "stirred up" the evil in Ahab.

Ahab Wises Up

1 KINGS 21:27–29 *So it was, when Ahab heard those words, that he tore his clothes and put sackcloth on his body, and fasted and lay in sackcloth, and went about mourning.*

And the word of the LORD came to Elijah the Tishbite, saying, "See how Ahab has humbled himself before Me? Because he has humbled himself before Me, I will not bring the calamity in his days. In the days of his son I will bring the calamity on his house." (NKJV)

Suddenly Ahab turns serious about Elijah's prediction and sincerely repents. Because of his gracious <u>mercy</u>, God accepts Ahab's humility. <u>Tearing</u> one's clothes and putting on <u>sackcloth</u> is the Jewish way of expressing grief and repentance. Only days before, Ahab had been sulking about Naboth's refusal to sell his vineyard. Now Ahab is saddened by God's prophecy about his death. God always recognizes a sincere, humbled heart.

As a result of Ahab's repentance, God decides to bring the judgment upon Ahab's house later through Ahab's wicked son, <u>Ahaziah</u>. But Jezebel doesn't repent, so God brings his judgment upon her. Over three years later, Ahab <u>dies</u> in battle after being wounded in his chariot. That day, <u>dogs lick</u> the blood left in his chariot in fulfillment of God's prophecy.

go to

mercy
2 Samuel 24:14

tearing
Esther 4:1;
Job 1:20

sackcloth
Genesis 37:34;
1 Kings 20:31–32

Ahaziah
1 Kings 22:40

dies
1 Kings 22:35

dogs lick
1 Kings 22:38

Jehu
2 Kings 9:2

what others say

Barbara Johnson

Once we admit our failures, we must relinquish ALL of them to God. Then we reach out and accept his cleansing forgiveness.[7]

God is always willing to forgive and show his mercy, even to the worst kind of sinner. Ahab, the worst king Israel had ever had, recognizes and repents of his evil, so God forgives him. God's mercy can be defined as "unlimited second chances." No matter how many times we ask him to forgive us, and no matter how wrong our actions, he will always forgive and restore us if we are sincere and humble ourselves.

the big picture

2 Kings 9:30–37

God uses Israel's newest king, Jehu, to execute God's judgment, which had been declared by Elijah several years earlier. <u>Jehu</u> orders Jezebel's attendants to throw Jezebel out of a window. Jezebel dies from the fall, and when Jehu sends men to pick up her body for burial, the men discover her body has already been eaten by dogs. Only a few of Jezebel's bones are left.

go to

Ahaziah
1 Kings 22:40

Jehoram
2 Kings 3:1

sons would also be killed
2 Kings 10:4–8

Jezebel's Death

Ahab's grandson, <u>Ahaziah</u>, reigns for two years in Israel. Then <u>Jehoram</u> (or Joram) reigns for twelve years, followed by Jehu. Jehu arrives in Jezreel to bring judgment upon Jezebel. Even in anticipation of her death, she takes pains to die in style: "She put paint on her eyes and adorned her head, and looked through a window" (2 Kings 9:30 NKJV). Her last actions, self-conscious and self-centered, reveal how evil controlled her.

When Jehu challenges the officials standing with her to show their loyalty to him, they cast her out the window. In fulfillment of God's judgment, she is killed and eaten by dogs. Her husband's death was kinder. Because of his repentance, he received God's mercy, but Jezebel never repented. She was arrogant to the end. Nothing was left of her except her skull, feet, and hands.

God's justice is completed through the deaths of Ahab and Jezebel. Shortly after Jezebel's death, all her <u>sons would also be killed</u> by Jehu. God had chosen Jehu to be the executor of justice.

> **what others say**
>
> **Liz Curtis Higgs**
>
> Even when we have a legitimate leadership role, there's no reason to make our employees miserable. Judging by the hasty way they shoved her out the window, Jezebel's servants were happy to get rid of her. Might those who serve beside us at work or at church feel the same way? If we've been given the skills and talents to lead, let's do so with grace and compassion.[8]

Although we may be horrified by the form of God's justice, we must remember that great evil was created by Ahab and Jezebel, with the death of Naboth being just one compelling example.

Many of the kings of Judah and Israel have the same names though they are different people. Some of the most common names are Jehoram and Ahaziah, while some kings have two names, for example, Jehoram is also called Joram.

A Chip off the Old Block (Athaliah)

2 KINGS 8:26 *Ahaziah was twenty-two years old when he became king, and he reigned one year in Jerusalem. His* *mother's name was Athaliah the granddaughter of Omri, king of Israel. (NKJV)*

2 CHRONICLES 22:2–3 *Ahaziah was forty-two years old when he became king, and he reigned one year in Jerusalem. His mother's name was Athaliah the granddaughter of Omri. He also walked in the ways of the house of Ahab, for his mother advised him to do wickedly. (NKJV)*

**Jehoram**
2 Chronicles
21:18–19

Athaliah, the daughter of Ahab and Jezebel, is given in marriage to Jehoram, a king of Judah, Israel's sister country. While this marriage is meant to bring the two countries together politically, the marriage also brings the worship of Baal to Judah. Jezebel brought Baal worship to Israel, and now her daughter brings Baal to the people of Judah and influences them to turn from Jehovah.

When <u>Jehoram</u> (Joram) dies from an intestinal illness, his son Ahaziah becomes king. Ahab's and Jezebel's evil influence continues as Athaliah encourages her son, Ahaziah, to do the wrong thing during his one-year reign.

> **what others say**
>
> **Herbert Lockyer**
>
> While [Jehoram] reigned, he was dominated by Athaliah who had the stronger character of the two, and who, having inherited from her evil mother strength of will and fanatical devotion to the worship of Baal, made Judah idolatrous.[9]

The evil bent of this family is deeply seated, despite having seen the consequences and judgment of God upon Ahab and Jezebel. God's predictions always come true. We all make choices that will affect our ancestors for a very long time. So when we make choices, we need to think about how our decisions will affect our children's children as well as the immediate consequences.

From Jezebel's example, we are reminded that when an evil heart continues in sin, turning that heart from evil gets harder and harder. Sin makes a person blind to its consequences until the person becomes unable to turn from evil.

Genealogical Table of Queen Athaliah

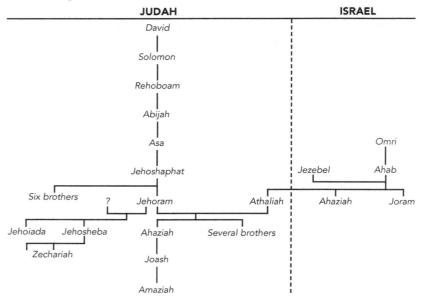

Athaliah Secures Her Throne

dies
2 Chronicles 22:9

2 KINGS 11:1–3 *When Athaliah the mother of Ahaziah saw that her son was dead, she arose and destroyed all the royal heirs. But Jehosheba, the daughter of King Joram, sister of Ahaziah, took Joash the son of Ahaziah, and stole him away from among the king's sons who were being murdered; and they hid him and his nurse in the bedroom, from Athaliah, so that he was not killed. So he was hidden with her in the house of the LORD for six years, while Athaliah reigned over the land. (NKJV)*

Ahaziah is wounded in battle and then <u>dies</u> in 841 BC. Normally a son of Ahaziah would take the throne, but Athaliah sees her chance to become queen. She attempts to kill all the heirs, even though they are her grandsons! Her evil has so blinded her spiritual conscience that she is willing to kill her own flesh and blood to keep her powerful hold over the land.

But one of her grandsons, Joash, has been hidden in the temple of God. So while his brothers are murdered at Athaliah's command, he survives. During the next six years Joash stays hidden, and Athaliah reigns as queen.

go to

rule
2 Samuel 7:16

temple
2 Chronicles
24:20–22

If Athaliah had been successful in destroying the royal line, the possibility of the Messiah coming from the royal line of Judah would have also been destroyed. God would not allow that to happen because he had determined that the descendants of David would <u>rule</u> over Judah forever. His sovereign and protective hand upon Joash guarantees his survival and, later, his success as king. And that guarantees the security of the line of David and the ancestors of Jesus. God's plans and purposes cannot be destroyed.

I'm Gonna Make You King, Joash

the big picture

2 Kings 11:4–16

The true king, Joash, is brought out of hiding from the temple by God's loyal priest, Jehoiada. Johoiada sends for the armies, and together, they plan a rebellion against Athaliah, Joash's wicked grandmother. After Joash is crowned the rightful king, Athaliah is killed.

Jehoiada, the high priest of Jehovah, arranged to have the little grandson Joash saved and hidden. Now Joash is seven years old, and Jehoiada arranges for him to be crowned as king. He stations Judah's military at several places in the temple and prepares to do a very dangerous thing: crown the young boy king to replace Athaliah's reign as queen. This happens on a Sabbath when as many people as possible will be milling around.

When Athaliah hears the celebration of the people, she arrives at the temple and sees Joash already crowned as the new king. She is livid but helpless to do anything about it. The military has abandoned her. After being arrested, she is removed from the temple area. Athaliah is going to be killed, and no one should be killed in the <u>temple</u>, a place of worship. Then Athaliah is put to death with the sword.

Hooray!

Mattan
2 Kings 11:18

the big picture

2 Kings 11:17–21

The people are thrilled to be rid of the evil queen, Athaliah. Joash is a godly king. For the next forty years of his reign, the people enjoy a peaceful time in their country.

The death of Athaliah ends the evil influence of the royal family. The people tear down the temple of Baal and the evil priests' altars and idols. The primary evil priest, Mattan, is killed.

Joash will reign in righteousness and the line of David will continue, as God promised. The people of the land enjoy a new godly freedom, knowing they are in the good hands of someone who serves God. The eventual outcome is the birth of the Messiah, a descendant of David and Joash.

Benefits of Righteous Leadership

Verse	Benefit
Proverbs 8:15	Just laws.
Proverbs 14:34	Righteousness exalts a nation.
Proverbs 16:7	The enemies of a righteous nation (or people) are made to be at peace with them.
Proverbs 16:10	A king with a divine revelation cannot voice a wrong judgment.
Proverbs 16:12	A throne is established through righteousness.
Proverbs 16:13	Righteous kings value honesty.
Proverbs 20:26	A wise king scatters the wicked and destroys them.
Proverbs 20:28	Mercy and truth protect a king and establish his throne.
Proverbs 25:5	Remove wicked people from the king's presence and there will be justice.
Proverbs 28:12	When righteous people triumph, there is great glory but wicked people in charge cause people to hide.
Proverbs 29:4	A country is built up through justice.

When Athaliah's evil influence no longer holds the people hostage, the people rejoice and enjoy the freedom of a righteous ruler. God's preference is that every country enjoy the leadership of godly people, but that isn't always the case. The book of Proverbs gives the benefits of righteous leadership.

Pretty Woman (Shulammite)

bride of Christ
Revelation 19:7

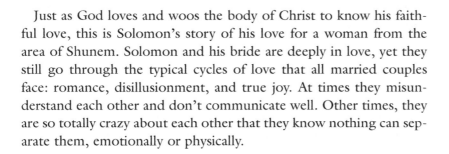

the big picture

Song of Solomon

This book of the Bible provides the story of Solomon's courtship and marriage to a woman; it is also an allegory of God's relationship with the church, the <u>bride of Christ</u>.

Just as God loves and woos the body of Christ to know his faithful love, this is Solomon's story of his love for a woman from the area of Shunem. Solomon and his bride are deeply in love, yet they still go through the typical cycles of love that all married couples face: romance, disillusionment, and true joy. At times they misunderstand each other and don't communicate well. Other times, they are so totally crazy about each other that they know nothing can separate them, emotionally or physically.

Elizabeth George

When it comes to the sexual side of your marriage, you are to give your all . . . freely, unashamedly, joyfully, heartily, regularly.[11]

This story is very explicit in its imagery of Solomon's and his bride's sexual passion for each other. The fact that this is in the Bible gives every woman and man the assurance that sex is a gift from God. Some people try to insist this book is only an allegory of God's love for the church, usually because they dislike the idea that sex is celebrated in the Bible.

For a married couple, reading aloud through the Song of Solomon can be an encouraging boost for any marriage. It can reaffirm a couple's belief that God brought them together to enjoy each other's love and sexuality.

Chapter Wrap-Up

- Ahab marries a very evil woman, Jezebel, and as a result, the country suffers from the wicked reign of the king. (1 Kings 16:29–33)

- Jezebel kills God's prophets and threatens the life of another one of them, Elijah. (1 Kings 18:1–19:2)

- Just as God predicted, Jezebel dies a violent death and her body is eaten by dogs. (2 Kings 9:30–37)

- Jezebel's daughter, Athaliah, has her grandsons killed so that she can reign as queen. But she only rules for six years before God provides the true king, Joash. (2 Kings 11:1–13)

- Solomon loves his bride, the woman from Shunem. In this story of their courtship, wedding, and marriage, we see God's approval of sexual love in marriage and an allegory for God's relationship with the church, the bride of Christ. (Song of Solomon)

Study Questions

1. Why did Jezebel take the deaths of the priests of Baal so personally?

2. How did Jezebel arrange for the death of Naboth?

3. What happens to Ahab and Jezebel, in fulfillment of God's prophecy?

4. What did Athaliah do that shows her evil heart?

5. What does God want to communicate through the Song of Solomon?

Chapter 9 Women of Wisdom

Let's Get Started

Let's look at the stories of three women of wisdom in the Bible. The first, the "Proverbs 31 woman," shows us balance; the next, Abigail, shows us how to handle a crisis with poise; and the third woman, Ruth, shows us her loving response to the grief of her depressed mother-in-law, Naomi.

The Proverbs 31 woman can intimidate us with her perfection, especially when we first read the twenty-two verses contained in Proverbs 31:10–31. This woman is perfect. If there's something worth doing, the perfect woman does it. She does it all. She does it all perfectly. But we must remember that some Bible experts think this description was written by a mother advising her son on how to pick a perfect wife.

If so, the mother is describing the daughter-in-law she wants her son to find! Certainly that kind of woman would be good to her mother-in-law! Others believe that this section of Scripture was written by <u>Lemuel</u> or <u>Solomon</u>, or someone else. We don't know the author of this portion of Proverbs, but we do know that God doesn't intend to frustrate us with the story of this wonderful woman. Instead of feeling that we must be like her, we should think of emulating her as a worthy and inspirational goal God has set for us. The woman of Proverbs offers a model example of how a very busy woman balanced all her responsibilities through faith in God. Then, as we look at Abigail, Ruth, and yes, even Naomi, we'll see women with faith in God's ability to give them insights into life and human character. From studying their lives we'll be inspired and guided.

go to

Lemuel
Proverbs 31:1

Solomon
2 Samuel 5:14

She Does Everything Right! (Proverbs 31 Woman)

> **PROVERBS 31:10**
> *Who can find a virtuous wife?*
> *For her worth is far above rubies. (NKJV)*

strong
Proverbs 24:5

acrostic
written so first or
last letters spell
another word

The word "virtuous" can also be interpreted as fine, <u>strong</u>, wealthy, and capable. When the writer asks, "Who can find?" he or she isn't saying such women don't exist, but that they are rare. In the book of Proverbs, wisdom is also compared to rubies: "For wisdom is better than rubies, and all the things one may desire cannot be compared with her" (Proverbs 8:11 NKJV). So we know that this woman is valued just as wisdom is valued. For those who say that God and Christianity don't value women, quote this passage as an answer. God does value women and godly women in particular.

what others say

Gien Karssen

Remember that the Proverbs woman is not a real person but a model—someone whose example we can follow.[1]

Liz Curtis Higgs

The very idea that the angelic woman of Proverbs 31 had great worth—in the Hebrew: "value, merchandise, or price"—was an incredible statement for that time and place when women were worth little more than cattle and were never worth as much as men.[2]

The twenty-two verses included in this passage are written as an alphabetical poem called an **acrostic**—the first letter of each verse spells the Hebrew alphabet in successive order. A common writer's pattern from ancient days, we find acrostic verse in Lamentations 1 and Psalm 119 as well.

apply it

As women, we all want to be considered priceless. Each of us wants to be loved, valued, supported, and appreciated. This Proverbs woman can inspire us to mold and fashion our lives in better balance, so we too can be more valued than rubies. Yet, thankfully, the evaluation of our worth comes not only from other people, but also from God. Because other people may not respond to us in a loving way, we can seek a far better source: God himself. We know that he considers us so important that he sent his Son, Jesus, to die on the cross and pay for our sins.

She Doesn't Tell Secrets

PROVERBS 31:11
The heart of her husband safely trusts her;
So he will have no lack of gain. (NKJV)

The husband of this noble, excellent, and capable woman trusts her completely. He knows she'll make wise choices for their home and family. Plus, when he reveals himself and his inner thoughts, she doesn't ridicule him. But she does laugh at his jokes! She listens and encourages him. She literally keeps his confidence when he shares something personal or revealing. He knows she won't <u>gossip</u> about him to her friends or mismanage their household funds.

gossip
Proverbs 11:13

listening
James 1:19

good
Proverbs 18:22

what others say

Ruth Peale

If I could give one piece of advice to young brides, and only one, it would be this: study your man. Study him as if he were some rare and strange and fascinating animal, which he is. Study his likes and dislikes, his strengths and weaknesses, his moods and mannerisms. Just loving a man is fine, but it's not enough. To live with one successfully you have to know him, and to know him you have to study him.[3]

Carole and Jack Mayhall

To listen and to be listened to is essential to communication. Only as we develop these traits will we really begin to understand each other and gain inroads into the mind and heart of the person whom God chose for us.[4]

<u>Listening</u> to husbands may not seem as important to men as it does to women, but even men want to be listened to. Women "overlap" their conversations by interrupting each other and consider that "contributing" to the conversation, but men don't regard interruptions as adding to the conversation. To men, overlapping comments seems rude and distracting, and these interruptions communicate disrespect.

She Can Be Trusted

PROVERBS 31:12
She does him good and not evil
All the days of her life. (NKJV)

The husband of this godly woman has confidence in her because he knows she intends to do that which is right and <u>good</u> for him.

pestering
Judges 16:16;
Proverbs 19:13

joy
Ecclesiastes 2:24

stress relievers
Proverbs 15:13;
17:22

And she will do it "for as long as they both shall live." Her commitment is for all her life. She's not going to give up when times get rough or when she doesn't feel in love anymore. Her commitment also means not <u>pestering</u> but instead being grateful for whatever good things he does—even when incomplete or imperfect.

Bringing "good" into someone's life means you have to find out what they consider good. Many people think they are loving their spouse, children, relatives or friends, but they're only doing what they would want—it might not necessarily be what the other wants. Truly loving a person means finding out what is significant and important to him and then acting accordingly, even if what is important to him has no value to you.

Treating your husband well also means realizing he can't be the source of all your happiness. Expecting him to meet all your needs will only make him feel like a failure. No person can meet all your needs. But as women we understand that God, and only God, can meet all our needs. He often does this through our husbands. Consequently, if we know all our needs will be met by God, we know not to demand too much of our husbands' available energy and joy.

She Makes Wonderful Things

PROVERBS 31:13
She seeks wool and flax,
And willingly works with her hands. (NKJV)

Not every woman enjoys working with her hands, but the Proverbs 31 woman does. Whether or not we sew or do crafts doesn't matter to God. What is essential is that we have eager, joyful hands in whatever we do. Many women do many wonderful things with their hands, but if they aren't working with a cheerful attitude, their handiwork isn't valued. God designed people to take <u>joy</u> in their work, whether we work inside or outside the home. The apostle Paul wrote, "And whatever you do, do it heartily, as to the Lord and not to men" (Colossians 3:23 NKJV). Everyone feels overwhelmed at times, but laughter and joy are great <u>stress relievers</u>.

Barbara Johnson

There are many articles and books about how healthy it is to laugh. On the physical side, laughter increases your breathing rate, which automatically increases the amount of oxygen in your blood, producing the aerobic effect usually associated with exercises like swimming and jogging.[5]

Apostle Paul on Work

Paul's Thoughts on Work	Scripture
Work should be done wholeheartedly and as unto the Lord.	Colossians 3:23
Work should be useful and result in giving to those in need.	Ephesians 4:28
Our work should not be a burden to others.	1 Thessalonians 2:9
Everyone should work.	1 Thessalonians 4:11

If we work only for the approval of others, we'll lose our joy and eagerness. But by doing the best we can while constantly growing and seeking God's approval of our work, we'll maintain our joy.

Bargain Shopper!

PROVERBS 31:14
She is like the merchant ships,
She brings her food from afar. (NKJV)

In ancient times, merchant ships brought unusual and fascinating merchandise from faraway places. This woman of Proverbs, like a merchant ship, seeks and brings her family the best. She shops far and wide to look for the best bargains for her household.

Liz Curtis Higgs

Few women could draw much encouragement from being compared to a "merchant ship": bottom heavy and in need of paint! All the translations of this verse were almost identical, though the Living Bible adds some insight: "She buys imported foods, brought by ship from distant ports."[6]

go to

prayer
1 Thessalonians 5:17

Early Riser!

PROVERBS 31:15

She also rises while it is yet night,
And provides food for her household,
And a portion for her maidservants. (NKJV)

This ideal, noble woman is organized. She doesn't mind getting up early to get started on her day. She most likely spends some of that early time quietly concentrating on God. That always makes a day go better. But before all the night people complain, we can emulate the Jewish day, which begins at sunset of the previous day. So night people can begin their "days" by having "quiet time" with God in the evening, well ahead of the morning people!

---

what others say

Jan Johnson

Our back-and-forth communication with God might take the time-proven "breath prayer" format, repeating a familiar prayer of nine or ten syllables or less that has great meaning. To those of us who have spent our energies reciting long lists of prayer requests, breath prayers may seem hackneyed and infantile, but they aren't.[7]

Liz Curtis Higgs

In other words, she got up early to give orders![8]

Tricia McCary Rhodes

It is difficult to be quiet long enough for God to speak. Our minds, jammed from signals from many frequencies, feel uneasy with silence, so we rush to fill its void. We can't get rid of this tendency by flitting here and there. Like a bee who penetrates the flower's depth, we must drink deeply of God's sweet nectar.[9]

Before we think this wonderful woman is fixing food for both her family and her servant girls, we need to know that the word "portion" actually means she apportioned or delegated the work of her household. Mothers without hired help can apply this instruction by including their children in the work of the home. Although children will complain, they will actually feel included, necessary, and important, plus they will learn valuable skills for later in life.

There is no way to get close to God without spending some portion of the day in communion with him. An effective "quiet time" often involves prayer, Bible reading or study, and committing to follow God in whatever that day brings. The Bible refers to both "arrow" prayers and extended times of prayer for communicating with God. Both are useful in different settings.

Moneymaker

PROVERBS 31:16
She considers a field and buys it;
From her profits she plants a vineyard. (NKJV)

This godly woman manages a field, makes a profit from its harvest, and invests it. Because her husband trusts her, she is given great freedom to build their income. Many men are not secure enough to allow their wives such freedom. And many wives have not earned the right. But when a secure man and an organized, wise woman form a bond, both are fulfilled by completing the purposes God assigns to them.

Liz Curtis Higgs suggests these questions for deciding whether or not to add a new responsibility:

1. Will this activity matter one week from today? One month? One year?

2. Is there someone who does it better than I do, to whom I might delegate this activity?

3. Does it satisfy a heart need for me or someone I love very much?

4. What are the ramifications if I don't do it?

5. What are the outcomes if I do do it?[11]

This verse also says she considers a new project before deciding whether or not to take on the additional work and responsibility. What a valuable caution for us today. We have only so much time, so if we accept a new responsibility or task, we must sacrifice something else. Our families and the important people of our lives must remain our highest priorities.

That Enthusiasm Again!

PROVERBS 31:17
She girds herself with strength,
And strengthens her arms. (NKJV)

Such a woman! Again, her joy in work is mentioned as vigorous and strong. Even though she has much to do, she enjoys it all. But that's true because she only takes on the work that God wants her to do—not everything offered to her or everything that everyone else thinks she should be doing. She's an example to us that we don't have to say "yes" to every opportunity. Remember, an opportunity is not necessarily God's open door. Be sure to ask God what he wants you to do, rather than depending on the opinions of others. An opportunity is not necessarily God's open door.

To maintain a vigorous sense of fulfillment in our work—whether in the home or outside it—we must choose to do only those things that God wants us to do. If we take on things that others should be doing, we're in effect saying we're indispensable and the only ones who can do it—and that's pride! Humility recognizes that God has something for everyone to do, but not any one person should do everything. If we take on things that others should be doing, we will be robbing them of the joy God intended for them.

She's a Night Person, Too!

PROVERBS 31:18
She perceives that her merchandise is good,
And her lamp does not go out by night. (NKJV)

This wonderful woman works at night as well as in the early morning. But she must be reasonable in her expectations of herself, for no one can continue burning the candle at both ends and stay sane and healthy! God intends for us to enjoy both work and relaxation. That's why he created the Sabbath for rest, and festivals, and time for enjoying a party! We all need time to get away from work and responsibility to spend special time with our mates.

Notice that this ideal woman isn't afraid to acknowledge that her efforts bring good results. People who have a wrong definition of pride might think she shouldn't be so aware of her accomplishments. She knows what she does, but that doesn't mean she is proud. Instead, she recognizes God's efforts through her and gives him the credit for her accomplishments. She shows us the correct definition of humility. Even the apostle Paul gave himself credit: "We, however, will not boast beyond measure, but within the limits of the sphere which God appointed us—a sphere which especially includes you" (2 Corinthians 10:13 NKJV).

If you are constantly encouraging your husband to accomplish things around the house, or if you are expecting too much from yourself and not putting time and effort into building your marriage, your marriage will suffer. Marriages need times of relaxation, togetherness, and fun. Playing together fuels love. Without times of playful pleasure, marriages run out of gas!

for your marriage

She Can Also Weave!

PROVERBS 31:19
She stretches out her hands to the distaff,
And her hand holds the spindle. (NKJV)

Bible experts aren't sure about the use of the words "distaff" and "spindle" since these words are not used anywhere else in the Bible. But obviously, this woman used her skills for weaving and sewing for her family and for her customers, whose payment benefited her family.

In Old Testament times, fabric was woven from flax to create linen for clothing and ships' sails. Making cloth was extremely time-consuming. After the flax was cut from the field, each piece was dried, cut, and its seeds removed. Then the pieces were soaked in water, before being dried in an oven. Finally the flax fibers were separated, wrapped around a spindle (see Illustration #15) and rotated. By rotating the spindle, the fibers were twisted into thread. Then the threads were put on a loom and woven into cloth.

Illustration #15
Woman Using a Spindle—After the flax fibers were clean and dry (see woman on the right), they were drawn out by hand and wrapped around a spindle. The spindle was rotated to twist the fibers into thread (see woman on the left).

<u>Thinks of Others</u>

PROVERBS 31:20
She extends her hand to the poor,
Yes, she reaches out her hands to the needy. (NKJV)

Our example of an ideal woman includes her sensitivity to the needs of others, especially the poor. God has blessed her materially, and so she shares some of her abundance with the <u>poor</u> people in her area. Wisdom says: "He who oppresses the poor reproaches his Maker, but he who honors Him has mercy on the needy" (Proverbs 14:31 NKJV). Money isn't specifically mentioned, so she might be helping others by listening to them and by being a good friend.

poor
Proverbs 19:17

what others say

Liz Curtis Higgs
It's ironic that one of the best remedies for impending burnout is to give yourself away.[12]

We all can reach out to the poor. Both community and worldwide programs need financial support, so our money can help fund worthy charities all over the globe. In addition to money, many programs desperately need volunteers to give their time to help, from feeding the needy to teaching someone to read to providing shelter for the homeless.

apply it

Quality Is Her Goal

PROVERBS 31:21–22
She is not afraid of snow for her household,
For all her household is clothed with scarlet.
She makes tapestry for herself;
Her clothing is fine linen and purple. (NKJV)

The fabric colors the Bible mentions most often are blue, scarlet, and purple. These may have been the basic colors available for clothing and fabric. Purple dye was the most precious because it was so costly to obtain. The dye was made from murex, a shellfish harvested from the eastern Mediterranean Sea. In one experiment in the early 1900s, more than twelve thousand murex shells were needed to produce just one and a half grams of purple dye. No wonder the dye was so expensive. Obviously, only the very wealthy could afford purple clothing, and the wearing of purple clothes was a sign of royalty and wealth.

Happily, the wealth of the Proverbs 31 woman does not distract her from her spiritual life. She is a person of quality and class. She represents wisdom.

women
Exodus 35:25

decorate
Exodus 35:30–36:1

values
1 Samuel 16:7

Lydia
Acts 16:14–15

city gate
Genesis 23:10

what others say

Gien Karssen

The Proverbs 31 woman strikes the balance between household and outside interests, and she seems able to do both naturally, without undue stress.[13]

God values quality and asks for skilled artisans—both men and women—to decorate his tabernacle with beautiful artistic designs in wood and cloth. God also wants us to dress ourselves attractively to best represent him; even more, he values the beauty of a godly life.

In the New Testament, a woman named Lydia sells purple clothes and cloth. Like the woman of Proverbs, Lydia does not allow her wealth to prevent her from seeking Christ. When the apostle Paul shares the good news about Jesus with Lydia, she immediately wants to be baptized and become a Christian. Then, in her generous spirit she invites Paul and his companions to stay in her home for a while.

For some people, wealth keeps them from seeking God because they depend on themselves, rather than God. But wealth is easily lost and cannot satisfy the spirit. Rich people, like people of every income, need to know God loves them and offers them a fulfilling spiritual life.

Behind Every Successful Man...

PROVERBS 31:23
Her husband is known in the gates,
When he sits among the elders of the land. (NKJV)

This woman's influence extends to her husband. Evidently, she contributes to his success in the community and to his standing as a respected member of the city leadership. Her husband and the others who rule the city and surrounding land carry out their civic duties at the city gate, a kind of city hall.

Even though this woman is active in her community, she doesn't try to control or replace her husband but builds him up and represents him well in the area.

go to

encouraging
Acts 14:22

And an Entrepreneur, Too!

Proverbs 31:24
She makes linen garments and sells them,
And supplies sashes for the merchants. (NKJV)

The godly woman of Proverbs 31 makes linen garments and sashes to sell, showing that any woman can find self-employment possibilities, if God directs. In this ancient time clothes were made from sheep's wool, goat's hair, animal skins, and linen. Ordinary people wore linen, but fine linen was a luxury item worn by the rich. Producing fine linen required a lot of skill. Evidently, she makes linen garments and sashes of such quality that people want to buy her work.

In the Old Testament, God directs Moses to outfit the new priests in fine linen garments: "He shall put the holy linen tunic and the linen trousers on his body; he shall be girded with a linen sash, and with the linen turban he shall be attired. These are holy garments. Therefore he shall wash his body in water, and put them on" (Leviticus 16:4 NKJV).

Whatever employment God leads us to, he wants us to do our best. Because everything we do is a representation of him, we should want to do our best.

apply it

Strength and Humor!

PROVERBS 31:25
Strength and honor are her clothing;
She shall rejoice in time to come. (NKJV)

This amazing woman certainly is a woman of strength and dignity. She is not critical, but <u>encouraging</u> of others. She expects the best, doesn't lower herself to destructive habits, and seeks that which builds up her life and the lives of others. She does not fear or worry

worry
Philippians 4:6–7

meditate
Philippians 4:8

about the future, and she doesn't dwell needlessly on the past. But most important, she has a sense of humor! Her trust in God allows her to regard life with joy, laughter, and flexibility.

---

what others say

Liz Curtis Higgs

What makes her godly attire especially attractive is the combination: strength and honor. The kind of women most of us long to be are both strong and honorable, clothed with the kind of power that comes from on high, certain of our value in God's eyes, definite in our calling, and moving forward with complete assurance.[15]

Barbara Johnson

Laughter is good for your mental health too. I heard one expert suggest that we should learn to laugh at our embarrassing moments in life. If we can't laugh about what has embarrassed us, we will remain embarrassed people. But if we can share our embarrassing moments with others, it achieves two things: first, we admit our imperfections, which helps other folks draw closer to us; second, it's a great way to find things to laugh about.[16]

Max Lucado

Worry will do that to you. It makes you forget who's in charge.[17]

Worry destroys. Worry steals our joy, makes us focus on ourselves, and diminishes our trust in God. Worry is actually a sin because worry is the opposite of faith. Nothing good comes from worry, a needless expense of energy that we could otherwise invest in worthwhile, productive activity. So let's not worry!

As soon as you begin to worry, imagine your item of worry riding on an arrow coming straight toward your mind. Grab hold of that arrow and throw it back out into space. Then meditate on those things that honor God and draw your attention to him. Immediately read or repeat any verse on trusting God.

Listen Up!

wisdom
James 3:17

PROVERBS 31:26
She opens her mouth with wisdom,
And on her tongue is the law of kindness. (NKJV)

When this lady speaks, people listen! They listen because they know what she says is spoken in love, insight, and encouragement. She's not the kind of person who tries to control or manipulate you. Instead, she calmly gives her opinion. Then she trusts God to do whatever work he wants in her life.

Her words fulfill the Bible's description of <u>wisdom</u>: pure, peace-loving, considerate, submissive, full of mercy and good fruit, impartial, and sincere. And those aren't all her qualities; she has verbal self-control!

---

what others say

Elizabeth George

I urge you to evaluate your speech patterns. Ask God to reveal if you are falling into the "contentious" category...or if you are articulating the sweet speech that marks you as a wife after God's own heart. Are you majoring on yourself or are you majoring on your husband—on helping, following, respecting, and loving him?[18]

Proverbs, the most practical book in the Bible, guides us on selecting words wisely. Look to these verses for advice on speaking with wisdom.

How to Speak Wisely

Words and Attitudes	Verse
Honest, truthful	Proverbs 4:24; 12:19
Life-giving, understanding, fitting	Proverbs 10:11; 10:13; 10:32
Few words, controlled, guarded	Proverbs 10:19; 13:3; 21:23
Healing, constructive	Proverbs 12:18, 25:12
Peaceful, gentle, pleasant	Proverbs 12:20; 15:1; 15:26
Encouraging, knowledgeable	Proverbs 12:25; 20:15
Patient	Proverbs 25:15

She Knows What's Going On

go to

needs
Philippians 4:19

PROVERBS 31:27
She watches over the ways of her household,
And does not eat the bread of idleness. (NKJV)

If there's anything this woman is not, it's idle! We get tired just reading about her. Thank goodness she is probably a composite—a person made from the wonderful talents and pieces of many different women. However, even if this woman really lived, remember that she did not do everything at once; she divided her work over the various seasons of her life.

In this verse, we are told that she knows what's going on in her family and home. She sees when a child needs attention. She is sensitive to her husband's discouraged frown when he returns from work. She notices a coworker's excitement and rejoices with that person. This type of woman even knows when it's time for the car to be serviced!

apply it

What all this means is this: because she's not focusing on herself every moment, she has time and energy to focus on others. She is "others-centered" rather than self-centered. A woman who trusts God to meet her <u>needs</u> is able to focus on others. If we don't have faith in God, our lack of faith forces us to concentrate on making ourselves happy.

She's Appreciated!

PROVERBS 31:28–29
Her children rise up and call her blessed;
Her husband also, and he praises her:
"Many daughters have done well,
But you excel them all." (NKJV)

All of us could use some appreciation and gratitude. Unfortunately, not many children say, "Thanks for giving me a time-out" or, "Mom, you're a blessing." Many husbands come home and say, "What did you do all day?" But as we are faithful, our children will grow up (maybe that's what "arise" means!) and be able to acknowledge our love and sacrifices. With time and prayer, our husbands will eventually see how much we accomplish in one day.

capabilities
Psalm 103:14

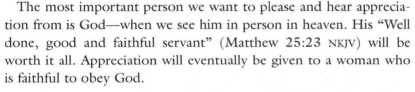

what others say

Liz Curtis Higgs

Maybe King Lemuel's mother meant her grandchildren would do the rising and the blessing. Maybe when our kids have kids, that's when they'll understand all we've sacrificed for them.[19]

Jean Fleming

I impart values, stimulate creativity, develop compassion, modify weaknesses, and nurture strengths. I can open life up to another individual. And I can open an individual up to life.[20]

The most important person we want to please and hear appreciation from is God—when we see him in person in heaven. His "Well done, good and faithful servant" (Matthew 25:23 NKJV) will be worth it all. Appreciation will eventually be given to a woman who is faithful to obey God.

God's expectations of us are much more realistic than those of our loved ones, who sometimes demand more than we can give. He sees our heart and knows our <u>capabilities</u>. He is patient and kind, wanting to provide the inner power and strength to obey him. If we turn to him, he will provide everything we need to be the women he wants us to be.

True Beauty

PROVERBS 31:30–31

> *Charm is deceitful and beauty is passing;*
> *But a woman who fears the LORD, she shall be praised.*
> *Give her of the fruit of her hands,*
> *And let her own works praise her in the gates.* (NKJV)

The beauty of this woman is inward as well as outward. She trusts in God for everything that has been previously described about her. She understands that physical beauty will deteriorate and charm will deceive. But a woman whose heart is intimately acquainted with God has an inner beauty that nothing can destroy.

Such a woman will be praised by others, both within her family and among her friends and acquaintances. Having a woman praised at the city gate was very unusual in the days of David and Solomon, so the author seems to be saying, "If this woman were real, she, of

Nabal
1 Samuel 25:3

promised
1 Samuel 16:13

all women, would be praised there!" Whether or not she is acknowledged at the "city hall," she will be rewarded generously in heaven.

This fear of God is not a feeling of fright or terror but of awe and reverence. With that kind of fear, a woman can believe that God is powerful enough to take care of every problem she might encounter. When she has that kind of confidence inside her, her outer countenance is peaceful and poised.

what others say

Elizabeth George

How lovely and how encouraging to see that where men congregate, where the leaders of the people meet in solemn assembly, her praise is sung and the highest honor ascribed to her![21]

One Smart Lady (Abigail)

the big picture

1 Samuel 25:1–44

Abigail's husband, Nabal, is about to get himself and his family killed by David for denying David's request for help. But, without her husband's knowledge, Abigail steps in and provides food and drink for David. As a result, David's anger diminishes. When Abigail tells her husband what she has done, this harsh man dies of a heart attack. David quickly sees Abigail's value and proposes marriage. She accepts and joins his band of followers.

Abigail's first husband, Nabal, is described as harsh and evil, while Abigail herself is described as intelligent and beautiful. David, whom God has promised the king's position, is hiding from Saul, who wants to kill him. David contacts Nabal's servants and asks for assistance, but Nabal replies harshly, "Who is David, and who is the son of Jesse? There are many servants nowadays who break away each one from his master. Shall I then take my bread and my water and my meat that I have killed for my shearers, and give it to men when I do not know where they are from?" (1 Samuel 25:10–11 NKJV).

Because of Nabal's refusal, David plans to kill Nabal and destroy everything he owns. Fortunately, a servant sees what's going on and alerts Abigail.

Abigail wisely prepares to meet David with gifts of food to ease his anger. Her gifts work. Later, when Abigail tells her husband what she did, her husband has a heart attack and dies ten days later. When David hears of Nabal's death, he sends a proposal of marriage to Abigail, and she jumps at the chance. She becomes his second wife and bears him a son.

lifestyle
Proverbs 19:19

what others say

Marjorie L. Kimbrough

Abigail had a calming effect on David. She had assured him about who he was, whose he was, and what he was to become.[22]

Remember Abigail: How to Cope with Difficult People

What Abigail Did	Scripture
Humbled herself	1 Samuel 25:23
Acknowledged her difficulty	1 Samuel 25:24
Asked to be heard	1 Samuel 25:24
Spoke the truth	1 Samuel 25:25
Gave reasons from a godly perspective	1 Samuel 25:26
Offered gifts	1 Samuel 25:27
Asked for forgiveness	1 Samuel 25:28
Acknowledged David's great purpose	1 Samuel 25:28
Recounted how God is using him	1 Samuel 25:29
Built him up by reminding him of his future	1 Samuel 25:31
Encouraged him to have no guilt about his actions	1 Samuel 25:31

Abigail can be viewed from two distinct viewpoints: either as a wise and resourceful woman, or as an enabler who rescues her husband behind his back. But the Bible doesn't consider her an enabler. Scripture describes her as intelligent, and God rewards her with marriage to David.

When we deal with difficult people, we should remember Abigail. She provides us with examples of ways to cope. See the chart above for a list of Abigail's responses, which we could imitate and apply to our own relationships with difficult people.

A person who enables another person to continue a destructive lifestyle is never thanked. Instead, the enabler will have to keep helping the other person over and over again. Better to ask to be heard, and then speak the truth.

Moab
Genesis 19:37

Naomi
means "pleasant"

True Friendship (Ruth and Naomi)

the big picture

Ruth 1:1–22

Naomi and her daughter-in-law Ruth, a Gentile, leave Ruth's home country, Moab, for Naomi's home country, Israel. Naomi is an Israelite, and the two women are returning to Israel because Naomi's husband and sons—one of whom was Ruth's husband—have died.

During the years detailed in the book of Judges, Elimelech and his wife, **Naomi**, leave Bethlehem because of a famine there. They travel to Moab, and while there, Elimelech dies. Both of Naomi's sons marry women of Moab. One son, Mahlon, married Orpah, and another, Chilion, married Ruth. In time, the two sons also die.

After ten years in Moab, Naomi prepares to return to Israel, but she encourages her daughters-in-law to stay behind in their own country. Orpah agrees, but Ruth wants to return to Israel with her mother-in-law. Ruth has become a believer in Naomi's Jehovah God and says the words that are often used today in a marriage ceremony:

> Entreat me not to leave you,
> Or to turn back from following after you;
> For wherever you go, I will go;
> And wherever you lodge, I will lodge;
> Your people shall be my people,
> And your God, my God.
> Where you die, I will die,
> And there will I be buried.
> The LORD do so to me, and more also,
> If anything but death parts you and me.
> (Ruth 1:16–17 NKJV)

Ruth's unconditional love and support overcome her mother-in-law's hesitation, and Naomi allows the young Ruth to return with her.

When Naomi and Ruth arrive back in Bethlehem, Naomi's old hometown, Naomi reveals her depression and grief over losing her husband and two sons. She tells everyone that God has afflicted her, and Naomi seems unable to get over her bitter loss. The townspeople notice Naomi's grief, but they don't seem to go to great lengths to minister to her. Perhaps if Naomi had returned rich, the townspeople would have responded with more attention. Or, they might have resented that Naomi escaped the famine while they had to stay and suffer. Perhaps some feel Naomi deserves to suffer now. In contrast, Ruth is a <u>true friend</u>, giving Naomi the attention she needs, regardless of any poor choices Naomi might have made.

true friend
Proverbs 18:24

Pentecost
Acts 2:1

levirate
Deuteronomy 25:5

levirate
the custom of marriage between a man and his brother's widow

what others say

Jill Briscoe

Ruth was a wise woman. It is in companionship that gives itself unselfishly, without looking for returns, that we receive the very things we are looking for ourselves.[23]

Steve Farrar

We need to remember in times of stress and hardship that "the angel of the Lord encamps around those who fear him, and he delivers them" (Psalm 34:7). I need time with the Lord to remind me that it's not my private battle, it's His.[24]

The book of Ruth is read on <u>Pentecost</u> by Orthodox Jews. No one knows when Ruth was written, or by whom. Since King David is mentioned in it, some Bible experts think it was written about 400 BC. During the time of this book, the people are morally and spiritually weak. Ruth's story is a contrast to that faithlessness, and her story encourages wise and loving choices. One possible purpose of the book could be to affirm King David's right to the throne through the lineage of Boaz.

When Naomi says to her daughters-in-law, "Turn back, my daughters; why will you go with me? Are there still sons in my womb, that they may be your husbands?" (Ruth 1:11 NKJV), she is referring to the **levirate** marriage rule. Under that rule, the next brother is expected to marry the childless widow of his deceased brother, and the first child of that second marriage is considered a descendant of the deceased brother and the child carries on the family line. This child also inherits the property originally belonging to the dead brother. Naomi is saying she can't have any other sons in her old age to replace the husbands that Orpah and Ruth have lost. She is telling them to turn around; there's no hope for them to continue on with her.

Ruth was from the land of Moab, which was east of the Dead Sea. The Moabites were descended from Moab, a son of Lot and Lot's eldest daughter. Moab was conceived when Lot's two daughters got

go to

Chemosh
Numbers 21:29

only way
John 14:6

everything
Isaiah 45:7

good
Romans 8:28

everyone
John 3:16

their father drunk and seduced him. As a result, both daughters became pregnant and had sons, Moab and Ben-Ammi. Each son headed a nation, Moab and Ammon, and the people of these lands, the Moabites and the Ammonites, frequently fought together against Israel. These ancient people lived in what is now the nation of Jordan.

The "god" of the Moabites was named <u>Chemosh</u>. By returning to her original family, Orpah returns to the worship of that false god. In contrast, Ruth chooses to worship Jehovah, the true God of whom Naomi and her family had spoken. Each of us has a choice of which "gods" we will worship in our lives. The only true God, the Almighty God whose Son is Jesus, tells us he is the <u>only way</u>.

Naomi is deeply depressed because of her great losses. But Ruth's unconditional love shows her, in time, how God loves unconditionally. True friendship shows that kind of acceptance. Ruth doesn't scold Naomi for her feelings, nor does she try to change Naomi. She accepts her and stands alongside her—exactly what a depressed friend needs.

apply it

Naomi attributes her afflictions and problems to God. That is by itself correct, since God is sovereign over <u>everything</u> that happens to us. But Naomi feels that God is out to "get her" and destroy her. As a result, Naomi calls herself "Mara," which means "bitter." God allows everything that goes on in our lives, but his desire is to make us not bitter but better! He wants to use everything we experience to make us depend upon him and see life from his perspective. He is able to use everything for <u>good</u> in our lives. To prevent ourselves from becoming bitter, we need to change any negative ideas we might have about God to the truth that he loves <u>everyone</u>. Contentment is not a place, but an attitude.

<u>Gather What We Need</u>

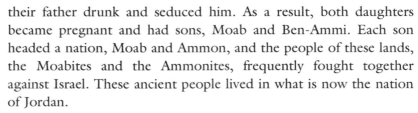

the big picture

Ruth 2:1–23

Ruth and Naomi first arrived at the beginning of barley harvest. Now that the harvest is over, Naomi instructs Ruth to glean or gather what is left in the fields after the harvest. Ruth happens to glean in the field belonging to a relative of Naomi's: Boaz. Boaz is attracted to Ruth and invites her to work only in his field.

Ruth continues to show love for Naomi by being patient in the midst of Naomi's depression and by seeking food for them by gleaning in the fields. Ruth must be attractive, for as soon as Boaz, a landowner, sees Ruth gleaning in his field, he asks about her. Boaz learns that she has returned with Naomi. Boaz instructs his field helpers to treat Ruth kindly and to provide easy gleaning for her. He speaks kindly to her and praises her for her kindness to Naomi. Ruth's character is being revealed through the difficulties she is facing. She shows herself to be generous in sharing her gleanings and to be a hard worker. Plus, her humility is evident for she doesn't shun the work of the poor.

instructing
Leviticus 19:9;
23:22;
Deuteronomy 24:19

Harvesting and gleaning are hard work. Reaping is accomplished by using a wooden sickle (see Illustration #16). The sickle has sharpened pieces of flint embedded to form a blade. Those who bind the grain follow the reapers and gather the grain into sheaves (see Illustration #17). The gleaners follow, gathering the stray stalks (see Illustration #18). All this is done as one stoops over in the hot sun.

As a foreigner, Ruth could have been subjected to abuse by the workers, but Boaz protects her. When Ruth returns to Naomi, tired at the end of the day, she tells Naomi that she was in the field of a nice man named Boaz. Naomi is pleased and praises God—maybe for the first time in a long time. Naomi explains that Boaz is a relative who can qualify as a redeemer and provide for them both. Naomi encourages her to return to that field the next day.

what others say

Jan Frank

After the threshing process removed the grains from the stalks, the mixture remained on the threshing-floor for the winnowing process. In the morning and evening, the breezes would blow more strongly. The farmer would take a winnowing fork with broad prongs, pick up a pile of chaff and grain, and toss it into the air. The heavy grains fell directly to the floor, while the chaff was blown away into another pile away from the good grain.[25]

God provides for the needs of the poor by <u>instructing</u> the nation of Israel to allow the poor to glean from what is left behind in the fields. God is always interested in providing for the needs of everyone. In Ruth and Naomi's case, Boaz even tells his workers to leave

redeemer
Ruth 3:9

key point

out more for Ruth than usual. God not only promises to meet our needs, but he frequently provides for our "wants" also.

Ruth could communicate with the people of this different country, Israel, because the language she spoke and the Hebrew language are very similar. That was proved in 1868 when the Moabite Stone was discovered, revealing that the Moabitish and Hebrew languages had few differences.

There are no coincidences for those who live in reverence to God. Ruth unknowingly "happens" to glean in the field of a man who is a relative of Naomi's family. But we know that God in his sovereignty has placed his loving hand upon Naomi and Ruth. God is about to show Naomi his unconditional love, even though she thinks he has abandoned her.

The friendship between Naomi and Ruth is solidified as they spend each evening together talking. Although we're not told this specifically, we can observe how Naomi is beginning to be pulled out of her depression through God's provision and through these long talks with Ruth. God will provide us with friends who are able to help us deal with our struggles.

> ### the big picture
> ### Ruth 3:1–18
>
> As Ruth prepares to return to the same field, Naomi tells Ruth how to signify to Boaz that she wants him to be their <u>redeemer</u>. Ruth obeys Naomi and follows her instructions, by lying at Boaz's feet in the middle of the night. When Boaz wakes up and discovers her, he immediately knows what is being communicated. He tells her to be patient. He is interested in fulfilling her desires.

Sleeping at Boaz's Feet

Because of the danger of robbers coming to steal the barley, the owner and his hired people sleep on the threshing floor to guard their crop. Also, they want to take advantage of the evening breeze to winnow the crop (see Illustration #19). The threshing floor is a level area, trodden into hardness, where the kernels of the grain are separated from the stalks by dragging a heavy slab over it or by the trampling of cattle (see Illustration #20). Naomi instructs Ruth to lie at Boaz's feet in the middle of the night because that is a way to

Illustration #16
Man Using Sickle—
Harvesters would
use sickles to cut the
wheat stalks.

Illustration #17
Man Gathering
Wheat into
Sheaves—After the
stalks were cut, they
were gathered into
"sheaves."

Illustration #18
Gleaning—Old
Testament Law
allowed the poor to
follow the harvesters
and gather the grain
that fell to the
ground during har-
vesting. This is what
Ruth did.

ask him to become her redeemer, called "go'el" in Hebrew. Naomi is thinking of their future when she instructs Ruth. According to Jewish practice and God's provision, a levirate marriage provides for the security of a widow who could otherwise become destitute. A widow can expect her dead husband's brother to marry her, to provide for her, and to give her children to carry on her dead husband's line.

If no brother exists, a distant male relative is required to become involved and is known as the "go'el" or her redeemer and protector. A group of potential redeemer kinsmen are called "goelim." The first son born to such a union is counted as the child of the dead husband and that son inherits his father's property. Naomi, who is past childbearing age, can't hope for such a levirate marriage, but she can sell her husband's property to bring in some money. The selling of the land owned by Naomi's husband, Elimelech, is necessary to provide money for Naomi to live. She prefers to sell it to someone in her family, so that the land will remain in the possession of her descendants.

Illustration #19
Winnowing—this lady is winnowing: separating the grain from the chaffe.

When Boaz notices Ruth in the middle of the night, he says he wants to "redeem" her, but first he must give the option to a closer relative. At morning's early light, he sends Ruth on her way with six measures of barley.

Illustration #20
Threshing—Before edible grains of ripe cereal crops could be separated from the stalks and husks, the dried stalks were first crushed with weighted, animal-drawn sleds that were pulled back and forth over the threshing floor.

wings
Ruth 2:12

wing
Ezekiel 16:8

what others say

Jill Briscoe

When Boaz covered Ruth with the corner of his garment, or the wings of his cloak, he was reminding her of the God of Israel, "under whose <u>wings</u> you have come to take refuge."[26]

A go'el (redeemer) had three duties: to purchase a family member's land when he was about to lose it through poverty (Leviticus 25:25); to represent a previously injured person who is now dead and doesn't have a son to receive the reparation for the original damage (Deuteronomy 25:5); and to execute justice upon a murderer who killed a family member, becoming the "avenger of blood" (Numbers 35:19; Deuteronomy 19:6).

A man placing his <u>wing</u> (a corner of his garment) over a maiden is a token of marriage among the Arabs. Ruth isn't doing anything immoral or wrong when she lies beside Boaz. She is following the custom of the day, and nothing sexual is involved in how she presents her request.

The spiritual application of the redeemer kinsman is that God offered to redeem each one of us by sending Jesus to die on the cross to free us from the things we do wrong. Claiming his death for our own restores us to friendship with God. In a sense, we each need to allow God to lay his wings over us so that we can take on God's righteous garment to cover our sins. We are told the great news that "in Him we have redemption through His blood, the forgiveness of sins, according to the riches of His grace" (Ephesians 1:7 NKJV).

key point

I Always Cry at Weddings

the big picture

Ruth 4:1–22

Boaz first gives the option of redeeming Ruth and Naomi's land to the closer relative. When he declines, Boaz completes the process and marries Ruth. Ruth bears him a child named Obed. Obed is the grandfather of King David. Therefore, Ruth is an ancestor of Jesus.

Boaz contacts the closest relative, who has the first opportunity to redeem Ruth, and he offers Naomi's land to him. That relative is at first interested, but when Boaz explains that he must also marry Ruth, the closest relative says he's not able to marry her.

The reason for his refusal is not explained, but some Bible experts suggest the following possibilities: he already has a wife and children, even though men in those days often had more than one wife; he fears the risk of losing the perpetuation of his own name in securing Elimelech's land; he doesn't want the financial drain of providing for both Naomi and Ruth along with the purchase price for the land; or, he superstitiously fears that marrying Ruth will cause his death, since both of Naomi's sons died. His reluctance is a relief to Boaz and Ruth, but it shows his self-centeredness in not wanting to fulfill God's plan of being the go'el. The closest relative tells Boaz that he, Boaz, can be the go'el.

King David's Family (simplified)

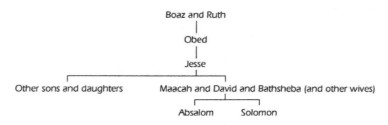

Boaz goes through the symbolic exchange of land when he receives the sandal from Naomi's closer relative (see Illustration #21). The transaction takes place in front of witnesses who sit at the gate—the "city hall." Boaz purchases Naomi's land, formerly owned by her husband, Elimelech, and also takes Ruth as his wife. Sometime later, Ruth bears Boaz a son named Obed. Naomi, who has been struggling with depression, is now overjoyed with having a grandson. Her friends bless her by pointing out how much her daughter-in-law loves her and is better than "seven sons," a comment of supreme blessing in a Hebrew family. The story closes with Ruth's ancestral line; Ruth is the great-grandmother of King David (see chart), and thus Naomi is the great-great-grandmother of Israel's famous king.

---

what others say

Shirley Rose

In our busy, self-absorbed culture, it takes time, commitment, and real effort to develop and nurture true and lasting friendships. If you make the effort, however, you will, like Ruth, always receive far more than you give.[27]

The reference in Ruth 4:7–8 to taking off a sandal to purchase land comes from the idea that when a man took possession of land, he planted his foot—and his shoe—onto the soil. The shoe became a symbol of ownership. When Naomi's first go'el hands his shoe to Boaz, he is saying, "You have ownership."

The people surrounding Boaz, as he makes the transaction, bless him by saying, "The LORD make the woman who is coming to your house like Rachel and Leah, the two who built the house of Israel; and may you prosper in Ephrathah and be famous in Bethlehem" (Ruth 4:11 NKJV). Rachel and Leah were the wives of Jacob, whom God later named "Israel." Along with Jacob's two other wives (his wives' maidservants), they gave birth to the twelve sons who became the twelve tribes of Israel. That is a significant blessing!

Naomi found renewed joy in seeing God's provision through Ruth's marriage and the birth of her grandson. Our ability to have joy shouldn't be dependent upon our circumstances but upon believing God wants only the best for us. God loves to give us good gifts, as Naomi experienced, but he desires that we delight in him—regardless of whether good or bad things happen.

apply it

Chapter Wrap-Up

- The Proverbs 31 Woman is described as an energetic and wise woman who supports her husband and provides generously for her family. (Proverbs 31:10–27)

- The Proverbs 31 Woman is a woman to be praised because she does everything from a sense of respect for God. (Proverbs 31:30)

- Abigail saved herself and her possessions by humbling herself in David's presence and thus placating him after he had threatened to destroy her husband, Nabal, and everything he owned. (1 Samuel 25:23–31)

- Ruth and Naomi returned to Israel destitute, but God provided for them by guiding Ruth to glean in the fields of Boaz. (Ruth 2:3)

- Boaz decides to "redeem" Naomi's land and marry Ruth, thus providing the way for the birth of their child who is in the royal line of King David and an ancestor of Jesus. (Ruth 4:9)

Study Questions

1. What are some of the characteristics of the Proverbs 31 Woman?

2. What was the Proverbs 31 Woman complimented for?

3. What did Abigail do to save herself and her possessions from destruction when David threatened to kill her husband, Nabal?

4. When Ruth wanted to return to Israel with Naomi, what was she saying about her spiritual beliefs?

5. What was the purpose of the "redeemer" or "go'el"?

Chapter 10 Women Victimized by Men

Chapter Highlights:
- Hagar
- Dinah
- Tamar, Er's Wife
- Bathsheba
- Tamar, Absalom's Sister

Let's Get Started

God never plans or desires for men or women to be abused, victimized, or used against his purposes. Yet, because this is a **fallen world** where sin temporarily rules many people's lives, these things do happen. God is grieved when they do. Knowing such unfortunate things will happen, he uses them for his glory and our good, as we turn our hurts and wounds over to him.

God never stands in heaven, wringing his hands, and lamenting, "Oh, no! I didn't anticipate this happening to my child. I don't know what in the world I'm going to do!" Instead, the Lord God Almighty stands alongside his hurting child, and weeps, and hurts with her or him. Then God puts his **redemptive plan** into practice. In this section, we will study biblical women who were victimized by men, and we'll see how God works to bring good out of bad.

Surrogate Mother (Hagar)

GENESIS 16:1–4 *Now **Sarai, Abram**'s wife, had borne him no children. And she had an Egyptian maidservant whose name was Hagar. So Sarai said to Abram, "See now, the LORD has restrained me from bearing children. Please, go in to my maid; perhaps I shall obtain children by her." And Abram heeded the voice of Sarai. Then Sarai, Abram's wife, took Hagar her maid, the Egyptian, and gave her to her husband Abram to be his wife, after Abram had dwelt ten years in the land of Canaan. So he went in to Hagar, and she conceived. And when she saw that she had conceived, her mistress became despised in her eyes. (NKJV)*

God has already <u>promised</u> Abram and Sarai that he will give them a vast family and, through that family, all the families of the earth will be blessed. As time goes on and Sarai doesn't become pregnant, their faith erodes until they take things into their own hands. Sarai makes her servant, Hagar, become a surrogate mother for her. Using human efforts, rather than God's efforts, to conceive a child,

promised
Genesis 12:2–3

fallen world
sinful world

redemptive plan
restoring

Sarai
the original spelling for Sarah

Abram
the original spelling for Abraham

hope
Jeremiah 29:11

has a bad effect. The atmosphere within their home deteriorates. When we try to fulfill God's promises our way, only chaos results.

Although their actions were acceptable within the customs of that day, this isn't what God wanted or planned. All three are responsible in some way for the sin:

1. Sarai didn't trust God (Genesis 16:2);

2. Abram didn't exercise his role as head of his home to resist doing the wrong thing (Genesis 16:2);

3. Hagar became arrogant (Genesis 16:4).

God Meets Hagar

> **the big picture**
>
> **Genesis 16:1-16**
>
> Hagar conceives a son. But, after becoming pregnant, the two women, Sarai and Hagar, do not get along. After being mistreated by Sarai, the pregnant Hagar runs away. The angel of the Lord meets her in the desert and promises that her unborn son Ishmael, will be the father of a great nation. The angel instructs her to return to Sarai and remain under her authority. She obeys. Her son, Ishmael, is born when Abram is eighty-six years old.

Hagar's immaturity and pain cause her to run away, but in God's great love, the angel of the Lord meets her in the desert. The angel tells her what lies ahead for her and her unborn son. Through no fault of her own, Hagar has been brought into a situation that doesn't honor God, yet God takes care of her. God understands her pain. The angel of the Lord sensitively asks her questions and gives her an opportunity to share her feelings. Then the angel gives her hope for the future by telling her what will happen for her son. As a result, Hagar worships God and obeys him, returning in submission to Sarai. In time, God's promise is fulfilled as Hagar's son, Ishmael, is born.

The impatience of Abram and Sarai brings generations of grief to their descendants. Hagar's son, Ishmael, becomes the ancestor of the Arabs, who have always been hostile to the Jews. Ishmael is the ancestor of Mohammed, the founder of Islam.

Sin doesn't affect just the person who sins, but it often has far-reaching effects. Even when we are forgiven, we may still suffer the consequences of our incorrect choices. In the case of Sarai and Abram, a lack of trust in God resulted in sin. This sin created conflict between Sarai and her servant, Hagar (Genesis 16:4); tension between Sarai and Abram (Genesis 16:5); and future generations of strife between Jews and Arabs.

key point

Kicked Out

When Ishmael is fourteen years old, a miraculously conceived son is born to Sarah and Abraham. About two years later, during the child's weaning party, Ishmael, who is now sixteen, makes fun of Isaac, the child. In response, Sarah demands that Ishmael and Hagar be driven from their home. This is part of God's plan so that the promise through Isaac will not be threatened. Though Abraham is saddened, God commands him to do what Sarah says.

Hagar, obviously believing that she and her son will die from thirst and hunger in the desert, leaves sobbing. But as before, God hears Hagar crying. In his faithfulness, he sends an angel and shows Hagar a well. Once again God takes care of Hagar and the boy, showing his concern for everyone and especially those who have been used for ungodly purposes.

God frequently poses questions to the people of the Bible, questions whose answers he already knows. Though God knows everything, he still asks questions to reveal things to us and to show his concern for us. Consider these examples:

1. Eve and Adam: Genesis 3:9

2. Cain: Genesis 4:6

3. Moses: Exodus 4:2

4. Elijah: 1 Kings 19:9, 13

5. Isaiah: Isaiah 6:8

6. Jesus and Woman with Issue of Blood: Mark 5:30

"Ishmael" means "God hears." His very name will continually remind Hagar that God heard her desolate, solitary cry in the desert. God always hears every cry we make or every joy we express. The psalmist said, "You comprehend my path and my lying down, and are acquainted with all my ways" (Psalm 139:3 NKJV).

God cares about each one of us and everything that happens in our lives. The mistreatment and misuse of Hagar don't disqualify her from being loved and cared about by God. Yet often a victim believes the lie that the abuse disqualifies her or him from receiving God's love. That's totally untrue, as Hagar's story shows.

Hagar may think God doesn't care about her struggles when she

is running away and years later when she and her son are thrown out of their home. But God meets her where she is and gives her the opportunity to express her feelings. Victims often have difficulty expressing their feelings. But when they learn to share what they're really feeling, they find greater freedom to work through their abuse. Though God always knows what's going on in our lives and doesn't really need the information, he asks us to share our hearts with him. That's a part of his love.

In two encounters with God, Hagar gained the courage and faith to do what seemed impossible: first, to return and submit to Sarah, and second, to go forth and raise Ishmael by herself. When we have staggering obstacles facing us, going to God and letting him share our struggle gives us the power to get through our troubles.

Paul's Analogy of Hagar

grace
Ephesians 1:6

self-effort
Ephesians 2:8–9

sets us free
Galatians 5:1

battles
Galatians 5:16–18

flesh
sinful nature

the big picture

Galatians 4:21-31

Many years later, the apostle Paul uses Hagar to represent the Old Testament belief that salvation is achieved through good works. He contrasts Hagar with Sarah, whom he uses to represent the ways of Christ and salvation through God's <u>grace</u>.

Many years after the days of Hagar and Sarah, the apostle Paul used the analogy of Hagar and Sarah to communicate a spiritual truth. Hagar, who gives birth to her son the ordinary way, represents the old way of the Old Testament: people have to earn God's favor by keeping the law. This old law system is based on <u>self-effort</u>.

But Sarah, who gives birth to her son at age ninety-plus, is extraordinary. She gives birth to a son through God's grace and her faith. That's why Paul used Sarah, who gave birth as a result of God's promise, to represent the new covenant through Jesus.

This new covenant <u>sets us free</u> from our own efforts to receive God's favor. Because of Jesus' death for our sins and salvation through God's grace, this covenant, Paul explained, is much better than the old one.

Paul's analogy also corresponds to the way the "old" **flesh** <u>battles</u> against the Holy Spirit in a Christian's life. The old flesh wants to be

go to

grieved
Ephesians 4:30

fruit
Galatians 5:22–23

intermarry
Deuteronomy 7:3

what others say

Herbert Lockyer

Hagar represents the Old Covenant and Sarah the New Covenant which is superior to the Old with its ordinances. Under grace all within the household of faith live by faith.[3]

in control and cause a believer to live dependent upon its own resources. But the best way—and only godly way—is to surrender to the control of the Holy Spirit and let him be in charge. When we don't surrender, the Holy Spirit is <u>grieved</u> by our actions.

When we are controlled by the Holy Spirit, we see the <u>fruit</u> of the Spirit in our lives: love, joy, peace, long-suffering, kindness, goodness, faithfulness, gentleness, and self-control. When we're tense, angry, worried, overwhelmed, doubtful, or tempted to do the wrong thing, we know we're being controlled by our flesh. Turning to God and asking for his help returns us to the control of the Spirit.

She's Just Lonely (Dinah)

GENESIS 34:1–5 *Now Dinah the daughter of Leah, whom she had borne to Jacob, went out to see the daughters of the land. And when Shechem the son of Hamor the Hivite, prince of the country, saw her, he took her and lay with her, and violated her. His soul was strongly attracted to Dinah the daughter of Jacob, and he loved the young woman and spoke kindly to the young woman. So Shechem spoke to his father Hamor, saying, "Get me this young woman as a wife." And Jacob heard that he had defiled Dinah his daughter. Now his sons were with his livestock in the field; so Jacob held his peace until they came. (NKJV)*

Perhaps Dinah, the only daughter of Jacob and Leah, is lonely for women her age. She has twelve brothers! Whatever the reason, Dinah goes to see what other people in her own country are doing. God has already told Jacob and God's blossoming nation (the sons of Jacob—soon to be Israel), that they are not to <u>intermarry</u> or make treaties with the people of the land, the Canaanites. Perhaps in Dinah's mind, just visiting with them can't hurt. And certainly, no law prohibits visiting those who didn't believe in Jehovah.

Unfortunately, her curiosity brings great pain to her and her family. One of the Canaanites, Shechem, rapes Dinah. This unthinkable, immoral act upsets her father, Jacob, and her brothers as well as her mother and herself. Thankfully, Dinah tells her father what happened. He doesn't take action until his sons come home from the field.

When someone is victimized, they often feel that they are to be blamed, so they don't tell anyone. They carry a secret that, if told, could stop the victimizer from hurting others. In addition to feeling guilty about being hurt, the victim carries a great deal of wounded pain. Sharing the secret and finding help for the problem bring healing.

apply it

Dinah's curiosity and restlessness brought great grief to herself and her family. Even so, her brothers must also be held accountable for their deception and brutality. The Word of God doesn't blame, though, it merely shares the story and expects us to learn from it.

Revenge with a Capital *R*

Schechem wants to marry Dinah, so he asks his father to arrange a marriage between him and Dinah. If trying to arrange a marriage after a rape sounds unusual, we need to remember that arranged marriages were the norm in the culture of the Middle East. Jacob knows this marriage, which would have been an intermarriage between a Canaanite man and his daughter, will not take place. God has already told Jacob and his people that they are not to intermarry

nature worship
Numbers 25:2

or make treaties with the people of the land, the Canaanites. Certainly, after being raped, Dinah cannot wish to marry Shechem, even if her father agrees to the intermarriage. But Dinah knows, if her father approves the marriage, she will have to marry him. Dinah must deeply regret looking for friends among the Canaanites, for after being raped, she is not available for marriage to any other man.

Shechem makes plans to marry Dinah, for he feels love for her. When he approaches Jacob's family to arrange a marriage, Jacob's sons require all of Shechem's male relatives and the men of the area to be circumcised. After the circumcisions are performed, the males are physically weakened and unable to protect themselves. That's when Simeon and Levi attack, killing Shechem's family. Then the Israelites rescue Dinah and take everything for plunder.

Tradition states through historian Josephus that Dinah went to the Canaanite annual festival of <u>nature worship</u>. She wasn't just visiting with other women, but watching heathen ceremonies.

God wants us to be content and not be tempted by the curiosities of the world. Whether watching movies with unnecessary violence or sex, or reading magazines about cults and the dishonesty of "safe sex," God wants us to be righteous beacons of his light in a dark world.

<u>Wanted One Husband (Tamar)</u>

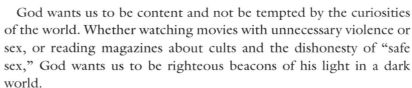

GENESIS 38:6–11 *Then Judah took a wife for Er his firstborn, and her name was Tamar. But Er, Judah's firstborn, was wicked in the sight of the LORD, and the LORD killed him. And Judah said to Onan, "Go in to your brother's wife and marry her, and raise up an heir to your brother." But Onan knew that the heir would not be his; and it came to pass, when he went in to his brother's wife, that he emitted on the ground, lest he should give an heir to his brother. And the thing which he did displeased the LORD; therefore He killed him also. Then Judah said to Tamar his daughter-in-law, "Remain a widow in your father's house till my son Shelah is grown." For he said, "Lest he also die like his brothers." And Tamar went and dwelt in her father's house. (NKJV)*

Judah, a son of Jacob (Israel), secured a wife, Tamar, for his first-born son Er. But the son dies, so Judah requires his second son, Onan, to fulfill the <u>levirate law</u>. According to the law, the brother of a dead husband must marry the widow and become her husband. In addition, the new couple's firstborn son inherits the land of the first husband.

go to

levirate law
Deuteronomy 25:5

But Onan doesn't fulfill his obligation, and God puts him to death. Because Judah has lost two sons, he fears giving his third son to Tamar to marry. He's afraid that son will die too. So, Judah puts off marrying his third son to Tamar.

> **what others say**
>
> **Carol Kent**
>
> I sometimes forget that God designed me to live in a perfect world, but because of sin I live in a "groaning" world.[5]

Keeping a promise is very important in God's eyes. God always keeps his promises, and he expects us to keep ours as well as not to make rash promises. If we make a promise, God expects us to keep it.

key point

Broken Promises

> **the big picture**
>
> **Genesis 38:12–30**
>
> When Tamar realizes Judah isn't going to keep his promise and give her his third son to marry, she devises a plan to fulfill the levirate custom. Evidently she's not trusting God to bring her justice so she takes things into her own hands by becoming available to Judah as a prostitute.

In time, Shelah, the third son, is grown, but Judah still doesn't make him Tamar's husband. When Tamar hears her father-in-law is in the area where she lives with her parents, she has an unusual plan ready. She dresses like a prostitute, covers her face, and makes herself available to Judah, who is now a widower. She requires payment for having sex with him, and he offers to send her a goat. She counters his offer by asking for something to show he'll keep his promise. He gives her his staff, his seal, and the cord he uses to hang the seal around his neck.

burned
Leviticus 21:9

line
Matthew 1:2–5

fruits
Galatians 5:22–23

Later, Judah tries to send the goat, but no one knows any prostitute in this area. Then Judah learns Tamar is pregnant. He is outraged and plans to have her <u>burned</u> to death, the law's consequences for prostitution.

In response, she confidently sends his seal, cord, and staff to him to prove her identity. He recognizes his things and calls her more righteous than I. Her plan works: she gets a husband, her father-in-law. Judah and Tamar marry. Tamar gives birth to twin sons, named Perez and Zerah. Zerah is in the <u>line</u> of King David, and then Jesus.

Tamar probably understood and believed God's promise that the Messiah will come through Judah. She didn't want the family line to end. Since Shelah wasn't going to marry, she needed to marry Judah. Tamar took action to keep the family line going. Although Tamar's desire to see God's law fulfilled is commendable, she forces it to happen in the wrong way.

what others say

Anne Graham Lotz

God's delays and his ways can be confusing because the process God uses to accomplish his will can go against human logic and common sense. The reason for this is to focus our faith, not in our friends . . . or ability . . . or resources . . . or knowledge . . . or strength . . . or anything other than him alone.[6]

Marie Chapian

I want always and forever to see God as he said he is: love. I want to maintain this truth whether or not he answers my prayers as I want him to.[7]

Faithfulness is an important characteristic in our lives. Judah doesn't exhibit faithfulness, but Tamar does, even though she takes things into her own hands. Faithfulness is listed as one of the <u>fruits</u> of the Spirit. God is consistently described as a faithful God, and he wants us to exhibit the same wonderful quality—faithfulness. God wants us to keep our promises.

God's Call to Faithfulness

Keep Your Promises About	Scripture
The truth	3 John 1:3
God's gifts	Matthew 25:23
Dedication	Romans 12:1
Representing the gospel	1 Corinthians 4:2
Obedience	Romans 2:8
Service and ministry	1 Timothy 1:12
Marriage vows	Hebrews 13:4
During persecution	Revelation 2:10

Tamar, like many others in the Bible, took action to try to fulfill God's promise. Yet God is never powerless or late. Although we don't know how God would have liked Tamar's situation to be solved, we can be assured he knows the plans he has for each of us in our struggles. Sometimes, we find waiting difficult, but God will work to bring good out of a bad situation and get us through our time of trial.

Why Wash? (Bathsheba)

2 SAMUEL 11:1–5 *It happened in the spring of the year, at the time when kings go out to battle, that David sent Joab and his servants with him, and all Israel; and they destroyed the people of Ammon and besieged Rabbah. But David remained at Jerusalem.*

Then it happened one evening that David arose from his bed and walked on the roof of the king's house. And from the roof he saw a woman bathing, and the woman was very beautiful to behold. So David sent and inquired about the woman. And someone said, "Is this not Bathsheba, the daughter of Eliam, the wife of Uriah the Hittite?" Then David sent messengers, and took her; and she came to him, and he lay with her, for she was cleansed from her impurity; and she returned to her house.

And the woman conceived; so she sent and told David, and said, "I am with child." (NKJV)

ritual cleansing
Leviticus 15:19–28

Although much is said about David's sinfulness in seeking Bathsheba, does a bit of the blame go to this wife of Uriah? We can't know. Certainly, in Jerusalem, the homes were low, with flat roofs, and if she was bathing in full view of surrounding homes and the palace, she would have attracted attention (see Illustration #22). She is not recorded as resisting David's advances, and her only righteous response was refusal. When she becomes pregnant after sleeping with David, she tells David instead of her husband.

But, in her favor, the Scripture doesn't say she was bathing in full view. She might have taken her bath in a well-hidden spot and was spied upon. In addition, saying no to a king would have been difficult, dangerous, or even impossible. Her pregnancy must have been a shock. How could she have explained a pregnancy to a husband who is away at war? Perhaps her difficulties are simply the result of being beautiful and being seen in the wrong place at the wrong time. But, God has a plan for her.

Illustration #22
The city of Jerusalem—Situated on Palestine's mountainous ridge, Jerusalem was the most important city of ancient Israel.

Evidently, her bathing is a part of her <u>ritual cleansing</u> after her monthly period. Perhaps Bathsheba could have made a wiser choice about where she chose to bathe, but perhaps not. We cannot know for sure.

Honesty develops and keeps trust in a marriage. Although confessing to her husband would have been very difficult for Bathsheba, God would have helped her to be honest, helped her husband to be understanding of her predicament, and provided hope for forgiveness and restoration.

More Deception

David calls Uriah home from the battlefield and commands him to go home, hoping that his reunion with his wife, Bathsheba, will convince Uriah he has made his wife pregnant. But Uriah sleeps at the palace instead; Uriah says his loyalty to his fellow soldiers prevents him from enjoying himself, especially sexually. Even David's efforts at getting Uriah drunk don't send Uriah home to Bathsheba.

Finally, David gives up on his plan to bring Bathsheba together with her husband. In a terrible deception, David sends Uriah back to the war front with a letter to his commander, Joab, saying to put Uriah in a deadly position. That's exactly what happens. After Bathsheba spends the appropriate amount of time mourning her husband's death, she is brought to the palace, becomes David's wife, and gives birth to David's son. We don't know what Bathsheba thinks about what has happened to her husband and to herself, but we can guess that she had to struggle to cope.

judgment
2 Samuel 12:15–18

Solomon
2 Samuel 12:24

separate
Romans 8:38–39

benefi
Isaiah 43:25

David
2 Samuel 5:4

Although most of Scripture doesn't comment on whether a person's behavior is good or bad, this incident causes the author of Samuel to write, "But the thing that David had done displeased the LORD" (2 Samuel 11:27 NKJV). In time, when David and Bathsheba's child is a week old, the Lord brings judgment and the child dies. David comforts Bathsheba, for they seem to have found happiness together. They have another son named Solomon. Later, she gives birth to three more sons of David.

Though David and Bathsheba are involved in sin, God, in his graciousness and forgiveness, allows them to be ancestors of the Messiah. Truly, there is nothing that can separate us from God's love—even sin, if we turn back to him.

Many people have trouble forgiving themselves for the things they've done wrong. But God wants us to forgive ourselves. That's the way he can have fellowship with us. In fact, he says forgiving us is to his benefit, not just ours. Forgiving ourselves may not be easy, but by choosing to forgive ourselves, by force of will, we will begin to believe in our forgiveness more readily.

God Makes Solomon King

the big picture

1 Kings 1:1–53

Many years later, David is about to die and his son, Adonijah, tries to establish himself as the next king. But God uses Bathsheba to make sure that their son Solomon, who is God's choice for king after David, is chosen by David as the successor before his death.

When we follow God's directions and state our opinion, God can bring the results he wants.

When King David is seventy, he becomes sick and feeble, and his fourth but oldest surviving son, Adonijah, tries to name himself the successor to the throne. Bathsheba is concerned because David wants their son Solomon to follow him on the throne. Not only does this threat to David's wish worry her, but she knows if Adonijah becomes king, her life and Solomon's life will be in danger. In this ancient time, a new king would kill any rival to the throne—certainly Solomon is a rival for the throne.

Bathsheba and the prophet <u>Nathan</u> alert King David, who is dying, to Adonijah's claim. David affirms that Solomon will be the next king and commands <u>Zadok</u> the priest and Nathan the prophet to anoint Solomon as king. That David listened to Bathsheba shows her great influence on him. Though David had several wives, Bathsheba must have been very special to him.

Over the years, beauty fades no matter how gorgeous the person. Obviously much more than her beauty has kept Bathsheba close to David's heart all these years. Nathan certainly recognizes her importance to David, and that's why Nathan asks her to make the first approach to David and to be the first person to tell David about Adonijah's plan to name himself king. Wisely, Bathsheba uses her influence upon King David to secure God's plan for her son Solomon.

After Solomon becomes king, the people of the land rejoice, but not Adonijah. Fearing for his life, he pleads for mercy. Solomon grants it. Bathsheba becomes the "Queen Mother."

Later, Adonijah asks Bathsheba to present the possibility of his marrying Abishag, who had nursed David in his last years. Although Bathsheba has great influence upon her son, Solomon <u>refuses</u> her request and has Adonijah killed.

Perhaps Bathsheba did not realize the political implications of such a union. Abishag had been King David's last concubine before his death. Although Abishag and David had never had sex, they had a relationship. In this ancient culture, a marriage between Adonijah and Abishag would show royal succession and provide a reason for Adonijah to challenge Solomon's right to the throne. Solomon understands this challenge, and that's why Solomon has Adonijah executed.

Nathan
2 Samuel 7:2

Zadok
2 Samuel 8:17

refuses
1 Kings 2:25

what others say

Beth Moore

I can't help but wonder what emotions filled Bathsheba. The crown would be taken from her husband and placed on the head of her son. Did she feel sadness and joy? Mourning and celebration? Bathsheba wanted nothing more than for Solomon to receive the crown, but was she prepared for David to have to lose it in order for Solomon to gain it? Being wife and mother can sometimes feel like two exclusive roles tearing one woman in half.[9]

The Bible is careful to blame David for the seduction, perhaps even rape, of Bathsheba. But Bathsheba did not let herself be destroyed by what must have been a most upsetting experience. Later, when they are married, she is able to see David's wonderful qualities and develop a strong relationship with him. Together, they had four sons. Bathsheba provides us with an inspirational example of a resourceful woman who worked with God to bring something good from a terrible experience.

From Lust to Hate (Tamar)

the big picture

2 Samuel 13:1–22

A young woman named Tamar is one of King David's daughters and is a godly virgin. She doesn't realize it but her stepbrother, Amnon, is filled with lust for her. But after he arranges for the household to be empty, he rapes her. His lust spent, he instantly hates her and throws her out of the room. She's willing to become his wife, but he refuses. Tamar is devastated and the resulting revenge by her brother, Absalom, creates a great divide in the family.

This Tamar, who is the sister of Absalom and daughter of King David, is young, beautiful, and <u>innocent</u>. Tragically, she is cruelly raped by Amnon, her stepbrother, even though she fights his advances verbally and physically, saying, "Do not force me, for no such thing should be done in Israel. Do not do this disgraceful thing!" (2 Samuel 13:12 NKJV). But he is too strong and forces himself on her. Although he initially claims he has raped her out of love, Amnon turns his passion from lust to hate. According to Hebrew law, Amnon is now <u>obligated</u> to marry her, but he refuses and throws her out of his room.

In her deep grief, she tears the beautifully decorated robe that signifies her virginity and puts ashes on her head. Her behavior tells her brother, Absalom, and her father, King David, that she has been violated. No more is said of Tamar, the loss of her innocence, and the terrible crime she endured.

Two years later, Absalom avenges the crime against his sister by killing the rapist, Amnon. We can consider Tamar an example of a woman who fights for what is precious, her virginity, and is crushed

go to

innocent
Deuteronomy
22:25–29

obligated
Deuteronomy 22:29

by the loss of it. Unfortunately, back in those days, a single woman who was no longer a virgin lost the opportunity to marry and have children.

Tamar is devastated by both the rape and the loss of her future as a wife and a mother. We assume she lives out her life in her brother Absalom's home, and we hope she lives in some contentment. Certainly her brother Absalom loved her, for he named his daughter, Tamar, after his sister. As a result of Amnon's crime against Tamar, King David's family is divided.

Even in today's society, a raped woman is often treated as if she is a criminal. But God's law protects a raped woman and considers her innocent.

what others say

Virginia Stem Owens

Hebrew has no noun for rape. When Tamar said it was "unspeakable" she meant it literally; she calls rape "the thing that ought not to be done." There is no verb for rape in Hebrew either. It employs the same term it uses to describe the enslavement of the Israelites by the Egyptians—"to humble."[10]

Chapter Wrap-Up

- Hagar was used wrongly as a surrogate mother for Abraham and Sarah, but God showed his love and provided for her needs and for her son's needs. (Genesis 16:1–16; 21:8–21)

- Because Dinah wanted to see what the other women of the land were doing, even though God had told the Israelites to keep separate from the unbelievers of the land, she came into contact with Shechem and was raped. (Genesis 34:1–5)

- Even though Judah was supposed to allow his third son to become Tamar's husband, he broke his promise after his two sons and her first two husbands died. Tamar used her own devices to secure her future instead of trusting God. (Genesis 38:6–30)

- Bathsheba became the wife of King David after David took her and then had her husband killed in battle. Despite the terrible beginning to their marriage, their relationship was very positive. (2 Samuel 11:1–27)

- Tamar was raped by her stepbrother Amnon even though she tried to both verbally and physically fight him off. His crime divides King David's family. (2 Samuel 13:1–22)

Study Questions

1. How was Hagar misused and yet God showed his love anyway?

2. Even though Dinah was an innocent victim of rape, what did she do that put her in danger?

3. What promise to Tamar did Judah break?

4. Why did Bathsheba become David's wife?

5. What did Tamar do after she was violated and why?

Chapter 11 Women Who Served Evil

Let's Get Started

No one begins life as an evil person. No one starts out with a plan to do wrong things. Yet, if we're not careful, we can easily slip in our commitment to righteousness and to obeying God. Perhaps the women described in this chapter did not know how ugly their attitudes and actions were, but their actions and attitudes were evil. We can be warned by their lives. Whether we're tempted to be with someone we shouldn't be with, to gossip, to be critical, discontented, or respond in anger, we should remember that God can help us resist. He would have empowered these women to do the same.

I'm Outta Here! (Potiphar's Wife)

the big picture

Genesis 39:1–20

Potiphar's wife is attracted to the new young slave her husband has brought into their home. That man is a Jew named Joseph, and she wants him to make love to her. When Joseph refuses, she accuses him of rape. Her husband believes her lie and throws the young man into prison.

Potiphar's wife is attracted to the handsome physical appearance and godly personality of Joseph, a Jewish slave her husband bought from the Ishmaelites. She tries repeatedly to entice him to make love to her, but he refuses. His rejection fuels her desire, and finally, she tries to physically force him. When he runs away to escape her desperate grasp, she tears his clothing and uses his torn clothing to claim to her husband that Joseph tried to rape her. Her husband believes her and throws Joseph into jail—just where God wants him. Although God used Potiphar's wife to fulfill his plan for Joseph and the Israelites, Potiphar's wife is still responsible for her evil actions and desires.

God works in mysterious ways—in ways that we might not under-

surprised
1 Peter 4:12

serving
Ephesians 2:10

circumcision
Genesis 17:10

anger
Proverbs 15:1

fruits
Galatians 5:22–23

stand, or even agee with sometimes. God wants Joseph to be put into prison so that Joseph can eventually be called before Pharaoh. God uses an insignificant woman, aimless and lustful, to imprison Joseph. God doesn't promise us a rose garden in this life, and he tells us that we shouldn't be <u>surprised</u> by our trials. God is able to use even evil people, like Potiphar's wife, to secure his purposes.

Potiphar's wife shows us the need for purpose in our lives. Because Joseph took care of everything in Potiphar's home, this woman had nothing of value to do. She felt lonely and useless, even though she could have used her time helping others. She lacked purpose and the positive self-esteem that come from accomplishment. Although we don't want to base all our self-esteem on our achievements, we know that God wants us to find purpose through <u>serving</u> him.

I'll Do It Myself! (Zipporah)

EXODUS 4:24–26 *And it came to pass on the way, at the encampment, that the LORD met him and sought to kill him. Then Zipporah took a sharp stone and cut off the foreskin of her son and cast it at Moses' feet, and said, "Surely you are a husband of blood to me!" So He let him go. Then she said, "You are a husband of blood!"—because of the circumcision. (NKJV)*

Zipporah, Moses' wife from the land of Midian, may not be familiar with God's Law and his command for <u>circumcision</u>. Or, perhaps initially she did not want their son circumcised. But God holds Moses accountable for the delay in circumcising the son and tries to kill Moses—we don't know how, but we know Moses' disobedience has led to a dire situation. Zipporah, probably in a panic to save her husband, circumcises their son herself.

Although Bible experts don't know the true meaning of the phrase "a husband of blood," Zipporah seems to use these words to refer to her disapproval of this bloody ceremony. But she does it anyway to save her husband's life.

Dealing with <u>anger</u> can be a struggle, but God promises that the Holy Spirit can strengthen us to be patient. In fact, patience is listed as one of the <u>fruits</u> of the Spirit. Consider these advantages of patience and disadvantages of anger from the book of Proverbs.

Great Reasons to Stay Calm from the Proverbs

Advantages of Patience	Disadvantages of Anger
Shows great understanding (Proverbs 14:29)	Shows foolish actions (Proverbs 14:17)
Produces a healthy body (Proverbs 14:30)	Brings hatred (Proverbs 14:17)
Turns away others' anger (Proverbs 15:1)	Produces diseased body (Proverbs 14:30)
Calms disputes (Proverbs 15:18)	Stirs up even more anger (Proverbs 15:1)
Shows a person has knowledge (Proverbs 17:27)	Invites violence (Proverbs 18:6)
Is persuasive (Proverbs 25:15)	Reveals greed (Proverbs 28:22)

go to

Samson
Judges 13:24

Anger never adds constructively to God's purposes. Although expressing anger can make us feel better temporarily, it usually creates guilt, shame, and pain. Anger doesn't build up, it only tears down. Instead, God wants us to control ourselves and follow his directions in a calm manner.

Nag, Nag, Nag! (Delilah)

> **the big picture**
>
> **Judges 16:4–22**
>
> Delilah is the latest love object of Samson—a man whose ministry was determined from birth. As a Nazirite, he is not to cut his hair, and as a result he has great strength in God's power. The Philistines are afraid of his great strength and enlist Delilah to find out the source of his great strength. Eventually, through great persistence, Delilah does find out, she tells the Philistines, and they destroy him.

Samson loves Delilah, but Delilah doesn't love Samson. In fact, she uses his affection to gain a reward of 1,100 shekels of silver, in return for finding the source of Samson's strength for his enemies, the Philistines. At first Samson won't reveal the secret of his strength, but Delilah keeps nagging him. He starts telling her incorrect reasons, but each one is proved false.

Delilah complains, "How can you say, 'I love you,' when your heart *is* not with me? You have mocked me these three times, and have not told me where your great strength lies" (Judges 16:15 NKJV). As a result of her persistent nagging and complaining, he

tension
Proverbs 21:19

finally reveals the source of his strength—staying pure from unclean foods and not cutting his hair. Once he reveals his secret, she gives the secret to his enemies, and the Philistines cut his hair, take him captive, and eventually destroy him.

> **what others say**
>
> ### Harold J. Ocknega
>
> It was not Samson's hair that was the source of his strength: it was the fact that the hair was the symbol of the covenant between him and God; and when he broke the covenant by sin, God removed the Spirit of Victory and power.[1]

Delilah got what she wanted by nagging, but nagging doesn't usually give us the results we want. Nagging can seem temporarily or occasionally to motivate a husband or boyfriend to accomplish a request, but ultimately nagging tears down the relationship and creates great <u>tension</u>. And the next time, more nagging is needed to accomplish the same result. Nagging never builds a relationship.

Sometimes we even nag God. He may answer no to our prayer request, but we keep asking him. If we truly believe he wants the best for us and surrender ourselves to his will, we can leave the results up to him.

Illustration #23
The Ark of the Covenant—This wooden chest held the most holy items in the history of Israel.

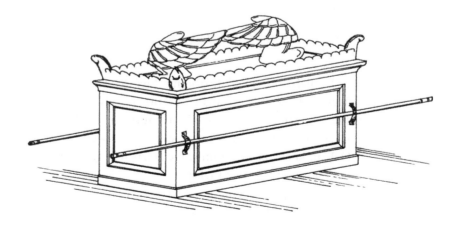

I'm Not Impressed! (Michal)

Michal and David have stormy times together. Michal, Saul's daughter, is given to David in marriage after David performs a heroic deed. Initially she really loves him. She even risks displeasing her father to protect David by hiding him when his life is being threatened by her father. But her feelings change. At one point, King Saul takes her away from David and gives her in marriage to another man. (That could certainly influence a woman's feelings.) Eventually David gets her back. But the final blow to the marriage happens when Michal observes him dancing and leaping through the streets of Jerusalem, in celebration of the return of the ark of the covenant (see Illustration #23).

She doesn't say why she hates what she sees, but for some reason David's actions really bother her. From then on, she hates David. Perhaps she was embarrassed by his display before everyone. She refers to him undressing himself for the celebration, but we don't have any evidence that what he did was indecent or incorrect. Maybe she is jealous and wants him only to herself. At that point, he had accumulated several other wives. We don't know why for sure but she never loves him again. Their unpleasant relationship keeps her from having children.

go to

builds
Proverbs 14:1

what others say

David and Claudia Arp

Nothing devastates loving communication as much as a mixed message of loving words spoken in a bitter tone of voice! So as you listen to your spouse, also listen to your own message and make sure your words, nonverbal communication and tone of voice convey the same loving message.[2]

All marriages cycle through three stages: romance, disillusionment, and true love. Michal and David definitely discovered disillusionment. We can move into true love by making a choice to love—even when we don't feel like it. That's how a wise woman builds her home. When your husband does something you disapprove of, don't get upset. Talk to him about it.

apply it

Summon Samuel! (Witch of Endor)

necromancy
Deuteronomy 18:11

spiritualists
Deuteronomy 18:10

necromancy
contacting the dead

apparition
ghostly appearance

God isn't communicating with King Saul because Saul isn't walking in fellowship with God. So Saul, with his identity a secret, contacts a witch and asks her to contact the late prophet Samuel. He hides his identity because witches have been expelled from the land, and they are not to practice their craft, including **necromancy** or the calling upon the dead. Despite that, the witch calls Samuel from the dead, although different Bible experts believe a variety of things about the **apparition** of Samuel. Some believe God in his sovereignty allowed Samuel to actually appear so that he could deliver God's message about Saul's downfall the next day. Other scholars believe it is a false spirit.

> what others say
>
> **Steve Farrar**
>
> The Christian view of meditation is exactly the reverse of its Eastern rival. In the Eastern version, you empty your mind by chanting some meaningless syllable, in the Christian practice, you fill it with the truth of God's Word in order to ponder the biblical ramifications for your life.[3]

God doesn't want us to seek truth through mediums or channelers. They are not God's righteous means for seeking him and his will. The power of mediums, spiritualists, or channelers comes from Satan. These people often worship Satan and give him credit for their power. The Scriptures say, "For all who do these things are an abomination to the LORD, and because of these abominations the LORD your God drives them out from before you" (Deuteronomy 18:12 NKJV).

God strictly forbids his children from participating in things like witchcraft, contacting the dead, practicing divination or sorcery, interpreting omens, or casting spells. Even playing what seems like a simple game of the Ouija board or reading your horoscope is detestable to God because it causes us to seek other things for help and strength rather than him.

No Way, Hosea! (Gomer)

the big picture

Hosea 1:1-11; 3:1-5

God tells the prophet Hosea to marry Gomer, a prostitute, as a visual picture of God's unconditional love for his people, Israel. Even though Gomer has children with Hosea, she continues to seek other men. Regardless, Hosea takes her back again and again.

God tells Hosea, a prophet, that he must marry Gomer, a prostitute. Such a marriage means Hosea faces the loss of his friends, the respect of his community, his reputation, and even his self-confidence. Having an adulterous spouse is always devastating to the other partner. Yet, God commands Hosea to marry Gomer, saying, "Go, take yourself a wife of harlotry and children of harlotry, for the land has committed great harlotry by departing from LORD" (Hosea 1:2 NKJV). God is using Gomer as a symbol of the unfaithfulness of the Israelites. This passage also suggests Gomer has children from previous relationships with unknown men. Gomer has been making terrible choices with her life, just like Israel!

God also tells Hosea that Gomer will continue to be unfaithful, even after their marriage. How difficult this marriage is for Hosea. For even after their marriage, Gomer continues to sleep with other men, and Hosea must take her back again and again and face the pain of her rejection again and again. But God, of course, has a purpose to this marriage. God is using Gomer's continual unfaithfulness as a way of showing the continual unfaithfulness of the people of Israel. God likens the people's rejection of him to spiritual harlotry to show the heartbreak God feels over the people of Israel. The Lord declares, "I will punish her for the days of the Baals to which she burned incense. She decked herself with her earrings and jewelry, and went after her lovers; but Me she forgot" (Hosea 2:13 NKJV). God, though sovereign and in need of nothing, shows his deep love for his creation. Just as God reveals his anger, disappointment, love, and delight, now he is showing his hurt and disappointment over the unfaithful people of Israel. Hosea provides us with a spiritual example of God's never-ending love.

equally yoked
2 Corinthians 6:14

what others say

Tricia McCary Rhodes

The book of Hosea is in many ways a parable of God's faithfulness. It tells of Hosea's unconditional love and commitment to his wife even in the face of her infidelity and rejection.[4]

God will go to great lengths to show us his love. Just as Hosea had to choose to love Gomer over and over again, despite her acts of self-hatred and her rejection of his love, God will forgive us again and again.

Gomer experienced great spiritual emptiness in her life because of her wrong choices. We will also feel hopeless and helpless if we turn away from God. God wants us to return to him so that he can take care of us.

God telling one of his children to marry a prostitute is very unusual and not bound to happen again. God wants us to be "equally yoked" with mates who also love him. Marriage is hard enough without adding the stress and conflict of someone who doesn't look at life from a spiritual standpoint.

Chapter Wrap-Up

- Potiphar's wife wanted to seduce Joseph and when she couldn't, she accused him of raping her. Joseph is thrown into prison, which fulfills God's purpose. (Genesis 39:1–20)

- Zipporah is angry at her husband, Moses, because his God requires him to circumcise their son. She's not used to that practice, and she performs the circumcision herself, perhaps in panic and anger, to save her husband's life. (Exodus 4:24–26)

- Delilah claims to love Samson but actually plans for his downfall by nagging him until he tells her the secret of his great strength. (Judges 16:4–22)

Study Questions

1. Why did Potiphar's wife lack purpose and a sense of value in her home?

2. What was Zipporah angry about?

3. How did Delilah finally get the truth out of Samson?

4. What made Michal so angry at David that she began to hate him, and why?

5. What ungodly activity did the Witch of Endor practice?

6. Why does Hosea marry Gomer, and what is God communicating with the story of their marriage?

Chapter 12 Women of Courage

Let's Get Started

We can't really plan to be courageous, but when we trust God and the time for courage comes, God can empower us to respond in a courageous way. The women in this chapter did exactly that. In moments of potential danger, they not only did the right thing, they did the courageous thing. Some put their lives in danger, which is about as courageous as you can get. As we review the stories of women in this chapter, we should expect that God is preparing us for similar acts of courage.

Not a Tent Peg! (Jael)

the big picture

Judges 4:17–22; 5:24–27

As usual, Israel is being attacked when Sisera, one of the military leaders of the enemy army, seeks help from an Israelite woman, Jael, in her home. Jael kills him by hammering a tent peg through his temple. As a result, she becomes a celebrated heroine.

In the days of Israel when Deborah is the prophetess and judge, a woman named Jael encourages Sisera, who commands the Canaanite enemy army, to enter her home. She pretends to care for her enemy and promises to protect him. But while he is sleeping, she hammers a tent peg into his temple. For her courage, Jael is immortalized in Deborah's mighty song praising God's victory.

what others say

Liz Curtis Higgs

When Jael saw the opportunity to subdue Sisera, she didn't run and get someone else to do it; she did what needed to be done. Leaders don't just point; they shoot. How often I'm guilty of seeing a need, then praying another person will handle it. Oh that I might have the courage of my ancient sisters and step forward![1]

go to

concubine
2 Samuel 3:7

covenant
Joshua 9:15–21

famine
2 Samuel 21:1

concubine
a low-ranking,
unmarried woman
who lives with a man

what others say

Herbert Lockyer

Any woman killing the country's enemy must be the friend of Israel, and so the method of Sisera's death mattered little to Deborah who doubtless thought that all was fair in time of war.[2]

Jael is praised for her courage in killing an enemy, but we might question her violent methods and the way she lured him into her home with promises of safety. Plus, in the customs of that time, if you give food to anyone, you are committed to protect them from harm. Jael gives Sisera milk to drink, yet she doesn't let that keep her from killing him. What do you think about Jael's actions? Is she courageous or deceptive? Right or wrong?

In those days, women pitched the tents; that's why Jael is so familiar with tent pegs and thinks of using one to kill her enemy. Because she does such hard work, she has the strength to hammer a tent peg through this man's head.

Protecting Past Death (Rizpah)

the big picture

2 Samuel 21:7–14

King Saul has been killed. Such a death usually means that almost everyone connected with him will also be killed, including the two sons of Rizpah, Saul's **concubine**. Rizpah's sons are killed, by hanging, and after their deaths, Rizpah watches over their bodies until they are buried.

Back in the time of Joshua, the Gibeonites made a <u>covenant</u> with the Israelites for protection and friendship. Saul violated that covenant, and so the Gibeonites demanded justice by killing Saul and seven of his sons, including the two that Rizpah bore him. Rizpah knows the bodies must not remain unburied, so she begins a vigil beside them and protects them from animals. We don't know how long she stays there, but some Bible experts believe she protected them about five months. When the rains come, ending the <u>famine</u> and drought, she is free to bury them. Her courageous devotion receives King David's attention.

go to

welcomed
2 Samuel 9:11

Virginia Stem Owens

Never did the Lord order David to accede to the Gibeonites' wishes for human sacrifice. Nor, for that matter, did David ask. Only later, after David heard of Rizpah's pitifully desperate measures, did it occur to him to follow suit and give his old enemy Saul and his heirs a "decent burial." And because of that long-delayed display for mercy, the land was healed.[3]

Just as Rizpah protects her sons, Mary Magdalene stands at Jesus' cross and then at the grave site. Both Rizpah and Mary might have believed in the resurrection of the dead.

Nurse to the Rescue (Mephibosheth's Nurse)

2 SAMUEL 4:4 *Jonathan, Saul's son, had a son who was lame in his feet. He was five years old when the news about Saul and Jonathan came from Jezreel; and his nurse took him up and fled. And it happened, as she made haste to flee, that he fell and became lame. His name was Mephibosheth. (NKJV)*

This nurse feels lovingly attached to Mephibosheth. She risks her life to rescue Mephibosheth from Saul's enemies after his father, Jonathan, and Saul are killed. Though she reacts with courage, she drops the child in her haste, and Mephibosheth is crippled for the rest of his life. She probably feels guilty about his injury, but Mephibosheth doesn't seem to have a bitter spirit about his handicap. Later in Scripture, Mephibosheth is <u>welcomed</u> into King David's court in honor of David's commitment to treat his friend Jonathan's family well.

Carol Kent

Our desire "to be all we can be" is from God. It is not essential that other people validate our success. It's encouraging when they do, but it is not what's ultimately important. When we walk in obedience and fix our minds on truth, our disappointments will eventually produce ruling passions that will result in actions that are honorable and holy.[4]

Just like Mephibosheth's nurse, we may take courageous risks that are either misunderstood or that bring unfortunate results. But mis-

rape
2 Samuel 13:14

exile
removal from your
homeland

understandings and poor results should not take away our joy in doing the right thing. We can still rejoice in God's power within us, even if the results of our actions are not all we had hoped for or expected.

The Power of a Well-Told Tale (The Woman of Tekoah)

> **the big picture**
>
> **2 Samuel 14:1–20**
>
> At the request of Joab, a woman tells a story, which is actually an analogy of King David's refusal to restore his relationship with his son Absalom. She performs in front of King David, and as a result of what he sees and hears, King David reaches out to Absalom.

Joab, David's friend, arranges for a woman to pretend she is in a similar situation to King David, and she presents her story as an analogy of King David's refusal to restore his relationship with his son, Absalom. She tells him, "Now your maidservant had two sons; and the two fought with each other in the field, and there was no one to part them, but the one struck the other and killed him. And now the whole family has risen up against your maidservant, and they said, 'Deliver him who struck his brother, that we may execute him for the life of his brother whom he killed; and we will destroy the heir also' " (2 Samuel 14:6–7 NKJV).

Her story is similar to David's life because his son Absalom killed his stepbrother in revenge for the <u>rape</u> of his sister, Tamar. Absalom had told his sister, Tamar, to be quiet and two years later, he arranged Amnon's death. Then Absalom fled the country and lived in **exile**. When David tells the woman he will do something to prevent the brother's being killed, she points out that he hasn't applied the same mercy to his own son. Instead, he has treated Absalom as if he were dead. Her reasoning as well as her powerful acting trigger a change of heart in King David, and he agrees to restore Absalom to his rightful place in the palace.

Not knowing King David personally, she may have wondered how he would react to the trick. In a sense, she is acting courageously because if he did become displeased, her life or her comfort may have been in danger.

> **what others say**
>
> **Joyce Meyer**
>
> Keep in touch with God today; stay tuned to His voice. You may have a plan for the day, but God may lead you in a totally different direction if you are sensitive to the Holy Ghost. Be brave enough to flow with what you feel in your heart God wants you to do.[5]

Find the Bad Guy (Wise Woman)

> **the big picture**
>
> **2 Samuel 20:16–22**
>
> A woman asks why Joab, David's military general, is attacking her city. She finds out that one of Israel's enemies, Sheba, is hiding there. She takes action and has the enemy killed.

The city of Abel Beth Maacah is being besieged by Joab and King David's military. Evidently the people of the city don't know why. When a woman, who describes the people of the city as "peaceable and faithful in Israel" (2 Samuel 20:19 NKJV), asks why the city has been surrounded by the Israeli army, Joab answers that their city is shielding an enemy of Israel named Sheba.

This wise woman talks it over with the people of the city. The people decide to decapitate Sheba, give his head to Joab, and end the siege. Obviously, Israel's army didn't communicate with the people of the town before beginning the siege. This woman's actions save the city.

> **what others say**
>
> **Max Lucado**
>
> One of the paradoxes of communication is that a word must be understandable to both parties before it is acceptable for use. Just because you understand a word or concept doesn't mean that the person with whom you are speaking does.[6]

This wise woman of Abel doesn't just make the decision herself to surrender Sheba. She involves the people of the city. When we involve as many as possible in the solution of a problem, we get more support and less criticism.

Sometimes our struggles stem from a lack of communication or miscommunication. The wise woman of Abel stops assuming what is going on and instead asks for the truth. When we assume we know what the cause of our difficulty is, or why someone is acting the way they are, or what God is really doing—without asking—we are operating in our own limited knowledge.

This woman asked, discovered the reason, and solved the problem. We can do the same.

She Found Even More (The Queen of Sheba)

> **the big picture**
>
> **1 Kings 10:1–13**
>
> A queen from a distant land hears about King Solomon's rule and his wisdom and wealth. Spurred by curiosity, she comes to see King Solomon for herself. She is very impressed and returns home with many gifts and with the benefit of learning from Solomon.

Sheba was a city located in what is now modern Yemen in Arabia. The city's queen is very wealthy herself, yet she travels about twelve hundred miles to Jerusalem to see whether the outrageous descriptions she's heard about Solomon's wisdom and wealth are really true. She seeks wisdom and when she encounters Solomon, she is completely satisfied, saying, "Your wisdom and prosperity exceed the fame of which I heard" (1 Kings 10:7 NKJV).

> **what others say**
>
> **Herbert Lockyer**
>
> The renown of such unparalleled wisdom drew her to Solomon and in going to him she revealed how wise she was. Possibly she had read some of Solomon's great proverbs.[7]

We hope Solomon shared the knowledge of his God, Jehovah, with the queen of Sheba. We hope when the Scripture states King Solomon "gave the queen of Sheba all she desired, whatever she asked" (1 Kings 10:13 NKJV), that Solomon did not merely give her possessions; we hope he gave her the fulfillment of her spiritual quest.

Just as this queen makes the effort to examine the truth about Solomon, we must make the effort to get close to God. Knowing him initially is a one-time choice of asking Jesus to <u>come into</u> our lives as Lord and Savior. At that point, we are <u>born again</u>. Our spiritual journey will probably resemble this queen's long and twisting twelve-hundred-mile journey. But when we arrive in heaven, we won't regret our long journey, for like this queen, we will see that our journey was worth any amount of time and trouble.

The queen could have sent ambassadors to check out Solomon, but she goes herself, for which she is richly rewarded. We can't "send someone else" on our behalf to get to know God. Even if our parents, siblings, or children know God personally, they can't be our ambassadors. We must personally meet with God and get to know him for ourselves.

come into
Revelation 3:20

born again
John 3:3

Helping Your Captor (The Captive Servant Girl)

> **2 KINGS 5:1–5** *Now Naaman, commander of the army of the king of Syria, was a great and honorable man in the eyes of his master, because by him the LORD had given victory to Syria. He was also a mighty man of valor, but a leper. And the Syrians had gone out on raids, and had brought back captive a young girl from the land of Israel. She waited on Naaman's wife. Then she said to her mistress, "If only my master were with the prophet who is in Samaria! For he would heal him of his leprosy." And Naaman went in and told his master, saying, "Thus and thus said the girl who is from the land of Israel."*
>
> *Then the king of Syria said, "Go now, and I will send a letter to the king of Israel."*
>
> *So he departed and took with him ten talents of silver, six thousand shekels of gold, and ten changes of clothing.* (NKJV)

A young Israelite girl works as a captive servant in the home of Naaman, who is captain of the army of the king of Aram. This courageous young servant girl shares her faith for her Jehovah and his power to heal. The servant girl speaks to Naaman's wife and this loving wife passes along the information. As a result, Naaman goes to Elisha, Jehovah's prophet, and is eventually healed.

go to

bravery
1 Corinthians 16:13

what others say

Beth Moore

People can easily be discouraged if they perceive God works mightily through others but never works through them. God does not play favorites. Anyone who cries out to him, he answers. Anyone who surrenders to his call, he uses.[8]

That young servant girl's <u>bravery</u> and lack of resentment greatly impact Naaman's life and many others'. She could have been fearful of speaking of God's power through Elisha, but instead, she speaks up, putting her love and concern for her master above any personal worries. She also doesn't think, "I'm only one person, I can't make a difference. God can't use me." Instead, she shows love in courageous action!

When we courageously stand up for God, we build our spirits by knowing we have obeyed him. Often we see great results, and that encourages us to grow even stronger in our faith and in our boldness to speak of God's great abilities.

Listen Up, Guys (Huldah)

the big picture

2 Kings 22:14–20

Huldah, a prophetess in the time of Jeremiah, is used by God to deliver an unpleasant message from God. Huldah must tell the people that they will be judged by God. She doesn't know how the people will respond, but Huldah courageously delivers her message. Fortunately, the people repent and turn back to the Lord.

Israel is operating without any spiritual foundation because God's Law is ignored. In fact, no one even knows where the Book of God's Law is. When the lost Book of the Law is found, the priest goes to a prophetess, Huldah. She courageously predicts national ruin for Israel because Israel isn't carrying out God's commands. Her courage is rewarded. The people repent of their sin and a national revival begins.

We won't always know the result of speaking out for God and encouraging people to turn back to him, but we can always have the courage to do so. God doesn't hold us responsible for the results, only our obedience.

God is always waiting to respond to his people's repentance. No matter how bad your sin or how distant you feel from God, remember, God will hear your cry of repentance and heal your hardened heart.

No Party for Me (Vashti)

the big picture

Esther 1:9–22

King Ahasuerus throws a huge party, lasting 180 days, with much eating and drinking. In the midst of the festivities, he calls for his wife, Queen Vashti, to show off her beauty. But when he calls for her she refuses to appear before all his drunken buddies. Because the officials of King Ahasuerus think her disobedience will provoke the wives of the land to disobey their husbands, the officials suggest that the king take away her position as queen. The king deposes Vashti.

God primarily uses Vashti's refusal to enable Esther to become queen and deliver the Jews. Some Bible scholars say Vashti's refusal to display herself at the king's drunken party can be seen as an example of a woman who courageously stands for purity and integrity. According to these Bible experts, she loses her position as queen, but she retains her dignity.

Other Bible experts believe that Queen Vashti made the wrong choice. They say she wouldn't have compromised her purity by attending the party. Scripture doesn't tell us, but God uses her removal for his will to be done.

what others say

Frances Vander Velde

So Vashti leaves the grandeur of the palace in obscurity, but not in shame, for in her refusal to be disgraced she shows dignity, nobility, and respect for the national custom which does not allow its women to appear unveiled in the presence of men, least of all, drunken, reveling men.[9]

submit
Ephesians 5:22

If her refusal to attend was her stand for purity, her faithful representation of good isn't rewarded. When we stand up for the good, we are not necessarily rewarded. But that doesn't mean we didn't do the right thing. Even if no one on earth agrees with our choice for righteousness, God does, and he's the One we really want to please.

In general terms, God wants wives to <u>submit</u> to their husbands, but if a husband asks her to do something dishonest, illegal, or immoral, she is to refuse.

Chapter Wrap-Up

- Jael is honored as a courageous defender of Israel by killing Israel's enemy, Sisera. (Judges 4:17–22)

- Rizpah courageously protects her sons' dead bodies after they are killed to satisfy the demands of the Gibeonites and to meet the requirements of a new ruler. (2 Samuel 21:7–14)

- Mephibosheth's nurse rescued Mephibosheth from being murdered, but in trying to whisk him away quickly, she dropped him and he became crippled. (2 Samuel 4:4)

- The woman of Tekoah is asked to present an analogy of King David's relationship with his son Absalom. As a result, the king makes efforts to reunite himself with Absalom. (2 Samuel 14:1–20)

- The wise woman of Abel asked why Joab was attacking her city and found out an enemy, Sheba, was hiding there. As a result, Sheba was killed and turned over to Joab; the city was saved. (2 Samuel 20:16–22)

- The queen of Sheba found out that everything she'd heard about Solomon and his reign was true, and she received all of her heart's desires by visiting him. (1 Kings 10:1–13)

- The wife of Naaman and his captive servant girl showed their true love by risking Naaman's disfavor to tell him about Jehovah, who could heal him. As a result, he sought out Jehovah's prophet, Elisha, and was healed. (2 Kings 5:1–4)

- As a prophetess, Huldah heard from God and revealed his message that there would be national ruin because the Israelites were not following God's command. Because of her courage, there was revival and repentance in the nation. (2 Kings 22:14–20)

- Vashti lost her position as queen because she refused to appear before a drunken party. (Esther 1:9–22)

Study Questions

1. How does Jael convince Sisera to trust her?

2. What courageous and dangerous action does Rizpah take for her sons and five others, and why does she take this action?

3. What did Mephibosheth's nurse do to help, and why? And, as a result, what unfortunate thing happened?

4. At the request of Joab, what did the woman of Tekoah do for King David?

5. How did the wise woman of Abel rescue her city?

6. Why did the queen of Sheba visit King Solomon?

7. How did Naaman's wife and his captive servant girl show their true love and concern for him?

8. What courageous thing did Huldah do?

9. What was the consequence of Vashti's refusal to attend the king's party?

Chapter 13 Women of Weak Faith

Let's Get Started

God has promised to never give us more than we can handle, yet the women in this chapter thought God gave them too much. For Lot's wife and his daughters, they find leaving their home and not looking back to be too much. For Miriam, having her brother Moses get all the credit is too much. And for Job's wife, losing sons and daughters in one fell swoop followed by her husband's painful illness is, as we can well sympathize, too much for her to cope with.

Yet, God's promises are true, regardless of how much we're going through. God would have preferred that these women trust his goodness and increase their faith rather than fall into destructive and hurtful thinking. Let's remember them the next time we think, "It's too much, Lord." We can trust God instead of forsaking him.

I Gotta Look (Lot's Wife)

the big picture

Genesis 19:12–38

Lot and his family live in a very wicked place, Sodom. Sodom is so bad that God has determined to destroy it. Because Lot is Abraham's nephew, Abraham prays that Lot will be spared. God sends angels to direct Lot and his family to leave the city and not look back. Lot's wife can't resist looking back, and she is killed. Lot's daughters seduce their father so they will have children.

Because of Abraham's intercessory prayer for the safety of Lot, who is Abraham's nephew, the angels lead Lot, his wife, and his two daughters out of Sodom before the city is destroyed. But the city keeps its hold on Lot's wife and, contrary to one angel's instructions, the wife looks back at her former home and is turned into a pillar of salt. Later, after Lot and his two daughters settle in the mountains, the two young women fear they'll never become mothers and continue the line of the family. Taking things into their own hands, they get their father drunk on two successive nights and trick

gold
1 Corinthians
3:12–15

him into having sex with one daughter each night. Impregnated, the daughters bear his children, Moab (the father of the Moabites) and Ben-Ammi (the father of the Ammonites).

what others say

Liz Curtis Higgs

Mrs. Lot not only looked, she hesitated, perhaps long enough for the edge of the maelstrom to reach her and wrap her head-to-toe in sodium chloride. At the southern end of the Dead Sea are literal mountains of salt. Such is the substance that whipped itself around Lot's wife, smothering her in seconds.[1]

Did Lot's wife want to see the destruction? Did she leave something valuable behind as the angel led her away? Why are her eyes focused more on wanting something destructible than something spiritual? We can struggle with the same things if we aren't truly convinced that God will take care of our needs.

When we focus on the wrong thing, like Lot's wife, our energy and efforts are put toward the things of the world, things that will be destroyed. Only what we build for eternity will last. God says that our efforts and focus on him produce <u>gold</u>, silver, and costly stones, but the things of this world will produce expendable wood, hay, or straw. Nothing on this earth is worth sacrificing heaven's blessings.

The battle against focusing on the things of this world is constant and long-term, but little by little, we can substitute the spiritual for the temporal. We might want to commit to watching less television in order to read our Bible more. Or we could read a Christian book instead of a secular romance or murder mystery. With exposure, our spiritual appetite for the things of God grows.

Can't I Be Leader Now? (Miriam)

the big picture

Numbers 12:1–15

Miriam, the sister of Moses, is a part of his important ministry. In the past, she has been part of a music ministry, giving praise to God in song. But jealousy overwhelms her, and she complains about her brother's leadership. As a result, God strikes her with leprosy until Moses prays for her healing.

Miriam, the sister of Moses and Aaron, has been <u>instrumental</u> in Moses' life. When Jochebed, their mother, puts baby Moses in the basket on the river, Miriam obeys her mother's instruction and watches to make sure the baby is safe. Miriam provides us with an example of spiritual leadership for she is active in a praise ministry.

Scripture says, "Then Miriam the prophetess, the sister of Aaron, took the timbrel in her hand; and all the women went out after her with timbrels and with dances. And Miriam answered them: 'Sing to the LORD, for He has triumphed gloriously! The horse and its rider He has thrown into the sea!'" (Exodus 15:20–21 NKJV).

But when the Israelites are wandering through the wilderness and complaining against Moses' leadership, Miriam and Aaron complain too. Miriam and Aaron are probably tired and hungry, but this brother and sister also complain out of jealousy and <u>envy</u>. God defends his humble servant Moses and strikes Miriam with leprosy. For seven days she stays outside the camp but is healed after Moses intervenes for her in prayer. Through this story, she provides us with an illustration of the danger of dissatisfaction. Later in the Israelites' wanderings, Miriam <u>dies</u> and is buried at Kadesh.

Many of us struggle with jealousy and envy, just as Miriam did. We may wonder why God doesn't use us in ministry like others. We may be jealous of a relative's good looks or abilities. We might envy someone's singing ability, while refusing to use our own gifts from God, whatever they might be. God knows how he wants to use every person in the **body of Christ**. We shouldn't be <u>dissatisfied</u>, even if we feel we're a toenail in that body, because God has a special purpose for each of us. Envy is saying God doesn't know what he's doing.

instrumental
Exodus 2:1–10

envy
Proverbs 14:30

dies
Numbers 20:1

body of Christ
1 Corinthians 12:12

dissatisfied
1 Corinthians 12:16

body of Christ
believers in Jesus

what others say

Jill Briscoe

It's what we have known of God's faithfulness in the past that will encourage us to have faith for the present.[2]

When Everything Goes Wrong (Job's Wife)

children
Job 42::13–17

> **the big picture**
>
> ### Job 2:9–10; 42:13–17
>
> Job and his wife are faced with the most horrible circumstances: the murder of their children, loss of all their possessions, and the illness that covers Job with horrible sores. Instead of trusting God as Job does, his wife wants him to curse God.

Job and his wife suffer any parent's worst fears—the death of their children. Job's wife experiences all the great losses that Job does, yet the Bible doesn't tell us if she is able to move from her pain to the lesson Job learns: trust God. She seems destroyed by their tragedies, while Job learns that God doesn't have to explain why bad things can happen to good people.

Job trusts in God's goodness, but she does not. She tells him, "Do you still hold fast to your integrity? Curse God and die!" (Job 2:9 NKJV). After Job goes through all these troubles, he is healed through God. While God offers no explanation for their troubles, God tells Job that human beings cannot understand God's purposes. Job's wealth is restored and he even goes on to have more children to rebuild a family. His wife is not mentioned again, but since they have more children, perhaps she too is healed from these tragedies.

> **what others say**
>
> **Carol Kent**
>
> Job reminds us that life is unfair and that being faithful to God does not mean our lives will automatically be filled with good health and happiness.[3]

After Job goes through a lengthy healing process, he has more <u>children</u>. No specific wife is mentioned in the account where those children are named, but since a different wife isn't mentioned, we hope that Job's original wife is still there and is a part of Job's restoration. God uses suffering for his own purposes and to benefit the person suffering. When we are suffering, we need to remember God's love and purpose for us. No matter how deep our grief, we should remember God knows and cares.

Men and women handle grief differently, but God doesn't want any of us to forsake our trust in his goodness during difficult times. When a husband and a wife experience tragedy or death, they might not understand each other's way of grieving. For instance, a wife may think her husband is uncaring or unsympathetic because he says little, while she speaks constantly about their loss. But everyone grieves differently, and acceptance of the differences will strengthen a marriage instead of destroying it.

Chapter Wrap-Up

- Lot and his wife and daughters are rescued by angels before Sodom is destroyed. But Lot's wife disobeys the angels' command not to look back. She looks and is turned into a pillar of salt. Later, Lot's daughters seduce their father, so that they can make sure they have children and carry on the family name. (Genesis 19:12–38)

- Miriam, Moses' sister and a spiritual leader in the Israelite community, becomes jealous of Moses' leadership and speaks against him. As a result, God strikes her with leprosy, but Moses prays and after seven days, she's healed. (Numbers 12:1–15)

- Job's wife is consumed with grief about the death of their children and about Job's suffering, so she tells him to curse God and then die. (Job 2:9)

Study Questions

1. How were Lot's wife and his daughters rescued before the destruction of Sodom?

2. What horrible thing did Lot's daughters do and why?

3. Why did Miriam complain along with the Israelites about the leadership of her brother Moses?

4. What consequence did Miriam pay?

5. How do Job and his wife experience grief? Why do you think their response to grief is so different?

Part Three
Women of the
New Testament

Chapter 14 Women Helped by Jesus

Chapter Highlights:
• Reaching with Faith
• Courage to Ask
• Receiving Forgiveness
• God's Love
• Receiving Unlimited Grace

Let's Get Started

Certainly these women, who experience personal contact with Jesus on earth, are especially blessed. Often, these women are touched by Jesus at a physical and an emotional heart level that goes beyond their greatest expectations and dreams. These women are healed from fatal diseases, receive spiritual forgiveness and cleansing, and see God's miracles. Jesus miraculously and uniquely intervenes in each woman's life.

Jesus does not operate in a cookie-cutter style. He doesn't treat each woman the same as the next, and he doesn't do the same thing for each woman. Instead, he reaches out in a caring and loving fashion to meet the particular needs of each. Today he still does the same thing for each of us.

If Only (The Woman with the Issue of Blood)

MATTHEW 9:20–22 *And suddenly, a woman who had a flow of blood for twelve years came from behind and touched the hem of His garment. For she said to herself, "If only I may touch His garment, I shall be made well." But Jesus turned around, and when He saw her He said, "Be of good cheer, daughter; your faith has made you well." And the woman was made well from that hour.* (NKJV)

Have you ever been ill for a period of time and felt so sick of being sick that you would have done almost anything to feel good again? That must be how this woman feels. She has been bleeding for twelve years straight.

Another passage says that she has spent everything she has on doctors, who have made her worse, not better. She must be so frustrated, and perhaps almost without hope of ever becoming well. Then she hears about Jesus. While she feels she doesn't deserve his full attention, she believes if she just touches the edge of his cloak, Jesus will heal her.

law
Numbers 15:37–40;
Deuteronomy 22:12

requires
Hebrews 11:6

father
Mark 9:23–24

That's exactly what she does and her expectations are met. She is healed. Jesus gives her the most powerful assurance: "Your faith has made you well" (Matthew 9:22 NKJV). Her faith in him has healed her. She is well! How she must have gone away rejoicing, telling everyone about this wonderful man, Jesus, who claims to be God. In her mind, she has proved that Jesus is God.

> **what others say**
>
> **Jan Johnson**
>
> According to Jewish <u>law</u>, this outer garment was supposed to have two fringes hung at the bottom and two hung over the shoulders where the cloak folded over. The woman probably touched the fringes on Jesus' cloak.[1]

Although Jesus rewards and <u>requires</u> our faith, he is also sensitive to our struggle in faith. When a man comes to Jesus for the healing of his evil spirit-possessed son, Jesus questions his faith and the desperate <u>father</u> replies, "Lord, I believe; help my unbelief!" (Mark 9:24 NKJV). Jesus delivers the man's child even though the father admits his faith isn't complete. Jesus sees our hearts and understands (see Mark 5:25–34 and Luke 8:43–48). God's goal is to help our faith grow.

A Crummy Miracle (The Syro-Phoenician Woman)

> **the big picture**
>
> **Matthew 15:21-28**
>
> A Gentile woman begs Jesus for the deliverance of her daughter from an evil spirit. At first he ignores her, but her comments show her faith and dependence upon him. Jesus delivers her daughter from the demon's control.

When Jesus takes a break from the religious leaders, he travels to the coastal town of Phoenicia, more than thirty-five miles away from Galilee. Gentiles or non-Jews live here. When one Gentile woman heard that Jesus was in Phoenicia, she went to him and asked him to deliver an evil spirit from her daughter. At first, Jesus ignored her. Then he said, "It is not good to take the children's bread and throw it to the little dogs" (Matthew 15:26 NKJV). She replied, "Yes, Lord, yet even the little dogs eat the crumbs which fall from their masters' table" (Matthew 15:27 NKJV). She was giving a wonderful picture of herself by comparing herself to a family dog who is content to have any morsels that fall off the table. Jesus was duly impressed by her faith and delivered her daughter.

loves
John 3:16

what others say

Marie Chapian

Our moments of testing are occasions to stretch our faith and confidence in God's love.[2]

Jesus came primarily to seek the house of Israel for salvation, but his sacrificial death on the cross is for everyone. God <u>loves</u> everyone and wants everyone to be saved. As Jesus showed this Gentile woman, all he requires is faith and dependence on him.

Jesus initially seemed to ignore her. Just as, at times, he might seem to be ignoring our prayers. But sometimes, he's just waiting for our faith to grow or for us to be humbled to accept whatever answer he gives us (see Mark 7:24–30).

what others say

Carol Kent

When God says, "Trust me with the impossible," we have an automatic impulse to use our human brain to figure out how God would do the job if he were in our position. At the root of that response is a lack of faith, trust, and assurance that God can be counted on, as well as a certain arrogance that our self-reliance is of any value whatsoever.[3]

How Did You Do That? (The Widow of Nain)

the big picture

Luke 7:11–16

A widow in the city of Nain is grieving over her son's death as she accompanies her son's coffin in his funeral procession. Jesus is standing near her. He feels for this widow, who, in addition to losing a husband, has now lost her only son. Moved by her grief, he raises her son back to life.

This widow must have been feeling absolutely hopeless. Her husband was dead. Her only son had just died. She walked alongside her son's coffin, grieving in the arms of her friends. Yet suddenly, Jesus was there and he stopped the funeral entourage. Then he called for the young man to rise up. She looks amazed while her son gets up. Her son is alive! Her gratitude and joy must have known no bounds!

Although faith is required in our requests to God, we can learn from this widow's experience that Jesus, in his sovereignty and compassion, will do great things even if we don't ask. Many of us have experienced wonderful things that we would have never considered requesting. That's God's generosity in action. We must be careful to always keep a heart of gratitude and not to take what he does for granted. God is generous—even when we don't ask.

key point

Party Crasher (The Woman Who Was a Sinner)

the big picture

Luke 7:36–50

A sinful woman anoints Jesus' feet with her tears and her perfume, and she receives Jesus' forgiveness. The people watching criticize the behavior of both Jesus and the woman. But Jesus uses this woman's devotion as an example of giving forgiveness.

A woman—perhaps a prostitute—crashes a party that was given in honor of Jesus by a Pharisee named Simon. (Could it be that she knows how to join this party because she's been there before on business?) When Simon and his friends comment on her arrival at the party, they learn a **parable** from Jesus. Jesus teaches them about forgiveness, saying a person who is forgiven much will love even more because of all the forgiveness received. Then Jesus turns to the woman and forgives her wrongs.

what others say

Tricia McCary Rhodes

A parable is a story that illustrates truth. Our task is to take hold of the story until it takes hold of us. Jesus was the master teacher of parables, although some parables were imparted through the prophets.[4]

Some Bible experts and Bible teachers believe that this woman is actually Mary, the sister of Martha and Lazarus. Does that seem likely? Compare the similarities and differences in John 12:1–11 and Mark 14:3–9.

Stand Up Straight!
(The Afflicted Daughter of Abraham)

the big picture

Luke 13:10–17

On the Sabbath, Jesus heals a Jewish woman who has been bent double for eighteen years. Jews aren't supposed to work on this day of rest. So the religious leaders criticize Jesus for working on the Sabbath.

After suffering from a disease for eighteen years and being bent over by its effects, a woman suddenly draws out of the crowds and stands near Jesus on the Sabbath. Jesus heals her. What happens when Jesus heals her on the Sabbath shows that God doesn't restrict his work to certain days of the week. But according to Jewish law, people aren't supposed to do any work on the Sabbath, and apparently that restriction includes healing. The synagogue officials criticize Jesus.

Of course, the woman doesn't care when she is healed—just that she is healed! She can now stand upright and enjoy the world from her improved perspective. Jesus isn't bothered at all by the criticism because he knows God loves to heal any day of the week.

Over the centuries, Jewish religious leaders have been adding rules to God's simple Law of love and, as a result, the Law has become complicated. This isn't what God intends at all. When Jesus healed this afflicted Jewish woman on the Sabbath, he shattered these old—

and new—regulations and showed us that these regulations are not important. What's important is demonstrating God's love and revealing his work. God wants to work in our lives all the time!

Some people have trouble knowing the truth about God and feeling close to him because they see God as a taskmaster and perfectionist. But God shows us through the story of the woman healed on the Sabbath that he's eager to make his wonderful love known.

After all, it was Jesus who said, "Come to Me, all you who labor and are heavy laden, and I will give you rest. Take My yoke upon you and learn from Me, for I am gentle and lowly in heart, and you will find rest for your souls" (Matthew 11:28–29 NKJV).

Friends with Jesus (The Woman at the Well)

the big picture

John 4:1-42

Jesus stops at a well as a part of his plan and encounters a Samaritan woman whom he engages in conversation. In the course of their conversation, Jesus reveals his identity as the Son of God and shows his total love and acceptance for this woman. Then she tells everyone in the town about Jesus, and many believe.

The Samaritan woman never expects that this, her usual daily visit to the well, will be anything special. But this day is very different. She is addressed by a Jewish man—who claims to be the Messiah. Initially defensive about herself and her sins, she tries to block his efforts to tell her all he knows about her life. Eventually she succumbs to his words of love and acknowledges him as the Messiah, her Messiah! In her excitement to tell the others in the village about him, she leaves her water pot at the well. She tells everyone in her village about this man, saying, "Come, see a Man who told me all things that I ever did" (John 4:29 NKJV). In her mind, she may have added "and he still cares about me."

Could the pot that the Samaritan woman leaves behind represent her old way of life? Jesus represents forgiveness and friendship with God. Her old way of thinking can no longer exist with these new ideas. We also need to leave behind any old, unbiblical ways of thinking as we encounter Jesus daily. To meet Jesus, we must seek the truth in God's Word, the Bible, and leave behind any unbelief, bitterness, anger, lies about God's nature, and other things that prevent us from enjoying a relationship with him.

good Samaritan
Luke 10:33

stoned to death
Deuteronomy
17:5–6

> ### what others say
>
> **Barbara Johnson**
>
> The key to shifting your attitude into positive gear is to rethink how you look at things.[6]
>
> **Patsy Clairmont**
>
> An ongoing source of oil for my lamp are the Scriptures, which are filled with light-giving counsel. The Word is often a flood-light searching into the corners of my heart. It fuels the passion of my faith. It's the wick that allows the light of Christ to be seen in my life. It steadies my faith and adds to my hope, as I wait on tiptoes for the skies to split open, the trumpets to shout, and heaven's light to immerse the earth.[7]

The Samaritan woman is surprised that Jesus is talking to her because Jews don't talk to the Samaritans. In fact, the Jews usually avoid going into areas where Samaritans live. Some Jews even travel the long way to avoid exposure to the "other side of the tracks." That's why Jesus' parable of the <u>good Samaritan</u> is so powerful—a Samaritan rescued and helped a Jew. At the time, everyone knew Jews never helped Samaritans. His story of the good Samaritan shows us that we need to go beyond our normal activities and prejudices to help others.

key point

Unlimited Grace (The Woman Taken in Adultery)

> ### the big picture
>
> **John 8:1–11**
>
> A woman is brought before Jesus and declared to have been caught in adultery. Jesus defends her by writing something in the sand. When her accusers see what he has written, they leave one by one. Jesus then extends his forgiveness to her.

When this woman is caught in the act of adultery, she knows her life is over. The law demands that anyone caught in the act be <u>stoned to death</u>. As the authorities push and pull her along the street, they keep repeating the name "Jesus" in their whispered plans of evil.

Before she knows it, she has been pushed to the ground at a stranger's feet, a stranger named Jesus.

She is amazed when Jesus doesn't condemn her but instead says, "He who is without sin among you, let him throw a stone at her first" (John 8:7 NKJV). In astonishment, she watches her accusers slink away. Then she hears the most wonderful words she ever had or ever will: "Neither do I condemn you; go and sin no more" (John 8:11 NKJV). She knows that she will never sin again.

Many people try to guess what Jesus wrote in the dirt for the angry men who are trying to force him into condemning this woman. Most Bible experts think he wrote their names and/or their sins. What do you think would have convinced you to change your mind and walk away?

God knows our sins but he wants to pass his hand over the ground where they are written and blot them all out. He'll blot them out, but he also tells us to stop sinning. Although he doesn't require us to be perfect, he does want us to grow in our faith and to sin less. What God forgives, he forgets—never to be remembered again.

Chapter Wrap-Up

- A woman who had been bleeding for twelve years without any relief believes Jesus can heal her. As soon as she touches the edge of Jesus' cloak, she is healed, and Jesus acknowledges her faith. (Matthew 9:20–22)

- A Gentile woman begs Jesus for the deliverance of her daughter, who is possessed by an evil spirit. Jesus delivers her daughter from the evil spirit, because of her great faith, even though the woman and her daughter are not Jews. (Matthew 15:21–28)

- A widow was accompanying her deceased son to his burial site when Jesus raised him back to life—even though she didn't ask! (Luke 7:11–16)

- Jesus uses a woman's wonderful devotion as an example of how a person who is forgiven much, loves much. This forgiven woman shows her love for Jesus by anointing his feet with her tears and perfume. (Luke 7:36–50)

- On the Sabbath, Jesus healed a woman who is bent over by disease. Working on the Sabbath was against the Jewish rules, and Jesus showed the Jewish leaders that God didn't approve of their misguided set of laws. (Luke 13:10–17)

- Jesus spends lots of time with a person he's not even supposed to be talking to: a Samaritan who is also a woman. But Jesus talks to her, and she becomes convinced that he is the Messiah. (John 4:1–42)

- Some men try to trick Jesus by bringing him a woman who was caught in adultery. Jesus forgives the woman and shows the men his awareness of their sins. (John 8:1–11)

Study Questions

1. How did the woman who bled for twelve years show her faith?

2. Why was the Phoenician woman unable at first to get Jesus' attention?

3. Why is the story of the Widow of Nain unusual?

4. How does a sinful woman become an object lesson for Jesus and how does she show him her devotion?

5. Why does Jesus' healing of the woman who is bent over by disease create a controversy with the Jewish authorities?

6. How was the Samaritan woman convinced that Jesus was the Messiah? What did she do that showed her new life?

7. How did Jesus stop the angry men from stoning a woman caught in adultery, and why did he stop it?

Chapter 15 Women Who Followed Jesus

Let's Get Started

Women were very important to Jesus and his ministry. In the Bible, faithful women, as well as the twelve disciples, followed Jesus and provided for his needs. Some women supported him financially and offered needed friendship. He loved and valued them all for the unique gifts they brought to his ministry. Jesus patiently and lovingly worked within their lives, even when he acted differently from the ways they thought he should. Today, we can have as close a relationship with Jesus as these women did, even though we can't yet see him face-to-face.

Who's Doing the Dishes? (Mary and Martha)

LUKE 10:38–42 *Now it happened as they went that He entered a certain village; and a certain woman named Martha welcomed Him into her house. And she had a sister called Mary, who also sat at Jesus' feet and heard His word. But Martha was distracted with much serving, and she approached Him and said, "Lord, do You not care that my sister has left me to serve alone? Therefore tell her to help me."*

And Jesus answered and said to her, "Martha, Martha, you are worried and troubled about many things. But one thing is needed, and Mary has chosen that good part, which will not be taken away from her." (NKJV)

We don't know how Mary and Martha, two very different sisters, first heard about Jesus or how they became his supporters. But he frequently visited their home in Bethany, two miles east of Jerusalem, and apparently their home was large enough to accommodate both Jesus and his disciples. Jesus probably traveled the road to Bethany often (see Illustration #7).

A quiet, soft-spoken, introverted person, Mary valued contemplation and solitude, while her sister, Martha, was just the opposite. Bible experts believe Martha was the older of the two and, perhaps as a result, Martha was opinionated, strong-minded, and busy, in her actions and her thoughts. Can you imagine these two very different women trying to live under the same roof?

We don't know whether the two women were once married and later became widows, or whether they had never married. From other Bible passages, we know that their brother, Lazarus, also lived with them, and the household seemed fairly wealthy. Perhaps the house belonged to all three, and it was their inheritance from their parents.

Perhaps Martha became annoyed with Mary, because Martha had waited too long to do her work. Or more likely, Martha started early but was not satisfied and kept doing jobs over again to make everything "just so." Martha obviously valued "doing" rather than "being" and was upset that Jesus didn't get Mary to help her.

The word "distracted" has the meaning of "pulled apart" or "pulled away." Martha was definitely pulled apart at her emotional seams, even though Jesus was very close to her. To her credit, she took her frustration to Jesus, to whom we can take all of our cares. Perhaps Martha was irritated because she wanted to be with Jesus, like Mary. But she was too much of a perfectionist to stop working.

Perhaps Martha was thinking, "I'd like to be relaxing, listening to Jesus too, but if I do, then who will take care of everything else?" The truth is that when we do what God wants us to do, everything else will fall into place. God may want to show us a different way to operate.

what others say

Anne Graham Lotz

Mary may have been the middle sibling. She was intuitively sensitive, deeply spiritual, and thoughtfully quiet. She seemed like a still pool that went deep. In spite of household demands, she made the time to sit at Jesus' feet and listen to His Word, a trait for which she received His encouraging, lasting commendation.[1]

Mary likes to have Jesus come so that she can listen to his wonderful words. The use of the Greek word for "listening" suggests that whenever Jesus visits, Mary spends her time listening to him. Certainly she looks forward to his visits, so perhaps she finishes her work before he arrives. When Jesus comes to her house, she wants to devote all her attention to him. Mary values Jesus' presence.

Mary doesn't try to defend herself. She is too focused on Jesus to care what Martha thinks. When we have our eyes focused on Jesus and gain his approval, the approval of other people won't matter as much.

Mary provides us with a wonderful example of the importance of time alone with God. We will always have many things to do in our busy lives, but concentrating on God must be something we choose to do. Even if other people don't value our time with God and criticize us for it as Martha did her sister, we need to remember our time with God pleases him. We also need to realize the benefits we receive from being alone with God.

Martha stands close to Jesus as she is serving the food, but she isn't close at heart. Her desire to provide an elaborate meal and build her self-esteem through serving, rather than soaking up God's words, causes her to be spiritually distant. Service, even within the church or in Jesus' name, can be a <u>distraction</u> if the work is not done with a heart full of love.

distraction
1 Corinthians 7:35

still
Psalm 46:10

Choose Your Priorities

LUKE 10:41–42 *And Jesus answered and said to her, "Martha, Martha, you are worried and troubled about many things. But one thing is needed, and Mary has chosen that good part, which will not be taken away from her." (NKJV)*

Jesus, in his tactful yet honest way, gently rebuked Martha. We don't know how his voice sounded, but he must have been patiently encouraging her to value the right thing: his presence. He identified her problem as worry, agitation, and being troubled. Listening to him was more important than making the meal, he explained. We all need time to commune with God.

what others say

Patsy Clairmont

When I stop whatever I'm doing (working, worrying, whining) and become <u>still</u>, I realize the Lord is with me—not always because I can feel his presence, but because he has promised it.[2]

Joyce Meyer

I can just imagine Martha in this scene. I am sure that as soon as she heard Jesus was coming to her house, she started running around cleaning and polishing and cooking, trying to get everything ready for his visit. The reason I find it so easy to picture Martha in this situation is because I used to be just like her...I needed to learn to be more like Mary and less like Martha. Instead of worrying and fretting, I needed to learn to simplify my plans, lighten up, and enjoy life![3]

Martha is worried and upset because her priorities are wrong. Jesus doesn't tell her not to do anything, but to choose the better thing: him. He isn't saying that she shouldn't fix dinner, but perhaps serving an elaborate meal isn't as important as taking the time to concentrate on him. He doesn't tell her not to provide for her guests, but to offer something more simple.

Jesus is never worried or troubled, because he always focuses on obeying his Father and believing that God has a plan. Jesus says, "Most assuredly, I say to you, the Son can do nothing of Himself, but what He sees the Father do; for whatever He does, the Son also does in like manner" (John 5:19 NKJV).

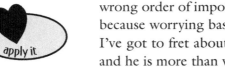

apply it

Our worry is often based on putting what we need to do in the wrong order of importance, the wrong priorities. To worry is to sin, because worrying basically says, "God can't handle this situation, so I've got to fret about it." But God is always in control of our lives, and he is more than willing to reveal the solutions we need and give us the power to obey him.

A Beloved Brother Is Ill

> JOHN 11:1–3 *Now a certain man was sick, Lazarus of Bethany, the town of Mary and her sister Martha. It was that Mary who anointed the Lord with fragrant oil and wiped His feet with her hair, whose brother Lazarus was sick. Therefore the sisters sent to Him, saying, "Lord, behold, he whom You love is sick."* (NKJV)

Some time later—we don't know how long—Mary and Martha are concerned about their brother, Lazarus. He is so sick that he might die, and the sisters' first thought is to find Jesus. The sisters know how much Jesus loves all of them, so they send a servant to get Jesus. They expect Jesus to come quickly to their home in Bethany and heal their brother, because of their faith in Jesus' love. Since Bethany is referred to as the "town of Mary and her sister Martha," some Bible scholars believe that their home was the largest and most important in the town and that Mary and Martha were the most significant people in Bethany.

pouring perfume
John 12:3

what others say

Anne Graham Lotz

Has your prayer for your "Lazarus" remained unanswered? Does God seem to be hiding himself from you? *Why does he delay?* Why does he allow you and your loved ones to suffer so? One reason for his delay seems to be to allow us time to exhaust every other avenue of help until we come to the conclusion, without any doubt, that we are totally helpless without him, and we rest our faith in him and him alone.[4]

Mary and Martha simply send a message saying their brother Lazarus is ill. They don't request anything from Jesus. They are so confident that Jesus will respond and that he has the power to heal Lazarus that they don't ask for help or give any further information. Their great trust in Jesus is the basis for their great faith, and they expect him to come quickly and heal their brother.

The reference to Mary <u>pouring perfume</u> on Jesus occurs in the next chapter of John—John 12. Evidently this story of Lazarus in John 11 was written after these events took place.

Telling God what to do, as opposed to making a request, is presumptuous and creates an attitude of "I know what's best for this situation." Only God knows best. Faith doesn't need to tell God what to do. Faith brings your concerns and lays them on the altar; faith trusts God to do the best thing.

What's Taking Him So Long?

JOHN 11:4–6 *When Jesus heard that, He said, "This sickness is not unto death, but for the glory of God, that the Son of God may be glorified through it." Now Jesus loved Martha and her sister and Lazarus. So, when He heard that he was sick, He stayed two more days in the place where He was. (NKJV)*

plan
John 5:19

stone
John 10:31

Everyone knows how much Jesus loves Martha, Mary, and Lazarus. Yet when Jesus receives the note about sick Lazarus, he waits two days. We can only imagine the grief and confusion as the sisters see their brother die. Some Bible experts suggest Lazarus was thirty years old when he died. They must have looked out their window several times a day to see if Jesus was hurrying along the dusty road. When Jesus finally arrived, he used Lazarus' death to show his power.

Jesus refers to a glory that includes the raising of Lazarus as well as his own death and resurrection, because the raising of Lazarus in Bethany helps to bring his own death. By going to Bethany and raising Lazarus, Jesus increases the hatred, envy, and fear that the religious leaders feel toward Jesus. The more his power is revealed, the more threatened the leaders are.

Jesus is operating on the basis of his Father's <u>plan</u> and sees the bigger picture. He knows that delays are not necessarily God's denials and that God will receive greater glory through this delay.

Danger Ahead

> **the big picture**
>
> **John 11:7–19**
>
> Sometime later, after he knows Lazarus has died, Jesus tells his disciples they'll return to Judea so that Jesus can wake him up (John 11:11). Although the disciples don't know what this means, they are immediately fearful because they know going to the Jerusalem area will get Jesus into more trouble and put him in more danger.

At first, the disciples may have thought Jesus delayed or refused to go to Lazarus' aid because of his concern for his own safety. When Jesus had been in Bethany before, people threatened to <u>stone</u> him. So when Jesus announces that they will return to the Jerusalem area (Bethany is two miles away from Jerusalem), they are surprised. They still do not understand that everything Jesus does is part of a big plan.

Jesus explains in a veiled way that he can go anywhere at any time and not be in danger. His life cannot be taken from him; he will surrender it in God's perfect timing, Jesus explains. "Are there not twelve hours in the day? If anyone walks in the day, he does not stumble, because he sees the light of this world. But if one walks in the night, he stumbles, because the light is not in him" (John 11:9–10 NKJV). He's saying that when someone walks in God's will, nothing can touch him without the Father's permission. But those who walk in darkness, walk in danger of evil because they are not protected by God.

go to

sleeping
1 Corinthians 11:30

ways
Psalm 103:7

Moses
Exodus 24:12

what others say

Frances Vander Velde

Mary was overcome with grief but Martha could shift the weight of her sorrow by keeping occupied with work.[5]

Jesus knows that Lazarus has died while he has delayed coming to Bethany. Yet Jesus knows he will raise Lazarus from the dead. That is why Jesus describes Lazarus as only "sleeping," indicating, as the apostle Paul does in later letters, that dead Christians are actually just waiting for the resurrection. Jesus' comment "I am glad for your sakes that I was not there, that you may believe" (John 11:15 NKJV) may sound insensitive, but Jesus knows the better plan will come from Lazarus' death. Of course, the sisters and the disciples don't know what God is going to do, so they are very confused by Jesus' actions and responses.

Many Jews have come from Jerusalem to Bethany to help console the sisters. They will witness Jesus' miraculous act and take back the news to the officials in Jerusalem. Their news will contribute to the determination and desire of the officials to get rid of Jesus.

When we don't understand God's actions, we must concentrate on his ways—his heart. Moses is described as knowing God's ways, whereas the Israelites knew his acts. Moses walked closely with God and came to know God's heart intimately—his motives and love, through meeting with him on Mount Sinai. The Israelites, who kept themselves at a distance from God and wanted Moses to meet personally with God, could only watch his acts. The Israelites often misinterpreted them because they didn't know God personally. God wants his children to know his ways, along with his actions. Even when we are disappointed by God's acts, we can trust his heart of love.

key point

"If Only"

live
Romans 6:23

JOHN 11:20–27 *Then Martha, as soon as she heard that Jesus was coming, went and met Him, but Mary was sitting in the house. Now Martha said to Jesus, "Lord, if You had been here, my brother would not have died. But even now I know that whatever You ask of God, God will give You."*

Jesus said to her, "Your brother will rise again."

Martha said to Him, "I know that he will rise again in the resurrection at the last day."

Jesus said to her, "I am the resurrection and the life. He who believes in Me, though he may die, he shall live. And whoever lives and believes in Me shall never die. Do you believe this?"

She said to Him, "Yes, Lord, I believe that You are the Christ, the Son of God, who is to come into the world." (NKJV)

Finally, Jesus arrives in Bethany. Martha and Mary must be happy to see him, but also sorry that he arrives after their brother's death. Yes, Jesus is actually there, but alas, his arrival is too late to help their already dead brother. In characteristic fashion, Martha goes to meet Jesus immediately while Mary sits still. They both believe their brother is gone forever, and they grieve in different ways: Martha through activity and Mary through solitude.

Martha gently rebukes Jesus in her grief and pain. It's doubtful that Martha is saying she knows Jesus will raise Lazarus from the dead. She is probably referring to her stated belief that Lazarus will be raised when other believers will also be resurrected.

> **what others say**
>
> **Carol Kent**
>
> Instead of experiencing guilt for feeling and expressing our negative emotions and thus denying our pain, we can admit the struggle involved in the Christian life. It is not a sin to struggle.[6]

key point

Martha gives Jesus the opportunity to give one of the most powerful self-portraits about himself: he is the resurrection and the life. He is in control of life and death. He has the power to raise people from the dead and cause them to <u>live</u> forever in heaven. He knows he is on the way to the cross where he will pay the price for all our sins, so that we can enter heaven if we trust in him.

In the Bible, Jesus gave seven "I am" revelations:

1. I am the bread of life. (John 6:35, 48)

2. I am the light of the world. (John 8:12; 9:5)

3. I am the door. (John 10:7, 9)

4. I am the good shepherd. (John 10:11, 14)

5. I am the resurrection and the life. (John 11:25)

6. I am the way, the truth, and the life. (John 14:6)

7. I am the true vine. (John 15:1–5)

washing
John 12:3

Just as Martha and Mary grieve in their own ways, they also respond to Jesus in different ways. Every person responds to struggles in a way unique to her or to him. We can't expect someone else to grieve or rejoice the same way we do. We each have a different relationship with God as we face a crisis or a happy event. Trying to change people or getting hurt by their reactions only brings worry, discouragement, or frustration.

At His Feet

> JOHN 11:28–32 *And when she had said these things, she went her way and secretly called Mary her sister, saying, "The Teacher has come and is calling for you." As soon as she heard that, she arose quickly and came to Him. Now Jesus had not yet come into the town, but was in the place where Martha met Him. Then the Jews who were with her in the house, and comforting her, when they saw that Mary rose up quickly and went out, followed her, saying, "She is going to the tomb to weep there." Then, when Mary came where Jesus was, and saw Him, she fell down at His feet, saying to Him, "Lord, if You had been here, my brother would not have died." (NKJV)*

Hoping for a private meeting, Mary slips away to see Jesus after receiving Martha's message, but her comforters follow her. When she sees Jesus, Mary is overcome with grief and falls at his feet. How characteristic of this woman. Mary either sits at his feet, falls at his feet, or kneels at his feet while <u>washing</u> him with perfume. Mary has truly surrendered to Jesus, even in this intense time of grief.

work
Philippians 1:6

Her words are the same as Martha's, and certainly these two sisters have been repeating these words to each other for the past four days. From their perspective, they can't understand Jesus' delay and their brother's death. It makes no sense. Their brother, Lazarus, has been lying around dead in his tomb for four days. What can be done for him now?

> what others say
>
> **Virginia Stem Owens**
>
> All well-informed Jews knew the soul only lingers in the vicinity of the body for three days, during which a healer might manage a miraculous restoration. But after four days, all hope is abandoned.[7]

Jesus doesn't rebuke the grieving sisters for their incomplete knowledge. Likewise, God is patient as he takes us from little faith to greater faith in our journey. He knows the work he's doing in us, and he neither hurries nor worries as we learn to know him better.

Take it from John: "And we have known and believed the love that God has for us. God is love, and he who abides in love abides in God, and God in him. . . . There is no fear in love; but perfect love casts out fear" (1 John 4:16, 18 NKJV).

Jesus Weeps

> JOHN 11:33–38 *Therefore, when Jesus saw her weeping, and the Jews who came with her weeping, He groaned in the spirit and was troubled. And He said, "Where have you laid him?" They said to Him, "Lord, come and see."*
>
> *Jesus wept. Then the Jews said, "See how He loved him!" And some of them said, "Could not this Man, who opened the eyes of the blind, also have kept this man from dying?"*
>
> *Then Jesus, again groaning in Himself, came to the tomb. It was a cave, and a stone lay against it.* (NKJV)

The Greek word that means "groaned in the spirit" and "troubled" in verses 33 and 38 also communicates the idea of "angered." Many Bible scholars believe that Jesus' anger is directed toward Satan and Satan's control over sin that brings death to people. Or, perhaps some of his anger in the second instance (verse 38) is in response to the people's lack of belief, demonstrated in their opinion that he can't keep someone from dying.

The weeping referred to in verse 35 is a kind of silent weeping, which is in contrast to the mourners of this time who wailed loudly and openly. Jesus isn't crying in the customary way; he is expressing deep emotions about a painful situation. He's not afraid of doing things that might be misunderstood by others.

go to

understands
Hebrews 4:15

praying
Romans 8:34

joys
James 1:2

---

what others say

Anne Graham Lotz

Jesus is emotionally involved in our lives. His love for us is displayed in his understanding of and identification with our suffering to the extent that he weeps with us.[8]

Jesus' humanity is clearly demonstrated in his emotional response. God's plan is for his Son to experience everything human—except sin—so that Jesus can identify with us. As a result, Jesus <u>understands</u> the trials and temptations we face. Such knowledge enables him, through the Holy Spirit, to help us as we experience similar things. Knowing Jesus understands our struggles gives us confidence that he will help us. And indeed, he is continually <u>praying</u> before God's throne, on our behalf. When we face sorrows, we need to remind ourselves that God is in control of everything in our lives. God is constantly at work, using both our <u>joys</u> and our sorrows to develop our endurance and patience.

But, Lord

JOHN 11:39–40 *Jesus said, "Take away the stone." Martha, the sister of him who was dead, said to Him, "Lord, by this time there is a stench, for he has been dead four days."*

Jesus said to her, "Did I not say to you that if you would believe you would see the glory of God?" (NKJV)

Martha, with her take-charge personality, feels compelled to remind Jesus, who knows everything, that Lazarus has been dead for four days and will smell. Jesus, as usual, gently reminds her of their earlier conversation. Jesus also reminds her that she will see the glory of God, and in the New Testament, Jesus is revealed to be our Lord of Glory. Glory is God's essential quality and is often described as brilliance and light. This glory requires our praise and worship. David celebrated God's glory in this poem that he wrote while in the desert of Judah: "O God, You are my God; early will I seek You; my

share
2 Corinthians 1:3–4

soul thirsts for You; my flesh longs for You in a dry and thirsty land where there is no water. So I have looked for You in the sanctuary, to see Your power and Your glory. Because Your lovingkindness is better than life, my lips shall praise You" (Psalm 63:1–3 NKJV).

what others say

Barbara Johnson

You will win, and after you're a winner, you can reach back and help along another suffering, stressed-out person who needs to hear the good news that she can be a winner, too.[9]

key point

Although Jesus will raise Lazarus from the dead, he wants to involve people in what they can do—roll away the stone. God can deliver us from any difficulty or temptation, but, just like Jesus' involving others to roll back the stone from the grave, God involves us as we are able. Most of the time, God wants us to participate in a process of growth that will teach us things that we can later <u>share</u> with others. If God always gave us an instantaneous deliverance, we would have nothing to share with others. God, in his power, always knows how he's going to deliver and strengthen us to face difficulties.

Lazarus Is Alive!

> JOHN 11:41–46 *Then they took away the stone from the place where the dead man was lying. And Jesus lifted up His eyes and said, "Father, I thank You that You have heard Me. And I know that You always hear Me, but because of the people who are standing by I said this, that they may believe that You sent Me." Now when He had said these things, He cried with a loud voice, "Lazarus, come forth!" And he who had died came out bound hand and foot with graveclothes, and his face was wrapped with a cloth. Jesus said to them, "Loose him, and let him go."*
>
> *Then many of the Jews who had come to Mary, and had seen the things Jesus did, believed in Him. But some of them went away to the Pharisees and told them the things Jesus did. (NKJV)*

Jesus calls the crowd's attention to his Father, Almighty God, so they will understand that God sent his Son, Jesus. The whole purpose of this event, from Lazarus' illness, death, Jesus' delay, and

Lazarus' return to life, is to bring glory to God and to solidify the people's faith and belief that Jesus is indeed God's Son.

Then Jesus again involves the crowd by commanding them to remove the grave cloths wrapped around Lazarus. With a sudden jolt of awareness of Lazarus' predicament, the crowd is motivated into action. The people have a choice: will they believe Jesus is God, or will they scamper back to Jerusalem with further evidence of why the authorities should have him executed?

What joy Martha and Mary must feel as they rush up to Lazarus. As the cloths are unwrapped, they probably pat his face; it is warm! They probably take his hand and help him overcome the stiffness; and his hand moves! They may rush over to Jesus and hug him, for they never expected their brother's resurrection. Some Bible experts believe Lazarus lived for another thirty years after his resurrection.

Lazarus is called from his temporary death because nothing can stop what God has ordained. They may have seen other miracles of Jesus, but we can always rationalize the miraculous. But no one can explain how a man buried for four days can come back to life.

God's delay has brought even greater glory. Now that they look back, Mary and Martha are glad that Jesus did not arrive until after Lazarus died. Never again will they doubt his goodness and love. Can we look back on our own lives and see God's hand for his glory?

God is never in a hurry. He never wrings his hands in exasperation, wondering what he's going to do about his child's latest struggle. He is in complete control and authority over everything that happens on this earth. If he doesn't answer our prayers in the way we desire or think is best, we can trust his loving nature to work in the right way—for his glory and our good.

something to ponder

what others say

Anne Graham Lotz

How pathetic it would have been had Lazarus been raised from the dead but remained bound. Don't blame or criticize a formerly dead person who has just been raised into life for not walking: start unwrapping![10]

This Spikenard Smells Great

JOHN 12:1–3 *Then, six days before the Passover, Jesus came to Bethany, where Lazarus was who had been dead, whom He had raised from the dead. There they made Him a supper; and Martha served, but Lazarus was one of those who sat at the table with Him. Then Mary took a pound of very costly oil of spikenard, anointed the feet of Jesus, and wiped His feet with her hair. And the house was filled with the fragrance of the oil.* (NKJV)

Some time after the resurrection of Lazarus, Jesus returns to Bethany and attends a dinner given in his honor. Unfortunately Lazarus' resurrection has created more envy and jealousy toward Jesus. His enemies decide he must be stopped, or soon everyone will believe in him. Jesus knows he is on his way to the cross, yet his mission to call believers continues. As usual, Martha serves while Mary is at Jesus' feet. This time, Martha isn't complaining about Mary sitting at Jesus' feet. Maybe she is so grateful for her brother's life that she wants to serve and has learned to be content in whatever God calls her to do.

Mary washes Jesus' feet with an expensive perfume called spikenard. She wants to express her great love. Mary can reach Jesus' feet because when they eat, the guests don't sit at a table. They recline on couches so that their feet are out to the side. Washing a person's feet was a common practice in those days, because the roads were dirty, and when the guests arrived, their feet were dirty.

Mary uses spikenard, a sweet-smelling perfume made from the spikenard plant grown in northern India (see Illustration #24). This very expensive spikenard has to be imported to Palestine, and that long journey adds to its costliness. Just like Mary, when we have a deep sense of what God has done on our behalf, we also want to honor him. We can do that by speaking of him to others, by serving him, by spending time with him, and by many other ways.

what others say

Virginia Stem Owens

Perhaps because she's so filled with gratitude that she needs the outlet of physical activity to express it. But also she now sees that this is work, not imposed, but freely chosen. Her own last supper with her Lord is her gift, not her duty.[11]

Illustration #24
Spikenard—The sweet-smelling ointment made from this plant was imported, at great expense, to Israel from India.

The scene of Mary washing Jesus' feet is very similar to the one related in Luke 7:36–50, yet many Bible experts do not think the two scenes describe the same incident. If we interpret the two scenes as descriptions of the same event, we make Mary the sinful woman described in the Luke passage. That doesn't seem likely. The situations are similar, but there are enough different details to make these two different incidents involving two different women who loved Jesus. But the situation described in Mark 14:1–11 does seem to be the same as this scene, since more details are similar. Mark's description identifies the scene at Simon the Leper's home. Perhaps Simon is related to Mary, Martha, and Lazarus, since again Martha is serving dinner—but in his home. Or, perhaps with her energy and take-charge personality, Martha helps wherever she goes.

Mary must have been overcome with gratitude at the return of her brother to life. Also, Jesus' display of his power probably so deepened her faith in Jesus as the Son of God, her Messiah, that she wanted to express her full devotion. Gratitude makes us seek God all the more.

Certainly there are times when we are like Mary and times when we are like Martha. We're like Mary when we love him through being meditative, and we're like Martha when we love him through serving him.

Money, Money, Money

JOHN 12:4–6 *But one of His disciples, Judas Iscariot, Simon's son, who would betray Him, said, "Why was this fragrant oil*

cattle
Psalm 50:9–10

sacrifice
Psalm 51:16–17

not sold for three hundred denarii and given to the poor?" This he said, not that he cared for the poor, but because he was a thief, and had the money box; and he used to take what was put in it. (NKJV)

Judas, the keeper of the finances for Jesus and the disciples, is more concerned about money than the love Mary is lavishing on Jesus. Maybe Judas envies her love for Jesus. Most likely, Judas is thinking that he'd like to have that amount of money for himself. Like the other disciples, Judas was chosen at the beginning of Jesus' public ministry and accompanied him for three years. Judas held a position of trust as treasurer for the group, but John tells us Judas stole from these funds. Evidently the only thing Judas feels passionate about is money, for he will soon betray Jesus to the authorities for a small amount of money.

Mary spent nearly a year's wages, about 300 pence or $60 in that day, for the perfume she used to wash Jesus' feet. But today, can you consider "throwing away" a year's worth of wages? That amount cannot be easily given away. Yet Mary does it.

what others say

Shirley Rose

Paul tells us in 2 Corinthians 9:7 that we should not give grudgingly or out of necessity, but give cheerfully. Wow! You mean, we not only have to give, but give cheerfully? Well, I'd say if you can't give with a joyful willing heart, give anyway. But if you want to milk it for the full blessing, give cheerfully.[12]

The amount of money Mary gives up might represent her life savings or her dowry. Who knows? Perhaps she still hoped to marry. With her sacrifice, she offers Jesus her hopes of the future. She has joyfully and gratefully given up everything for him.

God loves our passion for him. He is the owner of the <u>cattle</u> on a thousand hills, so he doesn't need money. But he loves <u>sacrifice</u> that expresses our devotion and love for him. However, he doesn't want sacrifice only for sacrifice's sake. The writer of Hebrews says, "Therefore by Him let us continually offer the sacrifice of praise to God, that is, the fruit of our lips, giving thanks to His name. But do not forget to do good and to share, for with such sacrifices God is well pleased" (13:15–16 NKJV).

The Final Hours

JOHN 12:7–11 *But Jesus said, "Let her alone; she has kept this for the day of My burial. For the poor you have with you always, but Me you do not have always."*

Now a great many of the Jews knew that He was there; and they came, not for Jesus' sake only, but that they might also see Lazarus, whom He had raised from the dead. But the chief priests plotted to put Lazarus to death also, because on account of him many of the Jews went away and believed in Jesus. (NKJV)

What a contrast! Jesus, who is about to be crucified and buried as a sacrifice for the sins of the world, is reclining at dinner alongside Lazarus, whom Jesus has raised from the dead. Mary doesn't realize it, but her sacrifice of expensive nard prepares Jesus' body for his coming crucifixion.

Let's not misunderstand this passage. Jesus is not saying that providing for the poor is unimportant; rather he says that he will not always be on earth. He will soon leave earth, but the poor will always be here and will have many more opportunities to receive help. As the final events of Jesus' life quickly unfold, the chief priests plan to kill both Jesus and Lazarus. They fear Jesus, because they worry that Jesus will take their power away from them.

The Power of Jesus

Jesus will call people instantly into the heavens at the Rapture.	1 Thessalonians 4:16
Jesus returns for the Old Testament saints.	Daniel 12:2
Jesus calls the Tribulation Saints to life.	Revelation 20:4, 6
Jesus delivers the dead from their sins into spiritual life.	Ephesians 2:1–10
Jesus forgives sins.	Matthew 9:6; 1 John 1:9
Jesus strengthens us when we abide in him.	John 15:5
Jesus prepares a place in heaven.	John 14:2

what others say

Frances Vander Velde

When a few days later the Roman soldiers pressed the crown of thorns on Jesus, the King of the Jews, Mary's spikenard was still in his hair, and when the soldier held his seamless robe it still diffused the sweet smell, the unusual gift of Mary's devotion.[13]

wisdom
James 1:5

seven demons
Luke 8:2

needs
Matthew 27:55–56

cross
John 19:25

resurrection
Matthew 28:1;
Mark 16:1;
John 20:1

God's power through Jesus is unlimited; therefore, he has sufficient power to strengthen his children for their problems and temptations. Nothing is too difficult for him to deal with, and he always wants us to call upon him for help and for <u>wisdom</u>.

Jesus' power is sufficient for every problem because he can raise people from the dead and give spiritual life to any who seek it. In the Bible, we find several examples of his life-giving power.

Talk About Gratitude (Mary Magdalene)

> **the big picture**
>
> **Mark 16:1–19**
>
> Mary Magdalene is faithful in following Jesus and providing for his needs. She is also a diligent supporter at the cross and is among the first to learn of Jesus' resurrection.

Mary, from the area of Magdala, was first touched by Jesus when he delivered her from <u>seven demons</u>. That part of her story isn't included in Scripture, however, with the exception of a quick reference. But her great deliverance from the demons gives birth to a woman completely devoted to Jesus. We don't know where her wealth comes from, but she travels around with Jesus, meeting his <u>needs</u>. She is one of several women who do this. No men, other than the disciples, are described in this way.

Mary Magdalene is faithful to the end. She is one of those who stand at the <u>cross</u>, most likely dumbfounded and incredulous about the horrible thing that is happening to her Lord. But three days later, she is among the very first women at the tomb to know of his <u>resurrection</u>. In her usual fashion, she is at the tomb to serve Jesus by applying spices to his body. But instead of having an opportunity to serve his dead body, she is given the blessing of finding out that Jesus is no longer in the tomb. He is alive!

The women may have been concerned about the tomb being protected by Roman soldiers, but their love for Jesus compelled them to go despite the soldiers (see Illustration #25). Their desire to take care of Jesus never ends, beginning first with financial support and ending finally with spices to apply to his dead body. These women truly represent faithful devotion.

Illustration #25
A Roman Soldier in Uniform—Roman soldiers enlisted in their empire's army for twenty years.

Mary Magdalene's great gratitude for her deliverance from seven evil demons fuels her service for God. The more we focus on what God has done for us, the more we'll serve him faithfully (see Matthew 27:56, 61; 28:1; Mark 15:40, 47; 16:1–19; Luke 8:2; 24:10; John 19:25; 20:1–18).

For My Children (Salome)

MATTHEW 20:20–23 *Then the mother of Zebedee's sons came to Him with her sons, kneeling down and asking something from Him. And He said to her, "What do you wish?" She said to Him, "Grant that these two sons of mine may sit, one on Your right hand and the other on the left, in Your kingdom." But Jesus answered and said, "You do not know what you ask. Are you able to drink the cup that I am about to drink, and be baptized with the baptism that I am baptized with?" They said to Him, "We are able." So He said to them, "You will indeed drink My cup, and be baptized with the baptism that I am baptized with; but to sit on My right hand and on My left is not Mine to give, but it is for those for whom it is prepared by My Father." (NKJV)*

travel
Matthew 27:55–56

sons
Mark 10:35–40

cross
Mark 15:40–41

tomb
Mark 16:1–2

Every mother wants the best for her children, and Salome, the mother of two of Jesus' disciples, is no exception. She does not ask for herself, but for her sons, John and James. (Salome's son James is the older of the two disciples named James.) Her sons have been serving Jesus, and so has she. Salome is among the women who <u>travel</u> from Galilee to minister to the needs of Jesus.

In another Scripture passage, her two <u>sons</u> are identified as actually asking the questions. If so, their mother most likely put them up to it! Later, Salome will taste some of the bitter dregs of the cup, mentioned by Jesus, as she stands at the <u>cross</u> and watches him die. But only three days later, she is a part of the victory party when she discovers at the <u>tomb</u> that his body is gone and Jesus is alive!

what others say

Max Lucado

Don't go to God with options and expect him to choose one of your preferences. Go to him with empty hands—no hidden agendas, no crossed fingers, nothing behind your back. Go to him with a willingness to do whatever he says.[14]

Jan Johnson

To be fair to James and John, they had left a prosperous fishing company to follow Jesus, a huge step of submission. What would they get for their obedience?[15]

Some Bible experts identify this Salome as the sister of Mary, the mother of Jesus. If this is true, then James and John are Jesus' cousins. Maybe this is one of the reasons why Salome believes her sons deserve even more honor: they are family!

We all want what's best for our children, but only God can determine what is best. Salome doesn't realize that her request will actually bring her sons great trouble. She only sees the end result of glory, but Jesus knows the painful path to get there. We need to be careful to pray for our children according to God's plan, not for our own desires.

key point

To Salome's great credit, she believes in Jesus so much that she fully anticipates Jesus' victorious reign in heaven. Jesus doesn't rebuke her for her inappropriate question, instead he sees her faith. When we come to Jesus with inappropriate prayers, Jesus looks, as he did with Salome, into our hearts and sees our trust in him, even if our passion is out of bounds (see Matthew 27:56; Mark 10:35–40; 15:40–41; 16:1–2).

Take Them, They're Yours
(Mother of Joseph and James)

Mary's son James is often called James "the lesser" or "the younger" to differentiate him from the other disciple named James, who is older than this Mary's son James. Mary, the mother of the younger James and the mother of Joseph, ministers to Jesus and stands at the cross along with the other women. Although we don't know much about this Mary, we know she gives untiringly of herself and even gives her two sons—Joseph and James, the lesser—to be disciples. Her faithfulness pays off when she rejoices with the other women and with the disciples at the resurrection of Jesus.

Witnessing in the Palace (Joanna)

LUKE 8:1–3 *Now it came to pass, afterward, that He went through every city and village, preaching and bringing the glad tidings of the kingdom of God. And the twelve were with Him, and certain women who had been healed of evil spirits and infirmities—Mary called Magdalene, out of whom had come seven demons, and Joanna the wife of Chuza, Herod's steward, and Susanna, and many others who provided for Him from their substance.* (NKJV)

Joanna, one of the many women who have felt Jesus' healing touch, gave generously of herself. As the wife of a palace employee, she most likely spoke about Jesus in the palace. Perhaps Herod heard of Jesus through her and other believers. Joanna remained faithful until the end and was among the blessed women who were the first to learn about Jesus' resurrection. Tradition says that because of her witnessing about Jesus, her husband, Cuza, was fired from his job.

Witnessing about Jesus doesn't guarantee that listeners will respond positively. Still, we must be faithful to share the good news about Jesus. If Joanna's husband lost his job, Joanna suffered as the result of her faithful witness for Jesus. But Joanna's sacrifice, like ours, shall be rewarded in heaven.

Chapter Wrap-Up

- Mary and Martha were two sisters with whom Jesus found love, support, and an opportunity to glorify God through raising their brother Lazarus from the dead. (John 11:41–46)

- Mary Magdalene was one of several women who supported Jesus financially and emotionally after he delivered her from demon possession. (Mark 16:1–19)

- Like every mother, Salome wanted the best for her two children who had become Jesus' disciples. She asked Jesus to allow her sons, John and James, to be enthroned at his right and left when in heaven. (Matthew 20:20–23)

- Mary, the mother of the younger James and Joseph, gave her best for the service of Jesus. She encouraged her sons to follow Jesus and served Jesus herself with money and support. (Matthew 27:55–61)

- Joanna was the wife of Cuza, who served as a manager in Herod's household. As a believer, Joanna supported Jesus and most likely spoke of her faith in Herod's home. (Luke 8:1–3)

Study Questions

1. Describe how Mary and Martha differed in personality and in their interactions with Jesus.

2. How did Jesus first change Mary Magdalene's life, and how did she respond?

3. What did Salome request for her two sons, and why?

4. How was Mary, the mother of the younger James and Joseph, rewarded for her faithful service to Jesus?

5. How did Joanna serve Jesus?

Chapter 16 Women in Ministry

Chapter Highlights:
• Serving with Your Hands
• Teaching the Young
• Serving with Wealth
• Having a Servant's Heart
• Working Tirelessly

Let's Get Started

Ever hear someone say women are not valued in Christianity? Begin by pointing this person to the women of the early Christian church. Many of these women started by serving Jesus, and after his resurrection, they continued to work to establish the new church. After Jesus' time on earth, other women joined them in building the early church.

In this chapter we honor all these women of the early church as ministers of the gospel. Not in an academic way, but in recognition that they gave sacrificially of themselves. They raised godly children, shared their wealth, and worked to build the church. The work of these women provides us with examples of ways to honor Jesus in practical, daily service.

Don't Stop Her Yet (Dorcas)

the big picture

Acts 9:36–42

Dorcas was well known for her service to others. She sewed clothes for many people and helped the poor in a variety of ways. As a result, she was much loved, and when she died prematurely, everyone was very sad. Because so many were grief-stricken over her death, the disciples sent for Peter, and Peter restored Dorcas to life.

Dorcas, who was also known as Tabitha, not only worked for the early church, but performed many charitable acts. Well loved, her death was a blow to many people. Because she was so loved, the disciples in their faith called Peter to restore her to life. After reviewing what a wonderful person she was, Peter raised her from the dead. We don't know, but we assume that after being restored to life, Dorcas continued her wonderful selfless service to others.

abounding
1 Corinthians 15:58

Lystra
Acts 14:6

By giving of ourselves to others as God leads us, we will feel less of a desire to focus on ourselves and our own problems. Selflessness benefits us in that it helps us forget ourselves and find joy.

Look at Him Now (Eunice and Lois)

ACTS 16:1 *Then he came to Derbe and <u>Lystra</u>. And behold, a certain disciple was there, named Timothy, the son of a certain Jewish woman who believed, but his father was Greek.* (NKJV)

2 TIMOTHY 1:5 *I call to remembrance the genuine faith that is in you, which dwelt first in your grandmother Lois and your mother Eunice, and I am persuaded is in you also.* (NKJV)

Timothy's mother and his grandmother powerfully influenced Timothy's life. The apostle Paul acknowledged their influence, forever giving Lois and Eunice credit for sharing their faith with Timothy. Timothy's mother, Eunice, and his grandmother Lois must have been thrilled to see how God used him, for Timothy became a valued member of the community of Christians.

Timothy's father was not a believer, so Lois and Eunice probably worried about the father's influence upon Timothy. But God's sovereignty overrode the father's influence and created a godly man who served Jesus for many years. Women whose husbands are not believers can take comfort in the experience of Eunice and her mother, Lois. With God, we always have hope, and we can know that he is sovereign—even over the influence of an ungodly parent.

This doesn't mean that God wants women to marry unbelievers. He specifically says we are not to marry <u>unbelievers</u>. But perhaps we married before we knew Christ, or perhaps we thought we could influence our husbands to know Christ. If this is our situation, we can find comfort in the fact that God will still influence our children and help them to become godly children.

Based on what Paul wrote to Timothy, it appears that Timothy was an intense person. Today we might call him a perfectionist. He also seemed to be <u>fearful</u> that his mother, Eunice, and grandmother Lois worried about his trait of perfectionism. All mothers can be tempted into worry about the imperfect temperaments of their children, but God can be trusted with these concerns. He doesn't want us to be worried about anything, even our children's struggles. Once they are adults, we can influence them with advice when they ask. But our main function is to pray for our children.

unbelievers
2 Corinthians 6:14

fearful
1 Timothy 4:12;
2 Timothy 1:7

You Go, Girl (Lydia)

the big picture

Acts 16:11-15

Paul leads a wealthy woman named Lydia to Christ. Paul first meets Lydia when he arrives in the city of Philippi. Later, Lydia becomes a very important person in the new community of believers in that city.

Lydia and other women are meeting by the riverside in the city of Philippi, an important city in Macedonia. These women worship God in the Jewish manner, even though they have no synagogue. Ten men are required to establish a temple; these faithful women lack the required ten men. Despite the lack of a temple, the women always meet to worship and to dream of building a temple. Paul comes looking for a gathering of the Jews in this area, and finds these women. After explaining to them about Jesus being the Messiah, they believe in him.

meetings
Acts 16:40

Because Lydia is so grateful for coming to know Christ's wonderful love and grace, she invites the apostles to her home to stay. From then on, she frequently has <u>meetings</u> in her home and generously shares the wealth God has given her for Christ's work.

We know that Lydia is wealthy because she is a "seller of purple [fabrics]." Such a business made a person wealthy because only the rich could afford to buy such expensive fabrics. The purple color comes from a shellfish, the murex, or from the root of a plant, and the rarity of these two sources made purple dye extraordinarily expensive.

apply it

Like Lydia, when we truly appreciate what God has done through our salvation, we will want to be generous in other areas of our lives. Knowing God is generous in providing for all of our needs and knowing we can never out-give God, we can lavishly give to others.

Come on Over (Mary)

ACTS 12:12 *So, when he had considered this, he came to the house of Mary, the mother of John whose surname was Mark, where many were gathered together praying.* (NKJV)

This Mary is the mother of John Mark, who joins Paul and Barnabas on one of their missionary journeys. In the incident mentioned in this verse, Peter is released from prison through a miracle. Paul comes to Mary's house, knowing everyone will be meeting there. Mary seems to be another woman who gives hospitality and support to the Christians, especially at first when the Christians are a small group.

Allowing Christians to meet in her home probably meant danger for this Mary because Christians were being persecuted at this time. Peter had to knock at the door. This knock seems to indicate that the door is kept locked to prevent enemies from barging in and arresting these early Christians.

She Delivers (Phoebe)

ROMANS 16:1–4 *I commend to you Phoebe our sister, who is a servant of the church in Cenchrea, that you may receive her in the Lord in a manner worthy of the saints, and assist her in whatever business she has need of you; for indeed she has been a helper of many and of myself also.*

Greet Priscilla and Aquila, my fellow workers in Christ Jesus, who risked their own necks for my life, to whom not only I give thanks, but also all the churches of the Gentiles. (NKJV)

epistle
letter

Although we don't know a lot about Phoebe, we do know that while on a business trip, she delivers the letter from Paul to the church at Rome. Being on a business trip seems to indicate that Phoebe is a prosperous businesswoman. Paul writes that the Christians are to help Phoebe in whatever ways she asks.

Paul truly trusted Phoebe, for he put his precious **epistle** into her care. Obviously, Phoebe has helped him and many others, and she has proved herself to be a valued contributor to the work of the early church.

The other detail we know about Phoebe is that she has come from Cenchrea. Cenchrea served as the east harbor of Corinth, an important commercial city in ancient Greece. What's important to note is that Phoebe is called not only a sister, but also a servant. The Greek word for "servant" is *diakonon* meaning "deacon" or "servant." "Some Bible experts say Phoebe most likely led a definite office in the church, and her role as church officer shows that women such as Phoebe, Lydia and Priscilla, did have significant leadership roles in the early church. (See references to Lydia in this book.)

what others say

Eugenia Price

She was the natural, balanced kind of woman who didn't need to panic and wonder and struggle in prayer for the success of her mission.[5]

We should not show favoritism based on whether a person is wealthy or poor. In God's eyes, what matters is our love for him. Since he owns everything whether we have much or little is not important. But what does matter is that we surrender everything we have to him for his use.

Wealthy people need to <u>be careful</u> not to become conceited or focused on their wealth as the source of security and contentment. Wealth is given by God for his purposes and not for our glory or vanity. If we aren't faithful to use wealth in God's way, we know he can choose to remove our riches.

Living Dangerously (Priscilla)

be careful
1 Timothy 6:17–19

expelled
Acts 18:2

tentmakers
Acts 18:3

journey
Acts 18:18

risked
Romans 16:3–4

meet together
1 Corinthians 16:19

the big picture

Acts 18:18–26

Priscilla and her husband, Aquila, help a young evangelist, Apollos, to preach Jesus with increased truth. The couple hear him, and when they realize that what Apollos preaches is incomplete, they gently correct him.

Priscilla and her husband, Aquila, become involved in the apostle Paul's ministry when they are in Corinth. They are living in Corinth because Claudius has <u>expelled</u> all Jews from Rome. Paul lives in their home for eighteen months. They all share a common occupation: they are all <u>tentmakers</u>.

We don't know how this Jewish couple come to know the Lord, whether through Paul or not, but they begin traveling with Paul when he leaves for his next missionary <u>journey</u> to Ephesus. Later, Paul will write that they <u>risked</u> their own lives for his safety and benefit.

While they are in Ephesus, Priscilla and Aquila hear a young evangelist named Apollos preach about Jesus. Although he is speaking truthfully about Jesus, his knowledge is limited. In a gentle and sensitive manner, Priscilla and Aquila give him more information by inviting him to their home—instead of correcting him in front of the crowd. Their home is often used for Christians to <u>meet together</u>.

In every instance where Priscilla is mentioned in Scripture, her husband is also named. Evidently they are inseparable and probably childless. In some descriptions of Priscilla and Aquila in the Bible, he is named first. Other times, she is named first. Some Bible experts believe that indicates she becomes more prominent in the Christian community than her husband.

When helping a person to consider something in a new way, we should make the suggestion privately. The person will be more open to receiving information and correcting his or her thinking, when our discussion is private.

They Never Stop (Tryphena and Tryphosa)

ROMANS 16:12 *Greet Tryphena and Tryphosa, who have labored in the Lord. (NKJV)*

All we know about these two women is Paul's mention of them in his letter. But they must have been cheerful workers and worthy of mention for their service because he points them out. Even though Tryphena and Tryphosa are mentioned just once, they are "sisters in the Lord" and eager to serve their Lord.

Some Bible scholars believe these two women, Tryphena and Tryphosa, were twin sisters because their names are so similar.

Chapter Wrap-Up

- Dorcas, a giving person who frequently sewed clothes and helped the poor, has died. But her friends call Peter, and he raises her from the dead. (Acts 10:36–42)

- Timothy's mother, Eunice, and his grandmother Lois are godly influences upon Timothy's life, even though his father is not a believer. (Acts 16:1; 2 Timothy 1:5)

- Lydia was a wealthy businesswoman who came to know Jesus through the testimony of Paul. She becomes an important influence in the early church. (Acts 16:11–15)

- Mary served the Lord by having groups of Christians meet in her home, even though offering a gathering place was dangerous because Christians were being persecuted at this time. (Acts 12:12)

- While on a business trip, Phoebe carried the letter that Paul had written to the Christians at Rome. (Acts 16:1–2)

- In the early church, Priscilla and her husband, Aquila, helped Paul, counseled Apollos, and risked their lives for the sake of the gospel. (Acts 18:24–26)

- Paul honored Tryphena and Tryphosa by mentioning how much they worked for God's glory. (Romans 16:12)

Study Questions

1. What kind of person is Dorcas?

2. Whose wonderful influence did Timothy have in his life?

3. What does Lydia prove spiritually about rich people?

4. How did Mary, the mother of John Mark, serve the Lord?

5. What remarkable thing did Phoebe do on her business trip?

6. How did Priscilla show a loving sensitivity to Apollos?

7. How does Paul honor Tryphena and Tryphosa?

Let's Get Started

Women are responsible for using their God-given talents for God's glory, yet many people choose not to. God challenges the six women of this chapter to make changes in their lives. To make these changes, they struggle with some of the same things we struggle with today: conflict, lies, evil, and the call to share the truth about Jesus. Even if these women do not make the right decisions, we can learn from their experiences.

Forgetting Names (Euodia and Syntyche)

PHILIPPIANS 4:2–3 *I implore Euodia and I implore Syntyche to be of the same mind in the Lord. And I urge you also, true companion, help these women who labored with me in the gospel, with Clement also, and the rest of my fellow workers, whose names are in the Book of Life. (NKJV)*

For unknown reasons, Euodia and Syntyche have trouble working together, and Paul addresses their conflict. Most likely their personality clash is not the only one that Paul must try to resolve in his work with the early Christian churches. In the ancient world, people's names reflected who they were. For example, Euodia's name means "fragrant," and Syntyche's name means "fortunate," but these two women are obviously not living up to their names.

Just as babies are given names that their parents hope will fit them, the many names for God describe who he is and what he is like. When we pray in Jesus' name or claim Jesus' name, we are acting out our dependence on the nature of Jesus.

what others say

Charles Stanley

Forgive! "That's impossible," you say. Oh really? Think about it; what makes it impossible? Really only one thing, your refusal to let go of the lie that somehow those who have wronged you owe you something. To forgive is simply to mentally release the offending party of any obligation.[1]

counselor
Proverbs 13:10

wash
Matthew 27:24

congregation
local church

intercede
to act on the behalf
of others

mediator
a person who brings
about an agreement

To help these women overcome their bitter feelings toward each other, Paul first urges them to live in harmony for God's sake and glory. When we truly want God's glory in our lives, we are more willing to let go of petty misunderstandings and unrealistic expectations. Next, Paul suggests that a man in their **congregation intercede** as a "<u>counselor</u>" and try to help the two ladies overcome their dislike for each other. Getting another person to act as **mediator** is a great way to help us solve our differences.

More Than Indigestion (Pilate's Wife)

MATTHEW 27:19 *While [Pilate] was sitting on the judgment seat, his wife sent to him, saying, "Have nothing to do with that just Man, for I have suffered many things today in a dream because of Him." (NKJV)*

Jesus is questioned by Pilate, the top Roman authority in the area, and is found to be guilty in a mock trial. While Pilate is conducting the trial, his wife sends him a note saying that she dreamed about Jesus, and based on her dream, she believes him to be innocent. Unfortunately, his wife's comment doesn't prevent Pilate from continuing the trial, but her note probably influences him to "<u>wash</u>" his hands of the verdict.

what others say

Max Lucado

To know God's will, we must totally surrender to God's will. Our tendency is to make God's decison for him.[2]

Although Pilate's wife does not succeed in convincing her husband that Jesus is innocent and should be allowed to go free, she rightly gives him her opinion. Spouses should regard their mates' input as valuable. Remember, our spouses bring us different perspectives, and considering the other point of view helps us see life with two sets of eyes instead of one.

Liar, Liar, Pants on Fire (Sapphira)

overcome
Revelation 12:11

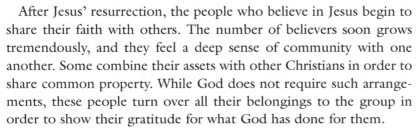

the big picture

Acts 5:1–11

Sapphira and her husband lie about the amount of money they received from selling some land. Then they contribute this incorrect amount of money to the local assembly of Christians.

After Jesus' resurrection, the people who believe in Jesus begin to share their faith with others. The number of believers soon grows tremendously, and they feel a deep sense of community with one another. Some combine their assets with other Christians in order to share common property. While God does not require such arrangements, these people turn over all their belongings to the group in order to show their gratitude for what God has done for them.

Ananias and Sapphira plan to contribute to the common property by selling a piece of land. They sell the land and pretend to give the full price to the group, though actually they keep some of the money for themselves. While they were never obligated to give the full amount, they are obligated to tell the truth. Their lie causes a serious problem. Somehow the leaders, especially Peter, find out that the couple has lied. When the leaders confront the husband Ananias and the wife Sapphira, both continue to lie. In that moment, their lives are snatched from them and they die.

what others say

Nancy Leigh DeMoss

A pursuit of holiness that is not Christ-centered will soon be reduced to moralism, pharisaical self-righteousness, and futile self-effort. Such pseudo-holiness leads to bondage, rather than liberty; it is unattrractive to the world and unacceptable to God. Only by fixing our eyes and our hope on Christ can we experience that authentic, warm, inviting holiness that He alone can produce in us.[3]

Beth Moore

Satan's worst nightmare is being overcome—particularly by measly mortals. He knows the Bible says we overcome our accuser in two primary ways. If he can do nothing about the blood of the Lamb covering the redeemed, what's a devil to do? Go for the word of their testimony![4]

hates
Proverbs 6:16–17

key point

Peter explains that, while they did not have to give all the money, they should not have lied about the amount. They were not only telling a lie to their fellow Christians but to the Holy Spirit. Their sin is so serious that they die on the spot. Lies are wrongs done not only to other people, but also to God.

God knows everything. When we lie, we aren't just lying to the people around us, we're lying to God. God says that he <u>hates</u> a lying tongue. In the case of Sapphira, God uses her death and the death of her husband to make a strong point against lying. Certainly their fellow Christians note the fatal consequence of Ananias and Sapphira and realize the seriousness of telling a lie. Their deaths sent a message to the people and spurred them to be more honest.

Bad Company (Herodias and Salome)

> **the big picture**
>
> **Matthew 14:3–12**
>
> Herodias the queen sees an opportunity to have her enemy, John the Baptist, murdered. She tells her daughter, Salome, to dance so erotically that she can request anything she wants from her stepfather, Herod Antipas, the king of Judea. After Salome dances and pleases Herod, Salome requests John's beheading.

Herodias, the granddaughter of Herod the Great, first marries her uncle, Herod Philip, and they have a daughter, Salome. Later, Herod Philip and Herodias host Herod Philip's brother, Herod Antipas, in their home in Rome. During this visit, Herodias and Herod Antipas have an affair and finally Herodias marries Herod Antipas, her former brother-in-law and the king of Judea under Roman rule.

Eventually, John the Baptist appears on the scene and Herod Antipas is fascinated with John's message. The two often get together to talk about God. John forthrightly tells Herod that he and his wife, Herodias, should not be married.

Herodias is threatened because she does not want to lose her position as queen. She schemes to have John the Baptist killed through her daughter. Salome sacrifices her daughter's modesty by having her daughter dance in such a way that her stepfather's lustful passions are aroused. As a result of her dance, Herod promises the girl anything she wants and after being coached by her mother, Herodias, she requests the head of John the Baptist. John the Baptist is beheaded.

what others say

Frances Vander Velde

From Josephus we learn that Salome married Herod Philip II, and we are told that she met a horrible death.[5]

Herodias receives what she wants—the head of John the Baptist. But later, Herod is banished from power so she is also banished. Herodias' schemes and choices get her nowhere. Doing wrong never brings us the satisfaction we crave.

Chapter Wrap-Up

- Euodia and Syntyche have helped the apostle Paul in the church but they can't get along with each other. Paul encourages the two women to resolve their conflict and get help from others. (Philippians 4:2–3)

- Pilate's wife does the right thing by sending a message to her husband. In the message, she tells him she thinks Jesus is innocent. (Matthew 27:19)

- Sapphira and her husband lie about the amount of money they received for the sale of some real estate. They didn't have to give all of the money to the Christian community, but they shouldn't have lied about the amount they received. The result is their prompt deaths. (Acts 5:1–11)

- Herodias tells her daughter, Salome, to dance sensually before her own stepfather, Herod, so that Salome can request the beheading of John the Baptist. (Matthew 14:3–12)

Study Questions

1. What does Paul suggest as a help for solving the conflict between Euodia and Syntyche?

2. What message does Pilate's wife send to Pilate, and where did she get her information?

3. Why do you think Sapphira and her husband lied, and how are they punished?

4. How did Herodias corrupt her daughter, Salome, and why did she use her daughter this way?

Chapter 18 Women of Faith

Chapter Highlights:
- Rejoicing in God's Work
- Believing God's Promises
- Giving All
- Sharing the Good News

Let's Get Started

God wants us to develop faith. When we have faith, our lives show it. We know who God truly is, and we trust him to do the right thing for us. This chapter highlights four women who, among the many in the Bible, have great faith. They believe God when he reveals his will to them. Today these women can help us believe God's messages to us, help us trust him with our money, and help us know he can do miracles! We've examined many biblical women throughout this book, and in this final chapter let's remember these women for the valuable examples they provide. These women tell us, "Believe in God and trust him. He loves you."

You're Gonna Be a Mom! (Elizabeth)

the big picture

Luke 1:5–25, 39–66

Elizabeth is the childless wife of Zacharias and the cousin of Mary, the mother of Jesus. God causes Elizabeth to become pregnant. She gives birth to John, who becomes John the Baptist.

Elizabeth, long childless, probably thinks she'll never become a mother. Then one day her husband, Zacharias, comes home from his time of service in the temple, and he can't talk. Somehow through sign language and writing, he tells Elizabeth that he saw an angel, who told him that they will have a child and the child's name will be John. Sure enough, Elizabeth is soon in seclusion because of her pregnancy.

While Elizabeth is still pregnant, her young cousin Mary travels the long distance to Elizabeth's door. In an instant, Elizabeth realizes that Mary carries the long-awaited Messiah in her womb. Elizabeth doesn't know how she knows, but she knows for sure. And

go to

cope
2 Timothy 3:16–17

as if to confirm her belief, the baby within Elizabeth leaps as if to rejoice in all that has happened.

At the appointed time and shortly after Mary has gone home, baby John is born. Elizabeth rejoices in God's blessing of a baby. As her child grows, Elizabeth can see God's special hand upon him. John, she realizes, has a unique ministry; he can call people to know God.

what others say

Tricia McCary Rhodes

God's Word is a love letter written for the heart of his beloved. It is a treasure—a gift like no other. He hopes we will hold it close, finding joy in every word day after day after day.[1]

We don't know how Elizabeth knows about Mary's special pregnancy, but God is able to communicate things to our spirits if he desires. Perhaps God sends us a strong impression in our minds or a sensation in our hearts. Some people report that receiving God's message is a "know that I know" kind of experience. God always wants to communicate with us, and he won't be held back from a relationship with us.

The best way for God to communicate to us is through the Bible, his love letter to us. In the Bible, he tells us about himself, how to <u>cope</u> with life, and how to grow closer to him.

There He Is! (Anna)

the big picture

Luke 2:36–38

For many years, Anna, a prophetess who serves in the temple, has been waiting to see the Messiah. She knows to wait because God has told her that she will see the Messiah. Finally Anna sees the baby Jesus. Immediately she knows he is the Messiah and rejoices.

Can you imagine waiting fifty, sixty, maybe seventy years for the fulfillment of a promise from God? That's probably how long Anna waits. God promised her that she will see—with her own eyes—the Messiah. We don't know when she first received that revelation, but most likely long ago. She has been serving in the temple for a long time and has seen many young couples arrive at the temple to dedicate their infants to God. How many times has Anna looked at a child and prayed, "Lord, is this the One?" We just don't know.

Suddenly, Joseph and Mary appear, and Anna knows their infant is the Messiah! She doesn't know how she knows but she knows, so she praises and thanks God. At age eighty-four, Anna knows God's promised Son has arrived for the salvation of all people.

God always keeps his promises because he doesn't change his mind. Sometimes he seems to delay, and we wonder if he's forgotten us or if we heard him wrong. Anna might have felt that many times. But God keeps his promise to Anna, just like God will always keep his promises to us. He's faithful and never makes a promise he won't keep.

go to

cheerful
2 Corinthians 9:7

> **what others say**
>
> **Carol Kent**
>
> Everything around me may change, but our God is changeless.[2]

Take It All (The Widow with Two Mites)

> **the big picture**
>
> **Mark 12:41–44**
>
> Jesus and his disciples are at the temple when Jesus points out a poor widow who gives sacrificially to the temple treasury. He uses her as an object lesson of selfless giving.

Jesus must know the widow is coming, for he uses her donation to show his disciples that God values wholehearted commitment. Soon the disciples will have their own commitment to Jesus tested. Will they be tempted to abandon Jesus, or will they remember her example? Their responses will vary.

Of course, the widow doesn't know she offers an object lesson to the disciples. She just knows she loves God. She is so grateful for his love that she wants to give all she has. She fully believes that he can provide for her in any way he chooses, so why not give him her all? She gives with <u>cheerful</u> abandon, and Jesus honors her. Jesus says that her gift is more valuable to God than all the huge amounts given by those who give out of their abundance. This widow gives out of the little she has.

Patsy Clairmont

I love that the Word of God is full of intrigue, love, mystery, family, prophecy, heresy, royalty, destiny, and much more.[3]

The widow gave two small copper coins. Each coin was the smallest bronze coin in circulation in Palestine at that time and was called a lepton (see Illustration #26). Two of these coins were probably worth less than one sixty-fourth of a Roman denarius (see Illustration #27). This story of the widow, who gave so generously, is often called the widow's **mite**. We wouldn't be surprised to learn that Jesus later finds this widow and gives her some money. What do you think of her actions?

You Ain't Gonna Believe This...(Rhoda)

the big picture

Acts 12:13–16

Rhoda is a servant girl in the home of Mary, the mother of John Mark. Gathered at Mary's home are Christians, and these Christians are praying for Peter, whom they believe is dead or imprisoned. Suddenly, Rhoda hears a knock at the door and Peter's voice. Knowing Peter has been delivered from prison, she tells everyone. At first, no one believes her.

Peter has been imprisoned for his witness of Jesus, and a group of believers are praying for his release in the home of John Mark's mother, Mary. Since everyone else is busy praying, the servant girl named Rhoda hears a knock and goes to the gate. She recognizes Peter's voice and becomes so excited to discover that their prayers have already been answered that she runs to tell the people inside the house and forgets to open the locked gate for Peter.

what others say

Joyce Meyer

I spent many years of my life mentally rehearsing what I was going to say to people. I imagined what they would say to me, then I tried to figure out what I was going to say back to them. If you are filled with anxiety, it may be a sign you think the outcome of the conversation depends upon you and your ability rather than upon the Holy Spirit and his ability.[4]

Who could believe it? Their prayers are answered, but they can't believe Rhoda's news. They tell Rhoda, "You are beside yourself!" (Acts 12:15 NKJV). They even think Peter is already dead and Rhoda is seeing his angel. Poor Rhoda, what a time she has convincing them. And then Peter arrives—in flesh and blood. Everyone is thrilled that Peter is alive and there with them. They realize their prayers were answered even when they had such little faith.

Rhoda faithfully tells the truth, but she can't convince anyone that Peter has arrived. We know what that is like. While we can't force anyone to change his or her mind, we, nevertheless, must obey God and tell that person the truth.

Illustration #26
Lepton—The widow's bronze coins may have looked like this bronze lepton from AD 6.

Illustration #27
Denarius—The denarius, the coin most mentioned in the New Testament, was a day's wages for the average workingman.

Chapter Wrap-Up

- Elizabeth is the cousin of Mary, the mother of Jesus, and though married, Elizabeth has been childless for many years. Then an angel tells her husband that they will have a special child named John. Their child becomes John the Baptist. (Luke 1:5–25)

- For many years, Anna has waited for the fulfillment of God's promise to her that she wouldn't die before seeing the Messiah. When Mary and Joseph bring Jesus to the temple, she sees Jesus and instantly knows he is the Messiah. (Luke 2:36–38)

- Jesus used the widow who gave two mites (two copper coins worth little) as an example of commitment and giving because the widow gave all she had. (Mark 12:41–44)

- Rhoda is so excited about hearing Peter's voice at the locked gate that she forgets to open the door and let him in. When she tells the Christians praying for Peter's release that Peter stands at the gate, they don't believe her. She has to try to convince them that Peter is alive and there with them. (Acts 12:13–16)

Study Questions

1. How does Elizabeth know Mary is carrying the Messiah as her child, and how does God confirm it through Elizabeth's own unborn baby?

2. Who was Anna waiting to see? How long did she wait?

3. What did the widow give to the temple treasury, and what did Jesus think of her action?

4. Who did Mary find at the gate, and why didn't the Christians at Mary's house believe Rhoda?

Appendix A - Time Lines

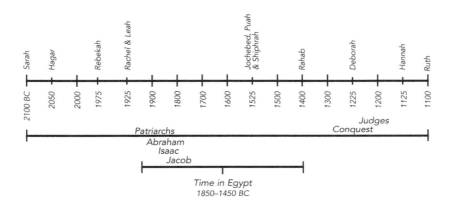

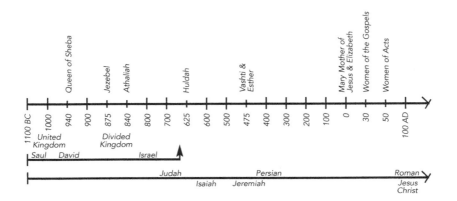

Appendix B - The Answers

CHAPTER 1

1. Adam could eat from any tree in the garden except from the Tree of the Knowledge of Good and Evil. If he did eat from the forbidden tree, he would die. (Genesis 2:16–17)

2. Adam named Eve. Eve means "living" and Adam was recognizing her ability to create a new life. He also called her "woman," in recognition of her similarity to him, "man." (Genesis 3:20)

3. The serpent questioned what God had said, giving Eve an opportunity to doubt God's directions and his goodness. (Genesis 3:1–5)

4. Eve saw that the fruit was good for food, attractive in appearance, and a source of wisdom. (Genesis 3:6)

5. Eve's consequences were pain in childbirth and a tendency to be ruled by her husband. For Adam, his job of taking care of the earth began to be painful toil and hard work. The serpent was now cursed and would crawl on its belly, eating dust. In time, the serpent, representing Satan, would be defeated totally. (Genesis 3:14–19)

CHAPTER 2

1. He tells them to leave their native country and after they move, God will bless them and their future heirs. (Genesis 12:1–3)

2. Abraham fears that if the pharaoh knows Sarah is Abram's wife, the pharaoh will kill Abraham in order to have Sarah for his wife. (Genesis 12:12)

3. Sarah has the idea, and Abraham cooperates with her plan to use Hagar as a surrogate mother. (Genesis 16:1–2)

4. God says, "Is anything too hard for the LORD?" (Genesis 18:14 NKJV)

5. Abraham is one hundred and Sarah is ninety. (Genesis 17:17)

CHAPTER 3

1. Eliezer prays that the woman God wants Isaac to marry will offer water to Eliezer and to his camels. Rebekah does exactly that, proving that she is God's choice of a wife for Isaac. (Genesis 24:12–27)

2. Isaac was out in the field meditating. (Genesis 24:63)

3. God determined that the younger would serve the older. (Genesis 25:23)

4. Rebekah made goat meat taste like venison, put Esau's clothes on Jacob, and covered his skin with goat's skin. (Genesis 27:14–17)

5. She never saw Jacob again after he fled for his life. (Genesis 28:2)

CHAPTER 4

1. The years seemed short, because he was working to gain Rachel, the woman he loved, as his wife. (Genesis 29:20)

2. A younger sister couldn't be given in marriage until the older sister had become married. (Genesis 29:26)

3. Leah hoped she could earn Jacob's love by producing children. (Genesis 29:28–35)

4. She gave her maid as a surrogate wife to Jacob. (Genesis 30:3)

5. Mandrakes are considered aphrodisiacs, and Rachel hoped the mandrakes would help her get pregnant. (Genesis 30:14–15)

CHAPTER 5

1. The angel Gabriel makes the announcement and calls her "highly favored." (Luke 1:26, 28)

2. If Elizabeth could become pregnant in her old age, Mary realizes that nothing is impossible with God, and this realization builds her trust. Therefore, God could do in Mary's life what he promised. (Luke 1:36–37)

3. Mary rehearses and remembers the many wonderful things that God has done through many generations. Remembering these things builds her faith as well as reveals her faith because she had learned those things from the Old Testament. (Luke 1:49–55)

4. They sacrifice a pair of doves instead of a lamb. (Luke 2:24)

5. Jesus lived a nomadic kind of life and he often didn't take time to eat. (Mark 3:20–21)

CHAPTER 6

1. The pharaoh wanted to prevent the Hebrew population from growing by killing their male babies, so to save her infant son, Jochebed put baby Moses into a basket in the river, where he'd be found by the pharaoh's daughter. (Exodus 1:15–2:10)

2. Rahab had heard of stories about God's mighty power from the people in her `surrounding area. (Joshua 2:10)

3. God had not yet allowed the Israelites to have kings. (Judges 17:6)

4. The Nazirites didn't drink alcoholic beverages, cut their hair, or touch dead bodies.

5. Elijah asks her to fix him a meal before she prepares one for herself and her son. (1 Kings 17:13)

6. Elisha tells her to get containers from her neighbors, and God fills oil in every one of them. (2 Kings 4:3)

7. She generously gives him food and a place to stay. (2 Kings 4:8–10)

CHAPTER 7

1. They want the queen removed, because they fear if she isn't deposed, other women will stop obeying their husbands. (Esther 1:22)

2. Esther found unusual favor with the person in charge of the women, Hegai. (Esther 2:9)

3. God brings Mordecai's action to the king's attention at just the opportune time to humiliate Haman. (Esther 6:12)

4. Esther says she will talk to the king if everyone fasts for her. She is willing to sacrifice her life to try to save the Jews. (Esther 4:16)

5. The word "purim" refers to the lot that was cast when Haman was seeking the best time to destroy the Jews. Since God used even the lot to further his plan, the Jews remember this "purim" with a festival. (Esther 9:26)

CHAPTER 8

1. The priests of Baal were her personal friends and usually ate dinner with her. (1 Kings 18:19)

2. Jezebel arranged for two men to lie and say that Naboth had cursed God. (1 Kings 21:13)

3. Ahab dies in battle, and dogs lick his blood. Jezebel is thrown out a window and dogs eat her body. (2 Kings 9:35)

4. She has her own grandsons murdered. (2 Kings 11:1)

5. God communicates his approval of marital sexual love. (Song of Solomon 1:2)

CHAPTER 9

1. The Proverbs 31 woman is loving, industrious, wise, generous, kind and ingenious. (Proverbs 31:10–27)

2. She is complimented for her fear of God. (Proverbs 31:30)

3. Abigail brought David food and humbled herself by taking responsibility and by reminding David of his great purpose. (1 Samuel 25:23–31)

4. Ruth was indicating that she believed in the God of Naomi, Jehovah. (Ruth 1:16–17)

5. He was to provide for a relative, who is widowed, by buying her land and by marrying her, so that the land stays in the family and the children carry the deceased man's name. (Ruth 3:13)

CHAPTER 10

1. God shows his love for Hagar, who is mistreated by Sarah and used as her surrogate mother for a child, by appearing to her and guiding her. (Genesis 16:4, 7; 21:17)

2. Dinah visited where she wasn't allowed to go, and she watched the pagan celebrations. (Genesis 34:1)

3. Judah was to give Tamar his third son in marriage, in accordance with the levirate law, but Judah refuses. (Genesis 38:12)

4. Bathsheba, a lone woman whose husband is away, probably has little choice but to go when King David summons her to his palace. He has sex with her, and she becomes pregnant by him. After trying unsuccessfully to get her husband home from war to dupe the husband into thinking the baby is his, David has her husband sent to the battle's frontline, where he is killed. Then David marries her. (2 Samuel 11:1–5)

5. After trying to fight off her stepbrother with both words and physical strength, Tamar tears her robe that once signified her virginity and puts ashes on her head. (2 Samuel 13:12–14)

CHAPTER 11

1. She had nothing she had to do, and her idleness made her restless and ready for any activity, including attempting to seduce Joseph. (Genesis 39:4)

2. She is furious. God is trying to kill her husband, Moses, since she and Moses have not yet circumcised their infant son. (Exodus 4:24)

3. Delilah wears Samson down by continually asking him the source of his strength and accusing him of not loving her. (Judges 16:10)

4. Michal saw David dancing in the street celebrating the Lord's victory, and for some reason, she is sickened by the sight and begins to hate David. (2 Samuel 6:20)

5. The Witch of Endor practiced necromancy, which is calling people back from the dead. (1 Samuel 28:13)

6. Hoses is commanded by God to marry Gomer, a prostitute who will be unfaithful throughout their marriage. God is using Gomer as a symbol of the unfaithfulness of the people of Israel. (Hosea 3:1)

CHAPTER 12

1. Jael gives him food, pretends to care about him, and offers protection. (Judges 4:17–22)

2. Rizpah protects their bodies from animals until King David agrees to bury them. (2 Samuel 21:7–14)

3. Mephibosheth's nurse rescued Mephibosheth from being murdered, but in whisking him away quickly, she dropped him and as a result, he is crippled for life. (2 Samuel 4:4)

4. The woman of Tekoah acted out an analogy of King David's relationship with his son Absalom. As a result, the king welcomed his son back to the palace and out of exile. (2 Samuel 14:1–20)

5. The woman of Abel asked why her city was under siege, and she finds out Sheba, an enemy, is hiding in the city. So the people of the city kill Sheba, and the city is saved. (2 Samuel 20:16–22)

6. She had heard about the wisdom of King Solomon, and she wanted to find out for herself. She discovered that not only was everything she'd heard about Solomon true, but his wisdom far surpassed what she had heard. (1 Kings 10:1–13)

7. The captive servant girl and the wife of Naaman show their true love for Naaman by risking his disfavor to tell him about Jehovah and how Jehovah God could heal his leprosy. As a result, Naaman sought out Jehovah's prophet, Elisha, and Naaman was healed. (2 Kings 5:1–4)

8. As a prophetess, Huldah heard from God. God told her that the Israelites were not following his command so destruction would follow. She courageously delivered the bad news, and as a result, the people repented. (2 Kings 22:14–20)

9. Vashti lost her position as queen by refusing to appear at her husband's party, because he is the king. We don't know why she refuses. Were her husband and his friends drunk and rowdy, so she feared for her purity? Or, didn't she want to leave her own banquet? What do you think? (Esther 1:9–22)

CHAPTER 13

1. Abraham asks God to intercede on the behalf of his nephew, Lot, and his family, so they are not killed when the city of Sodom is destroyed. Angels pull them away from the city, and all are saved but Lot's wife. (Genesis 19:16)

2. Fearing they'd never have children, the two daughters get their father drunk and each takes a night to seduce him. (Genesis 19:35)

3. Perhaps like the Israelites, Miriam was tired. In addition, Miriam was envious of Moses' leadership. (Numbers 12:2)

4. God caused her to have leprosy. (Numbers 12:10)

5. After all their losses, Job's wife tells her husband to curse God and die. Job trusts God; she does not. Besides, men and women often handle grief differently. (Job 2:9)

CHAPTER 14

1. She believed she would be healed if she could just touch the edge of Jesus' cloak. (Matthew 9:20)

2. She doesn't get Jesus' attention at first, because Jesus wanted to test her faith. (Matthew 15:21–28)

3. Unlike the others who make requests, this widow woman didn't even ask Jesus to raise her son from the dead, and yet he did out of sympathy for her plight. (Luke 7:11–16)

4. Jesus uses her wonderful devotion as an example of how a person, who is forgiven much, loves much. This forgiven woman shows her love for Jesus by anointing his feet with her tears and perfume. (Luke 7:36–50)

5. Jesus healed the woman on the Sabbath and working on the Sabbath, even to heal, broke the elaborate rules about keeping the Sabbath. The leaders of the temple were outraged and jealous of his power. But Jesus showed them that God didn't approve of their complex and enlarged version of God's laws. (Luke 13:10–17)

6. Jesus knew all about her life, things that only the Messiah could know. Overcome by faith, she left her water pot at the well and went to tell others about Jesus. (John 4:28)

7. He wrote in the dirt. We don't know what he wrote, but his words shamed the men and stopped the stoning. (John 8:6)

CHAPTER 15

1. Quiet and studious, Mary wanted to sit at his feet listening while Martha, a woman of action, wanted to serve Jesus by doing something, such as preparing a meal. (Luke 10:38–42)

2. Jesus delivers Mary Magdalene from seven demons, and she is transformed to a faithful and devoted follower. (Mark 16:9)

3. Salome wants the best for her children so she asked if her two sons could sit at Jesus' right and left while in the kingdom of heaven. (Matthew 20:20–23)

4. She was among the women to first learn of Jesus' resurrection. (Matthew 27:55–61)

5. Despite the fact that her husband works for King Herod, Joanna supports Jesus and speaks of him in Herod's home. (Luke 8:1–3)

CHAPTER 16

1. Kind and generous to everyone, Dorcas gives to others, particularly the poor. That's why her death is such a blow to the community. (Acts 10:36–42)

2. Timothy is fortunate to have the influence of his grandmother, Lois, and his mother, Eunice, both believers in Jesus. (Acts 16:1; 2 Timothy 1:5)

3. Lydia proves that rich people can come to know the Lord and serve him. (Acts 16:11–15)

4. This Mary hosts groups of Christians for meetings in her home. (Acts 12:12)

5. Phoebe carried Paul's epistle to the Christians in Rome, and by Paul's description of her, we can assume that Phoebe played a leadership role in the early church. (Acts 16:1–2)

6. Priscilla corrects him in private, not in front of his audience. (Acts 18:24–26)

7. Paul acknowledges their hard work for God. (Romans 16:12)

CHAPTER 17

1. Paul suggests that they agree to get along and that they ask someone to act as a mediator or counselor to help them resolve their conflict. (Philippians 4:2–3)

2. She tells him that, through a dream, she knows Jesus is innocent. (Matthew 27:19)

3. They are greedy or suddenly want some of the money for themselves, for they continue to lie about the amount of money received for the sale of property in order to keep some of the money. As a result, they are struck dead. (Acts 5:1–11)

4. She has her daughter dance sensually before Herodias' own husband, Herod, so that her daughter can ask for anything—even the head of John the Baptist. (Matthew 14:3–12)

CHAPTER 18

1. Elizabeth's baby leaps within her womb, in recognition of the Messiah Mary is carrying in her womb. (Luke 1:41)

2. For many years, Anna waits for the Messiah, because God promised her that she would see the Messiah before she dies. (Luke 2:36–38)

3. Jesus uses her as an example of generosity, because she gives all she has—two mites. (Mark 12:41–44)

4. She finds Peter at the gate, but the Christians praying don't believe her. They don't think God has answered their prayers, and they think what she sees is Peter's angel. (Acts 12:13–16)

Appendix C - The Experts

Arp, David and Claudia—Founders and directors of Marriage Alive International, popular speakers, and authors of many books.

Arthur, Kay—Well-known Bible teacher, best-selling author, and founder of Precept Ministries.

Briscoe, Jill—Popular international speaker and writer.

Carter, Jimmy—Former President of the United States and author of several books.

Chapian, Marie—Counselor, speaker, and coauthor of the bestseller *The All-New Free to Be Thin Lifestyle Plan.*

Chapman, Annie—Author and singer with husband, Steve Chapman.

Clairmont, Patsy—Author of many books and popular speaker.

Deen, Edith—Author, speaker, and former Women's Editor and daily columnist for the *Fort Worth Press.*

DeMoss, Nancy Leigh—host and teacher for *Revive Our Hearts* radio program and author of six books including *Lies Women Believe.*

Farrar, Steve—President of Point Man Leadership Ministries and author of several books including *Standing Tall: How A Man Can Protect His Family.*

Farrel, Bill and Pam—Counselors for couples since 1979, authors; Bill is a pastor and Pam is a speaker.

Fleming, Jean—Author, speaker, and a staff member with The Navigators serving in many different areas, both nationally and internationally.

Frank, Jan—Licensed marriage and family counselor and author of several books.

Freeman, Becky—Mother of four, popular speaker, and author of *Worms in My Tea and Other Mixed Blessings.*

George, Elizabeth—Popular teacher and speaker at Christian women's events and author of numerous books.

Heavilin, Marilyn Willett—Speaker and author on prayer, grief, family life, and spiritual growth.

Higgs, Liz Curtis—Award-winning speaker and best-selling author of over twenty books.

Hocking, Marion R.—Former teacher and missionary; now a freelance writer from Mesa, AZ.

Hybels, Bill—Senior pastor of Willow Creek Community Church and the author of many books including *Honest to God.*

Johnson, Barbara—Popular speaker and author of many best-selling books.

Johnson, Jan—Author of many books including *Healing Hurts that Sabotage the Soul,* speaker, mother, and wife of a pastor.

Karssen, Gien—The Navigators representative in Europe and author of several books including *Her Name Is Woman.*

Kent, Carol—Freelance writer and speaker, founder and director of "Speak Up with Confidence" seminars.

Kimbrough, Marjorie L.—Instructor in religion and philosophy at Clark Atlanta University and author of several books.

Littauer, Marita—President of CLASS (Christian Leaders, Authors, Speakers Services), author of many books, and international speaker.

Lockyer, Herbert—Author of the "All" series including *All the Women of the Bible.*

Lotz, Anne Graham—Daughter of Billy and Ruth Bell Graham, she is an international speaker and author of many books. She is also the founder of AnGeL Ministries.

Lucado, Max—Pastor, speaker, and author of numerous best-selling books.

Mayhall, Carole—Member of the The Navigators, missionary, author, and speaker with husband Jack.

Meyer, Joyce—Popular TV and radio teacher and best-selling author.

Moore, Beth—Teacher and writer of many best-selling Bible studies and popular women's coference speaker.

Nystrom, Carol—Author of more than fifty books and Bible study guides.

Ocknega, Harold John—Religious leader and educator, cofounder and first president of Fuller Theological Seminary, Pasadena, CA, and first president and one of the founders of the National Association of Evangelicals.

Omartian, Stormie—Best-selling author and popular women's conference speaker.

Owens, Virginia Stem—Director of The Milton Center at Kansas Newman College in Wichita, KS, and author of several books, including *Point Blank*.

Packer, J. I.—Professor of Systamatic and Historical Theology at Regent College in Vancouver, British Columbia, and autor of many best-selling books including *Knowing God* and *Keep in Step with the Spirit*.

Peale, Ruth—Author, director of the Norman Vincent Peale Foundation, and wife of the late Norman Vincent Peale.

Price, Eugenia—Internationally known speaker and author of many books, including *God Speaks to Women Today*.

Rhode, Naomi—Author of two books and past president of the National Speakers Association.

Rhodes, Tricia McCary—Speaker, writer, and worship coordinator for New Hope Church in San Diego, CA.

Rose, Shirley—Emmy-nominated TV host of *Aspiring Women*, which is syndicated in 100 cities in the U.S. and several foreign countries.

Sherrer, Quin—International speaker and award-winning author whose best-selling books include *A Woman's Guide to Spiritual Warfare* and *How to Pray for Your Children*.

Smalley, Gary, and John Trent—Popular speakers, authors, and coauthors of *The Blessing* and *The Language of Love*.

Stanley Charles—Senior pastor of the 12,000-member First Baptist Church of Atlanta and prolific author.

Taylor, William M.—Preacher at Broadway Tabernacle in New York City in the late 1890s and author of the series Bible Biographies.

Teal, Ricki—Homemaker, freelance writer, wife, mother, and grandmother with two grown daughters and four grandsons.

TerKeurst, Lysa—President of Proverbs 31 Ministries and author and speaker.

Vander Velde, Frances—Mother of eight, wife, and author of *Women of the Bible*.

Warren, Rick—Founding pastor of Saddleback Church, Lake Forest, CA, and popular best-selling author.

Endnotes

Chapter 1

1. Steve Farrar, *Point Man* (Sisters, OR: Multnomah Press, 1990), 122..

2. Jill Briscoe, *Running on Empty* (Wheaton, IL: Harold Shaw, 1988), 46.

3. Naomi Rhode, *The Gift of Family* (Nashville, TN: Thomas Nelson, 1991), 73.

4. David and Claudia Arp, *Marriage Moments* (Ann Arbor, MI: Vine Books, 1998), 19.

5. Bill Hybels, *Tender Love* (Chicago, IL: Moody Press, 1993), 15.

6. Warren, *The Purpose-Driven Life*, 206.

7. Jill Briscoe, *How to Fail Successfully* (Old Tappen, NJ: Revell, 1982), 27–28.

8. Beth Moore, *When Godly People Do Ungodly Things* (Nashville, TN: Broadman & Holman, 2002), 11.

9. John F. Walvoord and Roy B. Zuck, *Bible Knowledge Commentary, Old Testament* (Wheaton, IL: Victor Books, 1985, rep. 1987), 27.

10. Kay Arthur, *Lord, Heal My Hurts* (Sisters, OR: Multnomah, 1988), 24.

11. Ibid., 25.

12. Elizabeth George, *A Wife After God's Own Heart* (Eugene, OR: Harvest House, 2004), 64.

13. Jan Johnson, *Listening to God* (Colorado Springs, CO: NavPress, 1998), 14.

14. Harold Ocknega, *Women Who Made Bible History* (Grand Rapids, MI: Zondervan, 1979), 17.

15. Patsy Clairmont, *Normal Is Just a Setting on Your Dryer* (San Dimas, CA: Focus on the Family, 1993), 52.

16. Barbara Johnson, *Splashes of Joy in the Cesspools of Life* (Waco, TX: Word, 1992), 181–82.

17. Eugenia Price, *God Speaks to Women Today* (Grand Rapids, MI: Zondervan, 1964), 12.

18. Johnson, *Splashes of Joy in the Cesspools of Life*, 194.

19. George, *A Wife After God's Own Heart*, 29.

20. Marjorie L. Kimbrough, *She Is Worthy* (Nashville, TN: Abingdon Press, 1994), 12.

21. Briscoe, *How to Fail Successfully*, Introduction.

Chapter 2

1. Stormie Omartian, *The Power of a Praying Woman* (Eugene, OR: Harvest House, 2002), 90.

2. Edith Deen, *All the Women of the Bible* (New York, NY: HarperCollins, 1983), 11.

3. Omartian, *The Power of a Praying Woman*, 137.

4. Patsy Clairmont, *It's About Home* (Ann Arbor, MI: Servant/Vine, 1998), 76.

5. Rick Warren, *The Purpose-Driven Life* (Grand Rapids, MI: Zondervan, 2002), 194.

6. Anne Graham Lotz, *Just Give Me Jesus* (Nashville, TN: W Publishing Group, 2000), 205.

7. Marie Chapian, *A Confident, Dynamic You* (Ann Arbor, MI: Servant/Vine, 1997), 31.

8. Ibid., 32.

9. Lotz, *Just Give Me Jesus*, 200.

10. Max Lucado, *He Still Moves Stones* (Waco, TX: Word, 1993), 52.

11. Barbara Johnson, *Mama, Get the Hammer! There's a Fly on Papa's Head!* (Waco, TX: Word, 1994), 76.

12. Carol Kent, *When I Lay My Isaac Down* (Colorado Springs, CO: NavPress, 2004), 41.

13. Lysa TerKeurst, *Radically Obedient, Radically Blessed* (Eugene, OR: Harvest House, 2003), 37.

Chapter 3

1. Jimmy Carter, *LA Times*, Oct. 25, 1998.
2. Rick Warren, *The Purpose-Driven Life* (Grand Rapids, MI: Zondervan, 2002), 206.
3. Jill Briscoe, *Running on Empty* (Wheaton, IL: Harold Shaw, 1988), 19.
4. Patsy Clairmont, *It's About Home* (Ann Arbor, MI: Servant/Vine, 1998), 31.
5. Gary Smalley and John Trent, *The Blessing* (New York, NY: Simon and Schuster, 1990), 22.
6. Marie Chapian, *A Confident, Dynamic You* (Ann Arbor, MI: Servant/Vine, 1997), 38.
7. Cynthia Heald, *Becoming a Woman of Prayer* (Colorado Springs, CO: NavPress, 1999), 28.
8. Jan Johnson, *Enjoying the Presence of God* (Colorado Springs, CO: NavPress, 1996), 79.
9. Heald, *Becoming a Woman of Prayer*, 12.
10. Naomi Rhode, *The Gift of Family* (Nashville, TN: Thomas Nelson, 1991), 21.
11. Beth Moore, *A Heart Like His* (Nashville, TN: LifeWay Press, 1996), 209.
12. Rhode, *The Gift of Family*, 30.
13. Beth Moore, *A Woman's Heart—God's Dwelling Place* (Nashville, TN: LifeWay Press, 1995), 97.
14. Edith Deen, *All the Women of the Bible* (New York, NY: HarperCollins, 1983), 26.
15. Frances Vander Velde, *Women of the Bible* (Grand Rapids, MI: Kregel, 1957, 1985), 51.

Chapter 4

1. Beth Moore, *A Heart Like His* (Nashville, TN: LifeWay Press, 1996), 208.
2. Patsy Clairmont, *It's About Home* (Ann Arbor, MI: Servant/Vine, 1998), 22.
3. Shirley Rose, *A Wise Woman Once Said. . . .* (Gainesville, FL: Bridge-Logos, 2002), 79.
4. Cynthia Heald: *Becoming a Woman of Prayer* (Colorado Springs, CO: NavPress, 1999), 46.
5. Jill Briscoe, *Running on Empty* (Wheaton, IL: Harold Shaw, 1988), 29.
6. Stormie Omartian, *The Power of a Praying Woman* (Eugene, OR: Harvest House, 2002), 118.
7. Carol Kent, *Secret Longings of the Heart* (Colorado Springs, CO: NavPress: 2003), 187.
8. Max Lucado, *On the Anvil* (Carol Stream, IL: Tyndale House, 1994), 85.
9. Clairmont, *It's About Home*, 14.
10. Barbara Johnson, *Mama, Get the Hammer! There's a Fly on Papa's Head!* (Waco, TX: Word, 1994), 34.

11. Jan Frank, *A Graceful Waiting* (Ann Arbor, MI: Servant/Vine, 1996), 70.
12. Briscoe, *Running on Empty*, 35.
13. Naomi Rhode, *The Gift of Family* (Nashville, TN: Thomas Nelson, 1991), 12.
14. Kay Arthur, *Lord, I Want to Know You* (New York, NY: Random House, 2000), 25.
15. Moore, *A Heart Like His*, 102.

Chapter 5

1. Harold Ocknega, *Women Who Made Bible History* (Grand Rapids, MI: Zondervan, 1979), 172–73.
2. Max Lucado, *When God Whispers Your Name* (Waco, TX: Word, 1994), 58–59.
3. Beth Moore, *When Godly People Do Ungodly Things* (Nashville, TN: Broadman & Holman, 2002), 34.
4. Virginia Stem Owens, *Daughters of Eve* (Colorado Springs, CO: NavPress, 1995), 27.
5. Eugenia Price, *God Speaks to Women Today* (Grand Rapids, MI: Zondervan, 1964), 115.
6. Lockyer, *All the Women of the Bible*, 94.
7. Ocknega, *Women Who Made Bible History*, 174.
8. Pam Farrel, *A Woman God Can Use* (Eugene, OR: Harvest House, 1999), 133.
9. Shirley Rose, *A Wise Woman Once Said...* (Gainesville, FL: Bridge-Logos, 2002), 84.
10. Cynthia Heald, *Becoming a Woman of Prayer* (Colorado Springs, CO: NavPress, 1999), 66.
11. Omartian, *The Power of a Praying Woman*, 104.
12. Owens, *Daughters of Eve*, 29.
13. Ocknega, *Women Who Made Bible History*, 176.
14. Beth Moore, *A Heart Like His* (Nashville, TN: LifeWay Press, 1996), 207.
15. Carol Kent, *When I Lay My Isaac Down* (Colorado Springs, CO: NavPress, 2004), 109.
16. Joyce Meyer, *Be Anxious for Nothing* (Tulsa, OK: Harrison House, 1998), 57.
17. Max Lucado, *He Still Moves Stones* (Waco, TX: Word, 1993), 150–51.
18. Ocknega, *Women Who Made Bible History*, 72.
19. Farrar, *Point Man*, 138.
20. Frances Vander Velde, *Women of the Bible* (Grand Rapids, MI: Kregel, 1957, 1985), 141.
21. Price, *God Speaks to Women Today*, 129.
22. Vander Velde, *Women of the Bible*, 144.
23. Lucado, *He Still Moves Stones*, 147, 150.
24. Lucado, *He Still Moves Stones*, 43.

25. Owens, *Daughters of Eve*, 33.

26. Vander Velde, *Women of the Bible*, 146.

Chapter 6

1. Marjorie L. Kimbrough, *She Is Worthy* (Nashville, TN: Abingdon Press, 1994), 24.

2. J. I. Packer and Carolyn Nystrom, *Never Beyond Hope* (Downers Grove, IL: IVP, 2000), 76–77.

3. Kimbrough, *She Is Worthy*, 30.

4. Ibid., 34.

5. Naomi Rhode, *The Gift of Family* (Nashville, TN: Thomas Nelson, 1991), 39.

6. Kimbrough, *She Is Worthy*, 43.

7. Jan Johnson, *Enjoying the Presence of God* (Colorado Springs, CO: NavPress, 1996), 59–60.

8. Jill Briscoe, *Running on Empty* (Wheaton, IL: Harold Shaw, 1988), 65.

9. Barbara Johnson, *Mama, Get the Hammer! There's a Fly on Papa's Head!* (Waco, TX: Word, 1994), 46.

10. Marilyn Willett Heavilin, *I'm Listening, Lord* (Nashville, TN: Thomas Nelson, 1993), 26.

11. Max Lucado, *On the Anvil* (Carol Stream, IL: Tyndale House, 1994), 52.

Chapter 7

1. Shirley Rose, *A Wise Woman Once Said...* (Gainesville, FL: Bridge-Logos, 2002), 42.

2. Bill & Pam Farrel, *Marriage in the Whirlwind* (Downers Grove, IL: IVP, 1996), 25.

3. Kay Arthur, *Lord, I Want to Know You* (New York, NY: Random House, 2000), 35.

4. Marilyn Willett Heavilin, *I'm Listening, Lord* (Nashville, TN: Thomas Nelson, 1993), 87.

5. Carol Kent, *Secret Longings of the Heart* (Colorado Springs, CO: NavPress: 2003), 173.

6. Eugenia Price, *God Speaks to Women Today* (Grand Rapids, MI: Zondervan, 1964), 107.

7. Heavilin, *I'm Listening, Lord*, 130.

8. Virginia Stem Owens, *Daughters of Eve* (Colorado Springs, CO: NavPress, 1995), 177.

9. Patsy Clairmont, *It's About Home* (Ann Arbor, MI: Servant/Vine, 1998), 22.

10. Arthur, *Lord, I Want to Know You*, 157.

11. Heavilin, *I'm Listening, Lord*, 11.

12. Jan Johnson, *Enjoying the Presence of God* (Colorado Springs, CO: NavPress, 1996), 92.

Chapter 8

1. Herbert Lockyer, *All the Women of the Bible* (Grand Rapids, MI: Zondervan, no date listed), 74.

2. Virginia Stem Owens, *Daughters of Eve* (Colorado Springs, CO: NavPress, 1995), 181–82.

3. Jill Briscoe, *Running on Empty* (Wheaton, IL: Harold Shaw, 1988), 14.

4. Joyce Meyer, *Starting Your Day Right* (New York: Warner Faith, 2003), 40.

5. Max Lucado, *On the Anvil* (Carol Stream, IL: Tyndale House, 1994), 98.

6. Ibid., 69.

7. Barbara Johnson, *Mama, Get the Hammer! There's a Fly on Papa's Head!* (Waco, TX: Word, 1994), 66.

8. Higgs, *Bad Girls of the Bible*, 86.

9. Lockyer, *All the Women of the Bible*, 33.

10. Ibid., 33.

11. Elizabeth George, *A Wife After God's Own Heart* (Eugene OR: Harvest House, 2004), 69.

Chapter 9

1. Gien Karssen, *The Best of All* (Colorado Springs, CO: NavPress, 1982), 15.

2. Liz Curtis Higgs, *Only Angels Can Wing It* (Nashville, TN: Thomas Nelson, 1995), 17.

3. Ruth Peale, *The Adventure of Being a Wife* (New York, NY: Prentice-Hall, 1971), 27.

4. Carole and Jack Mayhall, *Marriage Takes More Than Love* (Colorado Springs, CO: NavPress, 1978), 73.

5. Barbara Johnson, *Mama, Get the Hammer! There's a Fly on Papa's Head!* (Waco, TX: Word, 1994), 11.

6. Higgs, *Only Angels Can Wing It*, 62.

7. Jan Johnson, *Enjoying the Presence of God* (Colorado Springs, CO: NavPress, 1996), 23.

8. Higgs, *Only Angels Can Wing It*, 78.

9. Tricia McCary Rhodes, *The Soul at Rest* (Minneapolis, MN: Bethany House Publishers, 1996), 102.

10. Elizabeth George, *Beautiful in God's Eyes* (Eugene, OR: Harvest House, 1998), 105.

11. David and Claudia Arp, *Marriage Moments* (Ann Arbor, MI: Vine Books, 1998), 42.

12. Higgs, *Only Angels Can Wing It*, 127.

13. Karssen, *The Best of All*, 67.

14. George, *Beautiful in God's Eyes*, 165.

15. Higgs, *Only Angels Can Wing It*, 163.

16. Johnson, *Mama, Get the Hammer! There's a Fly on Papa's Head!*, 11–12.

17. Max Lucado, *He Still Moves Stones* (Waco, TX: Word, 1993), 59.

18. George, *A Wife After God's Own Heart*, 48.

19. Higgs, *Only Angels Can Wing It*, 186.

20. Jean Fleming, *A Mother's Heart* (Colorado Springs, CO: Nav Press, 1982), 27.

21. George, *Beautiful in God's Eyes*, 243.

22. Marjorie L. Kimbrough, *She Is Worthy* (Nashville, TN: Abingdon Press, 1994), 47.

23. Jill Briscoe, *Running on Empty* (Wheaton, IL: Harold Shaw, 1988), 143.

24. Farrar, *Point Man*, 145.

25. Jan Frank, *A Graceful Waiting* (Ann Arbor, MI: Servant/Vine, 1996), 28.

26. Briscoe, *Running on Empty*, 148.

27. Shirley Rose, *A Wise Woman Once Said . . .* Gainesville, FL: Bridge-Logos, 2002), 116.

Chapter 10

1. Barbara Johnson, *Mama, Get the Hammer! There's a Fly on Papa's Head!* (Waco, TX: Word, 1994), 70.

2. Jan Frank, *A Graceful Waiting* (Ann Arbor, MI: Servant/Vine, 1996), 30.

3. Herbert Lockyer, *All the Women of the Bible* (Grand Rapids, MI: Zondervan, no date listed), 64.

4. Frances Vander Velde, *Women of the Bible* (Grand Rapids, MI: Kregel, 1957, 1985), 66.

5. Carol Kent, *Secret Longings of the Heart* (Colorado Springs, CO: NavPress: 2003), 85.

6. Anne Graham Lotz, *Just Give Me Jesus* (Nashville, TN: W Publishing Group, 2000), 205.

7. Marie Chapian, *A Confident, Dynamic You* (Ann Arbor, MI: Servant/Vine, 1997), 10.

8. Beth Moore, *A Heart Like His* (Nashville, TN: LifeWay Press, 1996), 132.

9. Beth Moore, *A Woman's Heart—God's Dwelling Place* (Nashville, TN: LifeWay Press, 1995), 204.

10. Virginia Stem Owens, *Daughters of Eve* (Colorado Springs, CO: NavPress, 1995), 114.

Chapter 11

1. Harold Ocknega, *Women Who Made Bible History* (Grand Rapids, MI: Zondervan, 1979), 72.

2. David and Claudia Arp, *Marriage Moments* (Ann Arbor, MI: Vine Books, 1998), 38.

3. Liz Curtis Higgs, *Really Bad Girls of the Bible* (Colorado Springs, CO: WaterBrook Press, 2000), 36.

4. Tricia McCary Rhodes, *The Soul at Rest* (Minneapolis, MN: Bethany House Publishers, 1996), 65.

Chapter 12

1. Liz Curtis Higgs, *Really Bad Girls of the Bible* (Colorado Springs, CO: WaterBrook Press, 2000), 64.

2. Herbert Lockyer, *All the Women of the Bible* (Grand Rapids, MI: Zondervan, no date listed), 71.

3. Virginia Stem Owens, *Daughters of Eve* (Colorado Springs, CO: NavPress, 1995).

4. Carol Kent, *Secret Languages of the Heart* Colorado Springs, CO: NavPress, 2003), 176.

5. Meyer, *Starting Your Day Right*, 3.

6. Max Lucado, *On the Anvil* (Carol Stream, IL: Tyndale House, 1994), 120.

7. Lockyer, *All the Women of the Bible*, 199.

8. Beth Moore, *A Heart Like His* (Nashville, TN: LifeWay Press, 1996), 186.

9. Frances Vander Velde, *Women of the Bible* (Grand Rapids, MI: Kregel, 1957, 1985), 126.

Chapter 13

1. Liz Curtis Higgs, *Bad Girls of the Bible* (Colorado Springs, CO: WaterBrook Press, 1999), 78–79.

2. Jill Briscoe, *Running on Empty* (Wheaton, IL: Harold Shaw, 1988), 22.

3. Carol Kent, *Secret Longings of the Heart* (Colorado Springs, CO: NavPress: 2003), 85.

Chapter 14

1. Jan Johnson, *Listening to God* (Colorado Springs, CO: NavPress, 1998), 88.

2. Marie Chapian, *A Confident, Dynamic You* (Ann Arbor, MI: Servant/Vine, 1997), 32.

3. Carol Kent, *When I Lay My Isaac Down* (Colorado Springs, CO: NavPress, 2004), 40.

4. Tricia McCary Rhodes, *The Soul at Rest* (Minneapolis, MN: Bethany House Publishers, 1996), 64.

5. Liz Curtis Higgs, *Bad Girls of the Bible* (Colorado Springs, CO: WaterBrook Press, 1999), 235.

6. Barbara Johnson, *Mama, Get the Hammer! There's a Fly on Papa's Head!* (Waco, TX: Word, 1994), 106.

7. Patsy Clairmont, *It's About Home* (Ann Arbor, MI: Servant/Vine, 1998), 46.

Chapter 15

1. Anne Graham Lotz, *Just Give Me Jesus* (Nashville, TN: W Publishing Group, 2000), 202.

2. Patsy Clairmont, *It's About Home* (Ann Arbor, MI: Servant/Vine, 1998), 30.

3. Joyce Meyer, *Be Anxious for Nothing* (Tulsa, OK: Harrison House, 1998), 30.

4. Lotz, *Just Give Me Jesus*, 203–4.

5. Frances Vander Velde, *Women of the Bible* (Grand Rapids, MI: Kregel, 1957, 1985), 170.

6. Carol Kent, *Secret Longings of the Heart* (Colorado Springs, CO: NavPress: 2003), 84.

7. Virginia Stem Owens, *Daughters of Eve* (Colorado Springs, CO: NavPress, 1995), 102.

8. Lotz, *Just Give Me Jesus*, 216.

9. Barbara Johnson, *Mama, Get the Hammer! There's a Fly on Papa's Head!* (Waco, TX: Word, 1994), 36.

10. Lotz, *Just Give Me Jesus*, 224.

11. Owens, *Daughters of Eve*, 104.

12. Shirley Rose, *A Wise Woman Once Said . . .* (Gainesville, FL: Bridge-Logos, 2002), 188.

13. Vander Velde, *Women of the Bible*, 179.

14. Max Lucado, *On the Anvil* (Carol Stream, IL: Tyndale House, 1994), 104.

15. Jan Johnson, *Listening to God* (Colorado Springs, CO: NavPress, 1998), 68.

16. Lockyer, *All the Women of the Bible*.

Chapter 16

1. Frances Vander Velde, *Women of the Bible* (Grand Rapids, MI: Kregel, 1957, 1985), 229.

2. Jan Johnson, *Listening to God* (Colorado Springs, CO: NavPress, 1998), 168.

3. Naomi Rhode, *The Gift of Family* (Nashville, TN: Thomas Nelson, 1991), 43.

4. Vander Velde, *Women of the Bible*, 24.

5. Eugenia Price, *God Speaks to Women Today* (Grand Rapids, MI: Zondervan, 1964), 185.

Chapter 17

1. Charles Stanley, *A Touch of His Freedom* (Grand Rapids, MI: Zondervan Publishing House, 1991), 51.

2. Carole and Jack Mayhall, *Marriage Takes More Than Love* (Colorado Springs, CO: NavPress, 1978).

3. Nancy Leigh DeMoss, *Holiness: The Heart God Purifies* (Chicago: Moody, 2004), 103.

4. Beth Moore, *When Godly People Do Ungodly Things* (Nashville, TN: Broadman & Holman, 2002), 12.

5. Frances Vander Velde, *Women of the Bible* (Grand Rapids, MI: Kregel, 1957, 1985), 188.

Chapter 18

1. Tricia McCary Rhodes, *The Soul at Rest* (Minneapolis, MN: Bethany House Publishers, 1996), 53.

2. Carol Kent, *Secret Longings of the Heart* (Colorado Springs, CO: NavPress: 2003), 101.

3. Patsy Clairmont, *It's About Home* (Ann Arbor, MI: Servant/Vine, 1998), 87.

4. Joyce Meyer, *Be Anxious for Nothing* (Tulsa, OK: Harrison House, 1998), 28.

Index

favoritism, 59, 61, 65, 295
fellowship, 100, 115
fermented, 130
fertility deities, 164
fervent, 132
fig leaves, 15, 23
Fleming, Jean, 195
flesh
    definition, 213
forbidden fruit, 14, 20, 22
forgiveness
    between Adam and Eve, 17
    condition for, 17
    definition, 16
Frank, Jan
    on contentment, 78
    on questioning, 212
    on winnowing process, 201
free will, 148
freedom
    between spouses, 185
    in Garden of Eden, 6, 10
fulfillment
    of God's promises, 41
    through relationships, 7
    in work, 186

G

Gabriel
    describes Mary's son in five
        significant ways, 92, 93
    "strength of God" or "man or
        hero of God," 87
Gad, 80
Galilee, 87, 88, 286
Garden of Eden
    illustration of, 4
    leaving, 24
Gehazi, 136
gender difference, 129
genealogies, 89
generosity, 133, 260
Gentiles, 258
George, Elizabeth
    on curse upon the soil, 22
    on girding of a gown, 186
    on intimacy, 15
    on Proverbs 31 woman, 196
    on sex, 177
    on your husband being your
        contribution to society, 191
    on your speech, 193
Gibeonites, 238
giving of a sandal
    illustration of, 206
gleaning
    illustration of, 203

glory, 41
God
    appreciation from, 195
    belief in, 31–32
    and creation, 3–4, 6
    dependence on, 83, 153
    discipline by, 74
    expectations of us by, 94, 195
    glory of, 107, 167
    human relationship with, 7
    nature of, 6
    obedience to, 11, 35
    as omniscient, 16
    personal relationship with, 100,
        136
    quiet time with, 184–85
    sovereignty of, 61
    theophanies of, 30
    trust in, 39, 91
    unconditional love from, 59,
        156
    as valuing women, 180
Godness, 13
God's ways are not man's ways, 58
go'el, 203
goelim, 203
Gomer, 234
Good Samaritan, 263
gossip, 78, 104, 181
grace
    in Mary, 90
    salvation by, 20
grace and mercy, 17
gratitude, 194, 260, 281
great nation, 30
grief
    of Abram and Sarai, 211
    handling, 253
    Jewish way of expressing, 171
    of Mary and Martha, 272
    of Naomi, 179, 198
growth
    process of, 278
guilt
    of Adam and Eve, 16
    from anger, 227
    definition, 17
    effect of, 17

H

hackneyed, 184
Hadassah, 144
Hagar
    apostle Paul's analogy of, 213
    God's promise to, 35
    surrogate mother for Sarai, 209
    theophany with, 35, 210

Haman, 147, 148, 149
handiwork, 182
Hannah, 131
happiness
    source of, 84, 182
Haran
    definition, 28
Harbonah, 156
harlotry, 233
harmony
    achieving, 77, 300
Heald, Cynthia
    on abiding, 54
    on deepened intimacy with the
        Lord, 72
    on intercession, 99
    on intimacy with God, 56, 57
heathen, 60, 65, 216
Heavilin, Marilyn Willett
    on creative ability, 135
    on prayer, 150
    on sticking with God, 159
    on waiting on the Lord, 153
Hebrew(s)
    as Egyptian slaves, 125
    male babies to be killed, 125
Hebrew alphabet, 180
Hebrew language, 202
Hebron, 43
Hegai, 144, 145
help
    seeking, 112
Herod, 64, 112–14
Herod Antipas, 302
Herod Philip, 302
Herodias, 302
Herodotus, 148
Higgs, Liz Curtis
    on burnout, 189
    on family, 195
    on kind of woman most of
        us long to be, 192
    on leadership, 172, 237
    on listening in silence and
        worshiping, 261
    on Lot's wife, 250
    on Proverbs 31 woman, 180,
        183, 184
holidays, 160
holy kiss, 69
Holy Spirit
    control by, 214
    patience from, 228
    role in Mary's pregnancy, 72,
        89, 95
honesty, 65, 221
Hosea, 233
house of Jacob

definition, 93
Huldah, 244
humanity,
    of Jesus, 277
humility, 91, 171, 186–87, 201
humor
    importance of, 192
husbands
        God's directions to, 20–21
Hybels, Bill, 9

I

idleness
    and temptation, 13
idyllic, 24
illness, 173, 249
immortalized, 237
immutable, 158
implication, 102, 223
impregnated, 250
inappropriate, 69
incredulous, 284
India, 138
industrious, 47
infantile, 184
infertility, 56, 131
infidelity, 104
inherited, 127, 167
innocence
    and good of Adam and Eve, 10
    loss of, 224
    of Tamar, 224
insignificance
    and God's glory, 88, 155
intercede
    definition, 300
intercessory, 249
interpretation, 11
introverted, 267
Iraq
    as Garden of Eden location, 4
irreversible, 157
Isaac
    and Abrahamic Blessing, 30
    God's promises to, 60
Ishmael
    casting out of, 42
Islam, 31, 211
Israel, 43, 84, 125, 127
Israelite Village
    illustration of, 134
Israelites, 214
    conquering of Jericho, 127
    fasting of, 151
    wandering of, 251
Issachar, 82

J

Jabin, 128
Jacob
    and Abrahamic blessing, 30
    betrothal of, 71
    birth of, 57
    birthright of, 58
    encounter with God, 67
    naming of, 57
Jacob's Journey to Haran
    illustration of, 68
Jael, 237
James (the older), 286–87
James (the younger), 287
jealousy, 59, 78, 250–51, 280
Jehoiachin, 145
Jehoiada, 175
Jehoram, 172
Jehosheba, 175
Jehovah
    definition, 92
    destiny and purpose are
        determined by God, 92
Jehu, 171
Jeremiah, 145
Jericho, 127
Jerusalem, 110, 112, 114, 115
Jeshua, 92
Jesus Christ
    as Angel of the Lord, 16
    birth of, 107
    brothers of, 118
    circumcision of, 111
    crucifixion of, 283
    devotion to, 281, 282
    fasting by, 150–51
    final hours of, 283
    followers of, 121
    genealogies for, 89
    healing by, 258, 287
    with Mary and Martha, 267–88
    meaning of name, 92, 276
    ministry of, 87, 88, 107
    miracles by, 87, 279
    presentation at Temple, 109
    as redeemer, 112
    relationship with Mary, 116
    resurrection of, 272, 278
    seven "I AM" revelations, 275
    as son of God, 281
    temptation of, 11
    trial of, 300
    weeping by, 276
Jewish day
    start of, 184
Jews
    edicts against, 157

in Jerusalem, 141
    kings of, 93
    and Mordecai's edict, 157
    Orthodox, 1999
    saved by Esther, 139
    war with Edomites, 57
Jezebel
    punishment of, 169
Jezreel, 167
Joab, 221
Joanna, 287
Joash, 175
Job
    wife of, 252
Jochebed, 125
John the Baptist, 94, 100, 290
    beheading of, 302, 303
    birth of, 103
Johnson, Barbara
    on attitude, 263
    on blame, 18
    on God's forgiveness, 211
    on grace, 20
    on hope, 40
    on laughter, 183, 192
    on our reaction to
        disappointments, 77–78
    on relinquishing our failures to
        God, 171
    on suffering, 133
    on winning and losing, 278
Johnson, Jan
    on breath prayer, 184
    on God creating us out of
        love, 16
    on Hannah's prayer, 132
    on huge step of submission,
        286
    on journaling, 160
    on Second Coming, 55
    on Timothy, 292
    on touching Jesus' cloak, 258
Jonathan, 239
Joram, 172–74
Jordan River, 127
Joseph, 55, 82
    ancestral line of, 104
    flight to Egypt, 113
    journey to Bethlehem, 104
    visitation by angel, 103
Joseph (Potiphar's slave), 227
Joshua, 127
journaling, 160
joy, 77
Judah
    tribe of, 89
Judas, 282
Judea, 87, 272, 302

judges, 128
justice, 65, 157, 172

K

Karssen, Gien
  on the Proverbs 31
    woman, 180, 190
Kent, Carol
  on "being all we can be," 239
  on Esther, 150
  on fairness, 252
  on following God's instructions,
    43
  on groaning world, 217
  on having an eternal purpose,
    105
  on our God's changelessness,
    307
  on struggle, 274
  on trusting God with the
    impossible, 259
  on ungodly responses, 75
Keturah, 55
Kimbrough, Marjorie
  on Abigail, 197
  on Deborah, 128
  on Eve, 23
  on God speaking to women as
    well as to men, 130
  on Hannah, 132
  on Jochebed and Moses, 126
King Ahasuerus's Palace
  illustration of, 142
King Darius, 139
King David, 93, 104, 105, 222–23
King Solomon, 164, 242
King Xerxes, 139, 144, 151
Kish, 145
kisses in the Bible, 67
kissing, 69

L

Laban
  God uses to refine Jacob's
    character, 75
  Jacob will be tricked and cheated
    by, 70
lack of purpose, 228
Lake of Gennesareth, 88
lamentations, 180
land laws, 167
laughter
  as stress reliever, 182–83
law
  definition, 104
Lazarus

death of, 273
raising of, 273
Leah
  children of, 77
  competition with Rachel, 77
  faith of, 76
  marriage to Jacob, 73
Lemuel, 179
leprosy, 250–51
lepton
  illustration of, 309
Levi, 74, 216
levirate
  definition, 199
life style
  destructive, 197
listening
  to God, 12
  to Jesus, 268–69
  to Proverbs woman, 189
  to spouse, 181
Living Bible, 183
Lockyer, Herbert
  on Ahab, 164
  on all's fair in time of war, 238
  on Athaliah, 173
  on God's purposes, 175
  on grace, 214
  on Lord's two natures within
    Mary's being, 96
  on Mary (mother of Joseph
    and James), 287
  on wisdom, 242
Lois, 292–93
Lord
  meaning of, 98
Lot
  family of, 249
  wife of, 249
lots
  casting of, 147
  definition, 148
Lotz, Anne Graham
  on blaming a formerly dead
    person, 279
  on focusing on Him alone, 218
  on God weeping with us, 277
  on Mary (Martha's sister), 268
  on realizing we are totally
    helpless without Him, 271
  on suffering, 39
  on unanswered prayers, 37
love
  of another, 176, 180
  for God, of Adam and Eve, 2
  of mother for children, 62
  as motivation, 12
  power expressed by, 162

love apple, 81
Lucado, Max
  on asking of God, 286
  on communication, 241
  on faithful, 40
  on Gabriel and Mary, 90
  on God's will, 300
  on physical family and the
    spiritual family, 118
  on relationships, 170
  on Satan, 169
  on talking to God, 106
  on us . . . we are not thump-
    proof, 136
  on what bothers us, bothers
    Him, 117
  on what you believe, 75
  on worry, 192
luscious, 13
Lydia, 190, 293
lying, 126, 302
Lystra, 292

M

Macedonia, 293
Machpelah, cave at, 43, 55, 84
Magi, 113
Magnificat, 100
magnify, 11, 100
Mahlon, 198
Man
  creation of, 3
  need for significance, 20
man gathering wheat into sheaves
  illustration of, 203
man using sickle
  illustration of, 203
mandrake
  definition, 81
  illustration of, 80
manger
  illustration of, 108
manipulation
  by Rachel, 81
  by Rebekah, 45, 64, 65
  by Sarah, 79
Manoah, 130
Mara, 90, 200
marriage
  of Abigail and David, 197
  abuse in, 22
  of Athaliah and Jehoram, 172
  at Cana, 119
  among Christians, 46,
  demands in, 182
  differences within, 6, 47
  of Esther and Xerxes, 144

God's principles for, 20–21
honesty in, 221
infertility in, 56
Jewish custom in, 88
levirate rule on, 198, 199
listening in, 181
of Michal and David, 231
nagging in, 230
reaffirming love in, 143
of Rebekah and Isaac, 46
sex within, 9, 177
of Tamar and Judah, 217
Mary and Martha, 267, 271, 279
Mary Magdalene
delivered from seven demons,
284
Mary, mother of Jesus
"bitterness," 90
the epitome of surrender,
sacrifice, and selflessness, 87
flight to Egypt, 113
Gabriel describes her son in five
significant ways, 92
God provides financially for His
people, 113
her song, 100
humility of, 90, 91
illustration of her journey, 114
and Jesus' crucifixion, 120
journey to Bethlehem, 104
pregnancy of, 103
she is His spiritual daughter, 116
song of praise by, 100
visitation by Gabriel, 89
visit to Elizabeth, 97–103
Mary, mother of John Mark, 294,
308
Mary Magdalene, 239
matriarch, 27
Rebekah as, 45
Mattan, 176
Mayhall, Carole and Jack, 181
media, 159
mediator
definition, 300
meditate, 110
meditating, 53
medium (spiritualist), 232
mentor, 95, 112
Mephibosheth
nurse of, 239
mercy, 17, 39, 171
Mesopotamia
definition, 28
Messiah
appearance to Anna, 111
birth of, 105
Simeon's prophecy of, 111

metaphor
Adam's rib as, 8
Meyer, Joyce
on anxiety, 308
on enjoying the fullness of God,
106
on learning to be more like
Mary, 270
on slingers, 166–67
on staying in touch with God,
241
Michal, 231
Middle East, 15, 34
midian, 228
midwives, 126
minimized, 292
minister, 48, 111, 198
ministry
of Jesus, 88, 116–18, 267
of Miriam, 251
praise, 251
miracles
by Jesus, 87, 257, 279
Miriam, 251
mission
from God, 139
mite
definition, 308
Moab, 199
Moabite Stone, 202
Moabites, 199
Moabitish language, 202
mocked, 170
Mohammed, 211
mohar
definition, 71
money, 281
Moore, Beth
on acknowledging God, 68
on Bathsheba, 223
on between wanting and getting,
221
on divided heart, 59
on fulfilling the works, 103
on God not playing favorites,
244
on God's perfect parenting, 61
on living in the past, 91
on Satan's two primary
motivations, 11
on Satan's worst nightmare,
301
on uncertainties, 83
Mordecai
edict of, 157
honor by king, 153
refusal to bow, 147
Mordecai's Edict, 157

mortality, 22
Moses
personal knowledge of God, 273
sister of, 249
wife of, 228
Moslems, 31
Most High
Jesus as, 83
mother of Joseph and James, 287
mother of Samson, 129
motives
judgment based on, 39
Mount Carmel, 165
Mount Tabor, 128
Muhammed, 31
mutual submission, 143

N

Naaman, 243, 244
Nabal, 196
Naboth, 167. 168. 172
nagging, 229
Nahor, 45
Nain
Widow of, 259
nakedness
shame of, 9, 14, 17
naming the animals, 6
naming of children, 58
Naomi
definition, 198
depression of, 198
instructs Ruth to lie at Boaz's
feet, 202
Naphtali, 80, 128
narcotic, 81
nard, 283
Nathan, 223
nature worship, 216
Nazareth, 87, 88, 90
Nazirite, 129, 130
necromancy
definition, 232
negative expectations, 90
Nehemiah, 141, 150
New Testament, 27, 32, 190, 277
Ninevites, 150
noble, 168, 181
Nystrom, Carol, 127

O

Obed, 205, 207
obedience
to God, 11, 35, 42
Ocknega, Harold
on Adam and Eve, 16

Wise Woman of Abel, 241
Witch of Endor, 227
witchcraft, 155, 232
witnesses, 169, 207
woman
    balance in, 190
    in Christianity, 180
    creation of, 8
    as helper for man, 6
    ministry of, 291
    need for security, 20
    Proverbs 31, 179
    self-employment for, 191
    Shulammite, 177
    Syro-Phoenician, 258
woman, bleeding, 256
woman of Abel Beth Maacah, 24
woman at the well, 262
woman taken in adultery, 262
woman of Shunem, 134
woman of Tekoah, 240
woman using a spindle
    illustration of, 188
woman who was a sinner, 260
woman with the issue of blood,
    256
woman with two mites, 306
womb, 40
women
    of courage, 236
    of faith, 304
    helped by Jesus, 256
    in ministry, 290
    of strong faith, 124
    very important to Jesus and His
        ministry, 266
    victimized by men, 208
    of weak faith, 248
    who served evil, 226
    who struggled, 298
    of wisdom, 178
wondrous, 107
work
    as fulfillment, 7
    as punishment for Adam and
        Eve, 21
    on Sabbath, 260, 261
worrying, 269, 270
wrath, 16
wrongdoing
    acknowledging, 18

X

Xerxes
    Esther as queen for, 144
    party of, 139

Y

Yahweh, 92, 198, 110
Yemen, 242

Z

Zarephath
    widow of, 133, 134
Zebedee, 285
Zebulun, 82, 128
Zerah, 218
Zilpah, 73, 80
Zipporah, 228

DISCARD

CPSIA information can be obtained at www.ICGtesting.com
Printed in the USA
LVOW03s1114300114

371651LV00001B/7/P

9 781418 509897